Undeserving yet Entitled

◇◇◇◇◇◇◇◇◇◇◇◇◇◇◇◇◇◇◇◇◇◇◇◇◇◇◇◇◇◇◇◇◇

A Metamorphic Transformation by Grace

Beautywood Books

Lisa Ann Samara Jones

Copyright © 2023 Lisa Ann Samara Jones
All rights reserved
First Edition

PAGE PUBLISHING
Conneaut Lake, PA

First originally published by Page Publishing 2023

ISBN 978-1-6624-7998-4 (pbk)
ISBN 978-1-6624-7999-1 (digital)

Printed in the United States of America

Contents

◇◇◇◇◇◇◇◇◇◇◇◇◇◇◇◇◇◇◇◇◇◇◇◇◇◇◇◇◇◇◇◇◇◇◇◇

Preface v
Chapter 1: The Promise 1
Chapter 2: What Is the Truth 16
Chapter 3: Who Has Righteousness? 30
Chapter 4: Saved by Faith 50
Chapter 5: Metamorphic Transformation 67
Chapter 6: Enemy of God 80
Chapter 7: Camping Out 99
Chapter 8: Armor of God 107
Chapter 9: Love 132
Chapter 10: Forgiveness and Judgment 142
Chapter 11: There Is a Way 157
Chapter 12: Purpose 172
Chapter 13: The Segue 183
Chapter 14: Black and Red Is Black and White 196
Chapter 15: Calling All Saints! 209
Chapter 16: Will You Worship the Dragon or Messiah? 221
Chapter 17: Still Going... 228
Chapter 18: It Is Done! 238
Chapter 19: Eternity 259
Abbreviated Version of A Time Line of the End-Times 267
A Time Line of the End Times 271
Bibliography 297

PREFACE

I remember, at the young age of thirteen, when I first became a believer, it seemed to me that I lacked a testimony. I felt inadequate as I listened to others tell of their sin-streaked lives and all they were delivered from once they believed. I knew I'd sinned, don't get me wrong, I knew I needed forgiveness even for the sins of a thirteen-year-long life under the shelter of two parents who kept us pretty much straight and narrow, but I didn't have anything extraordinary that God had to deliver me from and felt almost as though I were thought of as less by other Christians because of this.

I guess none of that mattered as time went on, and I got married, before my twentieth birthday, to another "believer"—whom I reluctantly left and ultimately divorced three and a half years later. Now I had a testimony on the wrong side of my conversion: a one-year-old daughter being raised by me, a single mother, and constant trips to a courthouse battling to keep custody of her.

No testimony was far better than having one after salvation it turns out because divorce is almost unforgivable in many Christian circles. I think I would have been more easily forgiven if I'd started popping pills, robbed a bank, or even killed someone, but divorce, that carries a far steeper and lifelong penalty in the Christian organization. I felt confident that I carried the equivalent to the scarlet letter. It didn't matter that we'd been virgins when we'd married and that I'd tried to be a great wife. It didn't matter that the man was crazy and still attached by his mother's umbilical cord with such a knack for lying that even he couldn't tell the difference. It didn't matter that we'd gone to pastors and marriage counselors who referred him to a neurologist to get brain scans—they were so sure there had to be something neurologically wrong with him—and who refused to see us together any longer because they believed he needed individual therapy before we could ever have successful marital counseling or that he wouldn't go to individual counseling because his mother told him he was fine. It doesn't even seem to matter that he chose his girlfriend over me.

I walked away from that marriage feeling as though I was damaged goods that God could do nothing with and nothing for. I watched my ex-husband, his new wife, and his parents destroy our daughter's life as they pulled and lied to get court judges to force me to compromise at each court-ordered session and wondered why no one noticed how they used the system to get their own way to the detriment of our daughter. I was told that his quick remarriage to a woman with kids made him look like the better parent because he had a family to offer and so found myself desperate enough to…marry again.

I wed a man who was no good, unavailable, and heinous in the way he fought me if I didn't comply with him but married nonetheless because I thought it was because I deserved to pay some form of penance for becoming divorced in the first place, and keeping my daughter was the forerunner of all my thoughts. I don't know how many affairs were had, what he did when he couldn't be found for hours or even days, and I surely didn't know what a narcissist was until about twelve years into this abusive hell and when all that remained to my life was only my breath. We had three children together and fourteen years of abuse. Still, I attended church regularly, read my Bible, praised God, worshipped him, but clearly, I had no merit to speak on the Creator's behalf. I'd lost any value I never started with because people knew what he was without knowing anything specific; my marriage to him made me an accomplice. Even more so was I disqualified in my Christianity when I finally divorced him and now had two ex-husbands in my wake.

Resigned to singlehood, I bought a farm, taught school, and lived alone with my three youngest children for a few years, content with life and my standing with God until I met a man full of wisdom, patience, love, loyalty, and the ability to see past the scarlet letter "D" prominently yet figuratively displayed upon my chest and… married again.

And while I see how God has blessed me beyond my wildest dreams, I'm still a woman who has had three husbands, four children by two different men, and am now married to a man who is father to none but who has taken on the daunting task of raising them with me. He's a man of God, a pastor, with godly discernment, who sees me as a redeemed woman of God.

In many circles, I still harbor a scarlet letter D. My first divorce was around twenty years ago, the second was so much more of a deliverance that I never considered myself as more tainted with that divorce personally. Instead, I felt rescued and saved by a God who loves me; a God who redeemed me by the blood of his Son, many years back, and never left my side even though I married men who would hurt me. I have a testimony! We serve an Almighty God who wants our love, affection, full attention, obedience, worship, and praise to him.

We also serve a God who divorced his first bride, Israel, described in Jeremiah 3:6–8, "The Lord said to me in the days of King Josiah, 'Have you seen what she did, that faithless one, Israel, how she went up on every high hill and under every green tree and there played the whore?' And I thought, 'After she has done all this, she will return to me,' but she did not return, and her treacherous sister Judah saw it. She saw that for all the adulteries of that faithless one, Israel, I had sent her away with a decree of divorce."

There are few pastors who want to discuss this aspect of God, but it's there. Israel spent the entirety of its existence worshipping pagan idols, following after false gods, and the ways of the neighboring pagan cultures, turning back to God and then falling away again. We can also see that while God hates divorce, it's not the actual decree of paper that he hates, it is the action of dismissing, giving over, letting down, casting out, etc. that God is against; it is "shalach" (https://www.bible-studytools.com/lexicons/hebrew/nas/shalach.html).

Malachi 2:16 says, "For I hate divorce, says the Lord, the God of Israel, and covering one's garment with violence, says the Lord of hosts. So take heed to yourselves and do not be faithless."

The New International Version puts it this way, "'The man who hates and divorces his wife,' says the LORD, the God of Israel, 'does violence to the one he should protect,' says the Lord Almighty. So be on your guard and do not be unfaithful."

The New Living Translation states it this way, "'For I hate divorce!' says the Lord, the God of Israel. 'To divorce your wife is to overwhelm her with cruelty,' says the Lord of Heaven's Armies. 'So guard your heart; do not be unfaithful to your wife.'"

I stayed in an abusive marriage for fourteen years because I didn't want to do something God hated (again). Stripped of everything, via emotional, physical, sexual, financial, and spiritual abuse, I had become nothing at the hands of a manipulative, unfaithful, unloving, scathing man and to my dying day will never see the divorce papers that I served him as the part of "divorce" that God hates but rather his heinous, violent, and overwhelmingly cruel treatment, contrary to God's desires, that were bestowed upon this child of God as the act of divorce God hated.

We serve a God of relationship who isn't legalistic. We are part of a religion that talks about grace, forgiveness, and relationship over law. It's okay for believers to take part in fornication, repent, break up with their lovers, and go on to marry another and be considered clean. The church can take pity on women who are beaten by their boyfriends, find refuge away from them, and later marry kind Christian men and never receive any reproof like a scarlet letter. It's the act of divorce, by Christian women who married, instead of fornicating—who ended up either bound to an abuser or marred and called to singlehood for the rest of their lives—and that doesn't make sense. If we serve a forgiving God, who wants our relationship, our worship, and our love, why does a legitimate divorce disqualify her while she sits in the same sanctuary with some who didn't marry before sex, are malicious gossips, drunks, or any other kind of sinner in current states of rebellion but behind closed doors?

In fact, I think of the story of the Samaritan woman at the well. "'I don't have a husband,' she answered. Jesus replied, 'You are right when you say you don't have a husband. You have been married to five men, and the man you live with now is not really your husband. You have told me the truth'" (Jn. 4:17–18). Our Savior was offering salvation to a woman married five times and living with another.

Notice Christ does not say she *has* but *had* five husbands. Her marriages to them were considered over by our Savior. It's true she didn't divorce on the wrong side of her conversion, but surely, if Christ can offer salvation to this woman…her divorces can't possibly be the unpardonable sins modern Christendom wants to call them. What's more if we can forgive our fellow believers for any number of backsliding offenses, abusing pain pills, theft, alcoholism, gossip mongering, etc. and celebrate their rededication to Christ in their lives, why can't an abused woman be forgiven by her peers for divorcing an abusive husband and finding deliverance and redemption even the blessing of remarriage to a godly man displaying the love of Christ for her every day?

I expect those who can't look past this unfortunate dissolution will stop reading now. For those who can find mercy and believes that God uses former murders (Moses, Paul), adulterers (David), prostitutes (Rahab), and divorcees (Lisa), this is the rest of my story and message from the Word of God.

As for me, my third husband and I share a small farm on the top of a little mountain, have six children between us, and are feeling a heavy calling from God.

So in obedience, not because of any sort of clout that would merit this endeavor, I'm writing this book. There's a burden within my soul that burns from my core. Writing this has been birthed from this place inside me. I've not gotten the whole Bible figured out or all the answers to every great mystery. I have the Holy Bible though and know that many messages preached from pulpits, being written about in books with catchy titles, and informally taught through small groups, intra-church relationships, and social media are completely wrong. They are topics that essentially lead to eternal life or death and the preparedness, or lack thereof, for believers still searching to fill a void. In this book, I speak of the "doctrine of grace" or this "era of grace" and essentially try to dispel its accuracy. The confusion lies in what George Orwell coined in *1984* as double speak.

There is a true doctrine of grace that is biblically founded. We will discuss grace and use scriptures to validate such, but this current notion of grace abounding and being used to teach believers that "striving" for anything godly is wrong and at the heart of what my burden to write is fueled by. To some who hear of others speaking of grace and God's forgiveness of sins may be grounded in their faith and not realize this "grace" being taught is not that which our forefathers preached on or that which is written in the word of God.

This false grace speaks to the weary souls who are physically tired of trying to look like they've got it all together in effort to manufacture a witness for Christ. Later in chapter 5, we will look at a quote used by believers to tell of the power of our Savior. We'll look at how it isn't literally happening for most of us today and why it's at the heart of recreating a "grace doctrine" that tells believers to abandon their "good works." There is a new religion coming alive with a focus on the word "grace" and redefining of many of the biblical words used to describe salvation. I've seen the verses in the book of James be twisted to say that the "good works" referenced by him meant a "one-time decision to accept Christ." The word repentance has been redefined to mean "changing one's mind about the identity and finished work of Jesus" (Andrew Farley, *Twisted Scripture: Untangling 45 Lies Christians Have Been Told*, May 2019. Salem Books, Washington, DC).

With such blaspheme within the body of Christ, we are battling to maintain the sanctity of Christianity. I read a post on Facebook months ago of a preacher's wife who was "ministering to her friends." She spoke of her years of "striving" to do what was right and how tired she'd become. She exclaimed that she'd finally found the true meaning of Christianity as she learned what grace means, "she can't do it and God doesn't expect her to." She exuberantly shared her new faith and said she finally understood Christianity and "would never weary herself again trying so hard to have good works." I keep stumbling across and listening to fellow believers confuse the concept of "law-based salvation" with "doing good works." They know that the law does not lead to salvation and quote various scriptures to illustrate this fact but immediately switch to a conclusion that alleviates them from "good works" and call it deliverance from a work-based religion. They claim doing any such good works is the denial of Christ who accomplished every good thing for us, and it is the epitome of believing salvation is only earned through good works.

I've been cut off by believers, of this type of religion, mid-sentence and accused of trying to earn my salvation through works. They claim that anyone living righteously is fake—hypocritical sinners who lack salvation and a relationship with God because one must only see him as a mean Father watching for them to slip up so he can zap them with a bolt of lightning. Through grace, Christ came to die for all those who would repent and believe in him.

The words of our Scriptures (New Testament included) tell of a transformed life for believers. The messages conveyed by apostles and disciples of Christ is to live righteously. This is not to be confused with striving for popularity, riches, keeping up with the Joneses, or some form of a prosperity gospel; striving for any of this is spoken against in Scriptures. But we can't confuse tiredness of trying to do these things with what the Bible speaks of as good works or good deeds. We can't "strive" to create an image of cultural success for ourselves, tire out, and come to claim that God doesn't want us to strive for righteousness. They are not the same thing and should never be the excuse to abandon what the Scriptures teach or create a new religion based on such.

Recently, I read a post on Facebook of a young pastor's wife, home with three children and pregnant with her fourth. She had a verse from Galatians quoted with a small commentary and connection to her personal life. She spoke of her tiredness. She elaborated on how she felt burned out, feeling like she had to balance everything perfectly and that this lifestyle had led to a shallow relationship with Christ. Her Christian settings were on what she called a "gospel plus" perpetrated by a "work based religion" and the solution was to go back to a simple "loving Jesus and admitting her need for him" sort of faith. There were others who responded to this post with suggestions for books to read. I went straight to Amazon to get my hands on many of these books. There was a theme running through these posts and a stigma attached to anyone trying to please God. They were called fakes and likened to tired, unhappy people lacking a true relationship with their Savior. The alternative was "grace" and what amounted to a group of people one upping the others as they bragged of their heinous sins. The authors spoke of a comradery and an acceptance felt in this true Christian club. Thinking specifically of this young, burned-out mother who authored the original post and the response to her reminded me of a passage:

"They are the kind who worm their way into households and captivate vulnerable women who are weighed down with sins and led astray by various passions, who are always learning but never able to come to a knowledge of the truth" (2 Tim. 3:6–7, BSB).

It is erroneous to strive for a cultural perfection. It is, however, natural for a mother to be tired while raising kids. It takes work and sacrifice. I'm still carving out time around the schedules of our six kids and being a wife to find time to write and study Scriptures. The more I seek for truth though, the more I pray for God to fill me with his Holy Spirit, the easier it is for me to do that which he's called me to do. I know the answer is not to abandon righteous living or the hard work that goes into training young kids up.

Grace is not "Jesus is perfect so I don't have to be." Grace is that Jesus is our Savior and has equipped us with what we need to do his will. The grace he gives revolves around the forgiveness of our sins, that we could do nothing on our own to deserve or earn, and the transforming power given to us mortals to live out his commandments. "…My grace is sufficient for you, for power [*dunamis*] is made perfect in weakness" (2 Cor. 12:9 NRSV).

I have come to write this book to share scriptures that will draw straight lines to our Lord and Savior. I desire to bring hope to the tired and weary who want to find the real truth! In fact, it is Christ alone who saves, and apart from him we are nothing. But when we are saved, we are not apart from him. The answer is not to give in to a life of sin that we should have repented from and call that grace. The answer is to be filled with the Holy Spirit of God and the power of a redeeming Savior who gives us the strength to do that which he's called of his saints to do. I've written this book to illuminate the endurance and preparedness required by our loving Father and revealed in his Holy Scriptures. This book will begin with the promise and end with eternity.

There are concepts that come to mind regularly, verses that jump off the page at me, and sermons from well-respected preachers that taunt me to look deeper, seek more determinedly, with a tenacity within me that keeps pushing me to find answers. Writing this book has been extremely hard to do. As verses came flying off the pages at me and the message of the whole gospel becomes abundantly clear, there was a constant contrast and bombardment of "grace" in our churches from the songs on the Christian radio station and from Christians in general that left me wanting to scrap the entire project. I had to dig deep into the scriptures to define grace, mercy, and even what the gospel is. It has been no easy feat to stare at verses that go against the very fiber of modern Christianity. I have felt alone and fearful that my own mind plays tricks on me as I draw conclusions that go against the norm. I could only pray for God to drive me forward or to stop me as I endeavored to finish this book.

Finding answers had to come straight from the word of God. Building truth came from aligning scriptures of the same nature. I made discoveries I wasn't expecting as I searched for passages to explain others. I listened to others share their beliefs and use scriptures to support their ideas. I found truth as well as new avenues to search. When single verses seemed to contradict vast portions of Scriptures but were used as arguments against what otherwise seemed obvious, it caused me to look harder, search out other scriptures to answer the differences.

I have prayed for myself and every person taking hold of this book that God would open our eyes, ears, and hearts to hear what the Lord on High wants us to know.

"If any of you lacks wisdom, let him ask God, who gives generously to all without reproach, and it will be given him" (Jas. 1:5, ESV).

"Yes, if you call out for insight and raise your voice for understanding, if you seek it like silver and search for it as for hidden treasures, then you will understand the fear of the Lord and find the knowledge of God" (Prov. 2:3–5, ESV).

"All Scripture is breathed out by God and profitable for teaching, for reproof, for correction, and for training in righteousness, that the man of God may be complete, equipped for every good work" (2 Tim. 3:16–17, ESV).

Lord, I lack wisdom. I want to know you! I don't know how to interpret your Scriptures alone. I want to know what your word speaks of, to understand all that you want me to know. I seek you like one seeks silver and lift my voice to the heavens to ask for your wisdom and understanding. In the name of the Lord, amen.

Together, we will embark on a biblical journey to uncover the details that God has given to us believers. Some of what we uncover will shock us and be contrary to that which we have read or heard for years, from godly pastors, commentators, and Facebook memes. Other discoveries will line up as we are expecting them to say, but most importantly, we need to find the truths God has given us so we are prepared and enduring to the end that we might be saved.

"For you have need of endurance, so that when you have done the will of God you may receive what was promised" (Heb. 10:36, ESV).

Chapter 1

The Promise

This is the promise which He Himself made to us: eternal life.
—1 John 2:25, BSB

We have been given access to this promise, by faith and grace, that which is eternal life. There are a plethora of doctrines surrounding this promise for eternal life regarding who can have it, what one must do to ensure it, and doctrine that explains nothing can be done by man himself to receive it. How then can we understand what the promise is, that we must remain faithful in endurance to receive, as promised? We will look at Scriptures ourselves to see what God has told us. We will not convolute it with man-made ideas or notions that require assumptions or leaps and jumps to conclude anything. We don't need commentators or scholarly writings to even explain something that is so clearly offered in our own Bibles. Here we go. Let's get our Bibles out, computers turned on, or phone apps ready to dive in and seek answers from our Lord and Savior.

The promise God made to us is for eternal life. It's the opposite of what God told Adam and Eve in Genesis 2:16–17, ESV "And the Lord God commanded the man, saying, 'You may surely eat of every tree of the garden, but of the tree of the knowledge of good and evil you shall not eat, for in the day that you eat of it you shall surely die.'"

Those of us who know the story of Adam and Eve know that they did not drop dead at the moment they ate the fruit or any time soon after; likewise, we know of or have heard of believers who have died and didn't live forever. As a child, hearing this story, I often cringed at this part, knowing that they didn't physically die but not wanting to consider God or the Bible were wrong. I silently wrestled with this dilemma.

Like me, some might wonder if these promises were broken; I assure you they were not. In order to understand "eternal life," however, we must first understand what "death" God spoke of in the garden of Eden. There are several verses throughout the New and Old Testament that speak of this death. Romans 5:12, KJV tells us that "Therefore, just as through one man sin entered into the world, and death through sin, and so death spread to all men because all sinned." The act of disobedience, by Adam and Eve, to the Creator of our universe is sin. Sin leads to death. The death referenced here is not the loss of breath and blood flow through the human body but rather a death of the spirit and an eventual eternity in hell or the lake of fire (referenced in several verses such as Revelation 21:8, Matthew 18:8, Revelation 20:15, Matthew 25:46, etc.).

Realizing this death is eternal and spiritual quenched that nagging worry that God had not fulfilled his promise but put an urgency in my soul to be saved from this sort of death.

I found the antidote for this fate in Romans 6:23, ESV "For the wages of sin is death, but the free gift of God is eternal life in Christ Jesus our Lord." As well as in 1 Corinthians 15:21, NASB "For since by a man came death, by a man also came the resurrection of the dead." I just didn't fully understand what this all meant. I started putting things together about the Bible stories my mother talked about as I was growing up, Jesus dying on the cross, and my mother's own story about her becoming a "born-again Christian."

My mother's a shy woman who was mostly a homebody, taking care of four children and keeping house. She told us that our Nana, her mother, had come to know Christ as her Savior watching a television show called the *700 Club*. I remember my mother telling us that her mom wanted her to watch the show and kept insisting she needed to know more about God than they'd ever learned in church growing up with her. I must have been around three or four when this was happening, and I know it without even asking my mother now because the *700 Club* came on while *Magic Garden* aired. This was my and my twin sister's favorite show, and we felt annoyed at the fact that our mother would switch to the *700 Club* occasionally, instead of letting us watch our favorite show.

As an older yet young thirteen-year-old, thinking about her story, I felt a little embarrassed at how much I couldn't stand it when she'd get our lunches made and then sit to watch this show, sandwich in her lap, and a mug of tea in her hand. I had little flashes of memories of us sitting with her in our bed hearing her tell of how God loves us so much that he let his Son die for us. The image my small mind created was of a boy being led away by someone with a rifle in his hand and a death by bullet; I don't think I actually paid close enough attention to what she told us specifically about his death because I hadn't put any further thought to her story and what I actually knew of Christ's death then. Nevertheless, I remembered her talking about needing to be forgiven and Jesus being the way to that remission of sins. The next part of her story that I recalled was of her getting baptized in the Hudson River and coming home to us, only to find my uncle there as well and how she "looked like a drowned rat," straight out of the water and wrapped in towels for the short drive home. She said she could hear her brother-in-law ask my dad "What happened to her?" and her typically shy and insecure demeanor melt away as she felt pride in getting baptized rather than embarrassed.

I'm sure that this part of her story was what made me first think of how my friend, Julie from school and church, would be sure to laugh at me if I got baptized in church and found the same overcoming spirit melt away any feelings of embarrassment I would normally have felt. I never said a specific "sinner's prayer," it was more of an open-ended dialogue with God. A conversation with the Creator letting him know I understood now and that I knew the next step in salvation biblically was baptism, more specifically though was that I needed to publicly claim him as my Savior. Most importantly, however, I knew that I was a sinner, in need of a Savior. I didn't know all the ways to describe being born again, but I knew I wasn't a Christ follower just because I went to church every Sunday. I was a sinner, and the thing missing in life was redemption from God through Christ.

To know what "eternal life" is, I had to understand sin. As we saw in the garden of Eden, the act of disobedience to anything God commands is sin. James 4:17, ESV tells us that "whoever knows the right thing to do and fails to do it, for him it is sin." Galatians 5:19–21, ESV lists specific sins, "Now the works of the flesh are evident, which are adultery, fornication, uncleanness, lewdness, idolatry, sorcery, hatred, contentions, jealousies, outbursts of wrath, selfish ambitions, dissensions, heresies, envy, murders, drunkenness, revelries, and the like of which I tell you beforehand, just as I also told you in time past, that those who practice such things will not inherit the kingdom of God" or have eternal life. The bottom line is "all have sinned and fall short of the glory of God" (Rom. 3:23, ESV). We are all born into a fallen world, "and the whole world lies in the power of the evil one" (1 Jn. 5:19, ESV).

Now, I was thirteen years old at the time and had not really had time to establish any of these sins in my life, but I knew I lied to my parents to stay out of trouble, had jealousy toward my sisters and little brother at times, and even initiated arguments with my siblings, but what was most valuable in my life at the time was the horse stable I volunteered at and the lives of the young twenty-somethings who worked there. I saw people who lived day-to-day but without God. I saw emptiness. This alone spurred me to realize that God was more than regular church attendance.

I suddenly saw the difference in the Christian life and a life spent apart from God, the variance of eternal life versus eternal death. My conversion was born from seeing that contrast.

Eternal life is for anyone who has faith in Christ Jesus. The most cited verse for salvation, or eternal life, is John 3:16, ESV "For God so loved the world that he gave his only Son, that whoever believes in him should not perish but have eternal life."

Biblically, we can read about repenting, turning from sin, apologizing to God for sinning against him, and making Christ the Lord of our lives. There have been tracts printed and "sinner's prayers" written, but those are not necessary for one to become saved and have the free gift of eternal life. All one must do is speak to the Creator, confess his sins, ask for forgiveness, and believe that the death of Christ was him taking our punishment and his resurrection proof of his deity as we make him Lord of our life. "I write these things to you who believe in the name of the Son of God, that you may know that you have eternal life" (1 Jn. 5:13, ESV).

My first name is Lisa, a derivative of Elizabeth, meaning "consecrated to God." I don't know if it was a prophetically given name or a prayer over me, but I am the definition of my name. I need to know more, to understand deeper, and to do my best at this life following Christ.

According to Merriam-Webster, "consecrated" means "dedicated to a sacred purpose" (https://www.merriam-webster.com/dictionary/consecrate).

As we delve into understanding Christianity, I feel the pull of this sacred purpose close to my heart and the passion behind finding and sharing the answers we can uncover in our Bibles. Mediocrity isn't a word I associate with myself too often. It is, however, the word that comes to mind as I listen to the preaching that comes from so many less-than-prepared and more-than-willing-to-follow-tradition preachers of today. I'm sure you will soon find in our thorough quest to find the pieces of this great puzzle that we can actively live out eternal lives in excellence instead of passively expecting eternal life while we live with mediocrity.

Coming to a saving faith is not the destination for Christianity, it's a starting place. While the promise for eternal life, which most people would refer to as spending our afterlives in heaven, is a fantastic incentive for becoming believers; it's not really the point. In fact, anyone who finds this supposed salvation and has no life change will miss eternal life and lives with a false sense of eternal security.

"This is the message we have heard from him and proclaim to you, that God is light, and in him is no darkness at all. If we say we have fellowship with him while we walk in darkness, we lie and do not practice the truth. But if we walk in the light, as he is in the light, we have fellowship with one another, and the blood of Jesus his Son cleanses us from all sin" (1 Jn. 1:5–7, ESV).

While it's easy to see that we can repent from our sins and find forgiveness, this passage in 1 John is explaining that God is good and light with no darkness. We can't walk in darkness and sin, not practicing the truth, and call ourselves saved Christians or expect eternal life. These verses have a clear mandate that we must actively walk in the light, have fellowship with each other in light, and this will assure us the cleansing of our sins.

This is where the waters get a little choppy. We live in this "era of grace." Christ was the final sacrifice for sin. There is no need for anyone to be sacrificing animals for forgiveness, such as the days of the old covenant, but this doesn't mean that we can continue in our lives as usual and carry on as sinners just because we have recited a "sinner's prayer" and asked Jesus into our hearts. We are all sinners and have already seen the verse in Romans 3:23, ESV "for all have sinned and fall short of the glory of God"; however, I contest that this doesn't mean we are to continue living in sin or as "sinners." This concept seems to be starkly different than the ideals of modern Christianity but written all throughout our Bibles.

As a newlywed to my first husband, I entered my first Pentecostal Church. I remember being enthralled at the display of what looked like love and worship until attending more regularly and finding that it was such commonplace that people knew what they were supposed to do, say, speak in tongues, and how they were to act singing worship songs, but it was still a dead church with sermons that fell on deaf ears, pride, arrogance, ignorance, with scores of extramarital affairs and porn addictions that were being swept under the rug. The teens in the youth group, led by a porn-addicted pastor, openly exposed their lack of belief and "acts" of false worship which fooled their parents and church families.

At the young age of nineteen, I was put in the hot seat and judged for not having spoken in tongues yet. It was this church that catapulted me forward in my Bible reading and studying. I thought it was good enough that I'd read my entire Bible through and a chapter a day before prayers. I began learning, however, to find scriptures and match them to other scriptures for a better clearer understanding. This was before internet was as predominant as it is today, so I sat with a *Strong's Concordance*, highlighters, and pen and paper to put God's word together to make sense. I began realizing that I was largely alone in my faith. Digging, searching, and pleading with God for answers, I kept turning to my Bible. Highlighting, coordinating, and tagging verses that pointed to something bigger than I'd been taught or read pushed my drive to find anyone I could Bible study with.

I felt alone and thought I was a freak, lost, and somehow tainted in my mind. Images of *A Beautiful Mind* flashed before my eyes as I continued highlighting and tagging verses that seemed to go together in a divine explanation of God's will that no one even wanted to look at, let alone study with me. I kept picturing the scene where John Forbes Nash Jr.'s (an American mathematician and Nobel Prize Laureate) wife, Alicia, walked into his shed and saw all the articles and texts tacked to his wall like wallpaper, overlapping, highlighted, put together like a crazy man to any person looking in on his work. I feared my Bible looked just like that wall, and only I saw the connections popping off the pages.

It seemed to me that our Bibles were made up of a multitude of books and verses that we were *not* supposed to read in order to fit in with modern Christians. I could hold a chunk of the good book and theoretically throw it away and no one would care; as long as the cliché verses about God always being with us, strengthening us, protecting us, etc. stayed, no one seemed to care or would have even noticed.

As I dig and seek God's Scriptures for his purpose and desires for his people, I continuously find that he desires more from us. Instead of scouring the Bible for verses that promise things to us, we need to search the Scriptures for verses that tell us what God desires of us. The problem I encountered was self-doubt. I concluded many times that I was a freak, stopped seeking, and went along with the crowd. I did the Christian thing, but I didn't do God's. Each time I walked away from what I knew God was pulling me toward, I felt my spiritual life drain. I didn't walk in the Spirit because I was busy doubting such a walk was even right. As I clung to the modern idea of Christianity, I made choices that were far outside of the will of God.

I lived for years with consequences to choices I made. I suffered immensely for it. But make no mistake, God was always there waiting for me to respond to that deep yearning he put inside of me. As I've come back to faith in God and not religion, or the things other people associate with Christianity, it is still a struggle to go forward in what feels like a lonely path. I am plagued with self-doubt, but I know what trying to be religious felt like. I see what the word of God says in contrast to what is being spread today and keep holding tightly to God. I press forward in lots of prayer and a genuine desire to please God.

When I come to crossroads and I'm not sure what the right thing to do is, I pray! I confess to God that it's hard to know and need his wisdom and power within me to do his will. I ask for the Holy Spirit to work through me, speak that which I don't know to say, and I press forward. I receive strength and direction with that burden to discover truth and share it, burning stronger. I am filled with physical discomfort as I see friends and other Christians post a few verses with a devotional that reads like an optimistic horoscope. They want to count on a promise from God and receive it as though God sees us as such worthless beings; he's going to give it to us no matter what sin we're in. They want to claim it and believe it because it feels good to hope for something wonderful. They've been listening to the same errant messages of grace being what God gives to us dirty, rotten, undeserving sinners. They want to claim all the promises from Scriptures as their own as though entitled to them because of grace because they prayed a prayer once, however, failed to make Christ their foundation (1 Cor. 3:11).

For every encouraging verse though, I see an "if-then" conditional statement. A logic problem reminiscent of my high school math days. If we will seek after God and repent, then he is a faithful God who rescues us.

"If-then" statements, "if this, then that," meant in math that the "if" part of the statement had to be fulfilled for the "then" part of the statement to also be true. For example, "If you pick apples, then I will make apple sauce." There is only going to be apple sauce if someone picks apples. We couldn't logically just take the part about apple sauce being made as a promise and expect it to be made without first picking apples. But this is what many Christian inspirational calendars and daily devotionals are made of. We want a feel-good religion with passive involvement while we hold onto promises and encourage each other by saying that "God is still in control" or "Faith over fear," but as long as we only look to God for his promises and never at what his desire for us is, we remain consumers and takers, rather than the servers we are supposed to be as believers.

Jeremiah 29:11, ESV is a frequently quoted "inspirational" verse that is the "then" part of God's promise: "'For I know the plans I have for you,' declares the Lord, 'plans for welfare and not for evil, to give you a future and a hope.'" Logically, we can't claim this as a promise for ourselves without looking at what our part to play in this is first, but with easy believism rampant that is exactly what Christians are doing.

There is an "if" part of this statement from Jeremiah 29, (If) "'you will call upon me and come and pray to me, (then) I will hear you. You will seek me and find me, when you seek me with all your heart. I will be found by you,' declares the Lord, 'and I will restore your fortunes and gather you from all the nations and all the places where I have driven you,' declares the Lord, 'and I will bring you back to the place from which I sent you into exile'"(Jer. 29:12–14).

Notice the last sentence in that section of scripture, "and I will bring you back to the place from which I sent you into exile." While we want to look at verse 11 and see God as a great big godfather in the sky who has great plans to prosper us and leave it at that for our own feel-good inspirational quote, we overlook the fact that this same God sent his people into exile prior to this, and only after they repent and sought God with *all* their hearts was God to be found and restored by him.

You see, the Old Testament is all about God's chosen people falling away from him, worshipping other gods and being guilty of idolatry, then being punished and allowed to live the consequences for such, and being brought back to God the Father through repentance. 1 Corinthians 11:31–32 echoes the same sentiments "that God disciplines His Children so that we may not be condemned along with the world." When we read Jeremiah 29:11 as an isolated verse and promise for us, we leave off our responsibility. We leave off the desire God has for us to repent, seek him, and walk in his statutes, instead continuing in this "grace-filled era" of "God is love," "is with me always," and "I can keep living my life as I want to with a special God the Father who will prosper me no matter what because I can never please God anyway." Basically, many believe they are "undeserving yet entitled" rather than in our Lord, full of truth and grace.

As I battled my way through family court over my daughter from my first marriage, I was barraged with an overflowing quiver load of positive scriptures to encourage me from well-meaning friends. I kept being told that God was with me, and yet the trauma associated with going through family court with a vindictive ex-husband and his family looked identical to nonbeliever's plights. It was nice of people to try to encourage me with these uplifting scriptures, but it didn't change the fact that at best, the promises being offered in these verses were no more than abstract. I felt as though God was a fast-moving car speeding away from me and I was holding onto his bumper flying in the wind doing everything I could do to hold on.

I was going to church, praying, reading my Bible, and praying the Psalms against my ex-husband. I was living as a "good Christian," and yet these promises didn't seem to pertain to me (was all that I could gather) as they didn't come to fruition. Ultimately, I came to feel as though God didn't hear me, didn't care about me, or that I wasn't valuable to him. I spent over a decade holding onto false hope and missing the key elements of Christianity and from the relationship God desired I have with him because I was focused solely on what God was supposed to be doing for me. Salvation isn't about us; it's about the Lord.

In fact, I spent eighteen or more years in a state of begging God for help and rescue without a response. It took another ugly fight with my second husband and a fear of being near him that sent me to the closet with a flashlight, my Bible, and a twenty-five-cent book that I'd just found in a thrift store. The author of this book wrote about a different kind of Christianity than I'd ever heard preached. He laid out scriptures that spoke of demons and spiritual battles that I'd never heard about. He wrote of people who were healed, saved from horrible situations, and cured with verses that didn't line up with any sermon's I'd ever heard. I was sure his verses were not real and miswritten to make a point he was making up, but I found them to be true. I was shocked at the misrepresentation of Christianity I'd had my entire life and lurched forward to piece scriptures together to find more truth. During the next four months, I poured over my Bible, using Google searches, and put together a ninety-thousand-word document that uncovered some of what I'm writing about in this book.

I was seeking. After almost fourteen years of marriage to a porn-addicted, violent, and volatile abuser, whom I'd pleaded with God to rescue me from for more than a decade, while financially destitute and unable to leave with four kids and no money, a plan to safely escape forged and was fulfilled over the span of a few months. I wasn't rich but prospered, was able to get my state-teaching certification, and a teaching position that led me to buying a farm and being able to raise my kids in ways I'd only dreamed of as his wife. It was truly miraculous. I knew that it was my seeking after God that gave me the favor needed to see these inspirational verses actually come true. As we've discussed earlier, we all know God hates divorce, and I'm sure many fellow believers are cringing at the idea that God delivered me from this marriage, but I'm telling you, it is no coincidence that once I fulfilled the "if" part of God's promises, that God's promises were fulfilled in my life.

"Ask not what your country can do for you but what you can do for your country" (John F. Kennedy's Inaugural Address, January 20, 1961) is a famous quote from our late president. I think we could change a few words and find our own Christian maturation begin to take hold within many: "Ask not what your God can do for you but what you can do for your God."

When the year 2020 hit and COVID-19 spread worldwide causing a global pandemic, more verses started getting quoted in pieces. By now, I saw these logical statements in scripture quite regularly, so as another frequently quoted scripture from Psalm 91:3–10 promising protection from pestilence and evil kept popping up on Facebook; it was all that I could do not to rant all over social media about the importance of the "if you do" part of that statement found in the first two verses. "He who dwells in the shelter of the Most High will abide in the shadow of the Almighty. I will say to the Lord, 'My refuge and my fortress, my God, in whom I trust'" (Ps. 91:1–2).

If we serve God, Christ is the Lord of our lives. We worship him, we think of Him and are obedient to him, then we are promised protection from pestilences. God hasn't filled this book with hyperboles. I strongly and firmly believe that if I have my mind, actions, and service in line with the will of God, I will receive his protection. These verses being quoted as encouragement and promises of God without also citing our part in the promise are giving empty words, empty hope, false hope for people who only want the promises without having to actively worship our Creator. I know it left people who lost loved ones or suffered from this pandemic in a quandary. They proclaimed "faith over fear" and paraded around as though they were invincible in the name of their Christianity, but no one did anything outside of their obligatory church attendance, including after churches were closed because they said "no one was going to stop them from worshipping!" But they still suffered from pestilences and diseases. I'm sure many felt as empty and forgotten as I had when I was given inspirational quotes as encouragement to get through a never-ending family court battle and a miserable second marriage and saw nothing like the promises delivered.

In light of the time we are in, 2 Chronicles 7:14, BSB has been quoted more frequently as well, "And if my people who are called by my name humble themselves and pray and seek my face and turn from their wicked ways, then I will hear from heaven, forgive their sin, and heal their land."

This verse is always quoted intact. The sad and frustrating fact is that the first part of this verse is intentionally overlooked. It's read but disregarded and believed that the first part doesn't actually apply to us. It is specifically because there is a doctrine being taught and shared throughout the body of believers that we are supposed to make a choice between trusting God and pleasing him. They divide Christians into two groups. There are those "with fake smiles, masks, and false Christianity." These are the supposed "God pleasers." They are described as the ones who have good intentions but feign perfection while they keep sinning the same sins persistently and focus on self-effort. They are mocked for trying to satisfy a God they cannot please.

    The second group are of the sinners who know they are sinners. They are the ones who want to proclaim to the world that they are *not* fine, that if you knew half their thoughts, they'd be kicked out of the club. These are the ones who compete to expose their failings and make light of the Christian's compulsive sin in the name of "grace" and "humility/" These are the ones described as "trusting in God." When we equate trusting God with the concept that "he loves us anyway" and "we can never please God," it's no wonder that the latter camp assumes the first must be faking their Christianity and neck-deep into their own sins. It's unfathomable for them to believe that there are believers who are leading lives with integrity and righteousness defined by Scriptures and possible only by the power of God through Christ who strengthens us. Then they look at a verse like 2 Chronicles 7:14 and rebelliously believe we do not need to humble ourselves or seek his face. Their religion is based on a notion that since humanity can never please God, we are only "striving" in vain and, therefore, have no obligation before God except to "trust" him, have "faith" in him, and believe his "grace" and "love" will forgive our sins and heal our lands and doing anything except this actually turn us to our wicked ways.

    We are absolutely called to humble ourselves, find refuge in the Lord, trust in him, *repent*, and *seek* his face. We can't do this by singing a few songs or reading a couple inspiring verses daily. We can't repent and seek the face of God if we fall prey to the idea that God is unsatisfiable and any effort to do such is denying God's grace. Repentance requires a turning from our sins, not an acceptance of them. Seeking God requires prayer for wisdom and reading of his word to glean truth, knowledge, and understanding. Neither of these are faking Christianity, wearing a mask, or trying to earn salvation through works. They are done in obedience to the Word of God because we love him so much we want to please him.

"But thanks be to God, who always leads us triumphantly as captives in Christ and through us spreads everywhere the fragrance of the knowledge of Him. For we are to God the sweet aroma of Christ among those who are being saved and those who are perishing" (2 Cor. 2:14–15, BSB). Let no one deceive you dear brothers and sisters in Christ; we can please God through the power he puts in us upon our conversion in faith. We are a sweet fragrance to him when we share the knowledge of the gospel of Christ. Certainly, this is satisfying to the Lord.

"For you have need of endurance, so that when you have done the will of God you may receive what was promised" (Heb. 10:36, ESV).

Brothers and sisters in Christ, we have to realize that there is a requirement for endurance and doing the will of God that we may receive what is promised. If we endure and do the will of God, then we will receive the promise. We cannot lackadaisically pray for forgiveness once and fallaciously believe we are saved and free from any evil coming our way. We can't claim our way into favor, pray our way in, or expect this promise just because we exist. That is not the grace our Bibles talk about.

Titus 2:11–14 (NRSV emphasis added) says, "For the grace of God has appeared, bringing salvation to all, *training us to renounce impiety and worldly passions, and in the present age to live lives that are self-controlled, upright, and godly*, while we wait for the blessed hope and the manifestation of the glory of our great God and Savior, Jesus Christ. He it is who gave himself for us that he might redeem us from all iniquity and purify for himself a people of his own who are zealous for good deeds."

"No weapon formed against you will prosper, and you will refute every tongue that accuses you. This is the heritage of the servants of the Lord, and their vindication is from me" (Isa. 54:17, BSB).

A servant of the Lord is a seeker who follows the precepts, commandments, and directions of the Lord. The heritage for these active participants of Christianity is that no weapon formed against them will prosper… We need to be free from simplistic and double-minded thinking and seek truth: "and you will know the truth, and the truth will set you free" (Jn. 8:32, ESV).

Chapter 2

What Is the Truth

We know that Christ died so our sins can be forgiven. We know that we have a role in our Christianity, but let us seek after truth so that we can fully understand how to marry these two concepts together without being too far on the side of grace or too far on the side of works (without salvation). After all, we need to keep our minds on endurance and doing the will of God to receive the promise.

Pastors tell us that "Jesus is truth." Churches offer altar calls to those wanting to be set free with the "truth." Preachers teach "truth" from the pulpit. There is a *truth* that often gets sought after through reading "trusted" commentaries, but exactly what is this "truth"? Many preach the concept that separation from God makes it impossible to find truth on our own. But if we turn from our sin, God will show us the ultimate truth that is found in Jesus Christ. "If we would just accept Jesus into our hearts, then we will be free," they say. Supporting these sermons are scores of verses: "Jesus answered, 'I am the way and the truth and the life. No one comes to the Father except through me'" (Jn. 14:6, NIV).

Easily, we can see that Jesus is the root of what *truth* is. Every believer knows that Jesus Christ is the only son of God and that he died for our sins. Is that what this verse means? Should this scripture be isolated and interpreted simply to mean that Christ is the only way to the Father? Is that the whole "truth"?

"The Word became flesh and made his dwelling among us. We have seen his glory, the glory of the one and only Son, who came from the Father, full of grace and truth" (Jn. 1:14, NIV).

"For the law was given through Moses; grace and truth came through Jesus Christ" (Jn. 1:17, NIV).

There it is. For those of us who believe, we now have truth.

But what does this mean?

In preparation of this chapter, I listened to various sermons about truth, dug deeply into my vast reservoir of memories learned from church, and heard the same message. "Those who are lost can't fathom truth, but those who have a saving relationship, through grace from God, which is belief in Jesus Christ, are given a special insight into truth. Jesus is truth. When we know Christ as our Savior, we know truth." Sermons often go on to include many more verses, noting that the Messiah is truth, and quote celebrities, philosophers, and even Buddha as searching for truth as they do not know Christ. These preachers stand at their pulpits pleading with a congregation to believe in our Savior so they can receive the truth and be set free.

While these sermons are fantastic and at the foundational level of Christianity—essential messages to convert more to the believing faith of Christ—what does it mean? What is the "truth" that believers are given upon conversion? Am I the only one who can't see the emperor's new clothes (*The Emperor's New Clothes* by Hans Christian Anderson)? Am I the only one who "got saved" but still see that the emperor isn't wearing anything but his skivvies? I didn't automatically understand what "the truth" was upon conversion.

Ask someone to explain, and you're sure to be told it's about faith, grace, and a relationship with our Lord and Savior, and I'm not arguing that it isn't about that. But to end here? To simply call it one of those "faith things" and pretend that we all see beautiful clothes on an emperor who is clad in nothing but his underwear is a lie; otherwise, someone would be able to put this thing called *truth* into words.

These messages come illuminated with plenty of fancy words, loads of scriptures, and stacks of commentaries to explain how faith in a God, who gives us salvation through his only Son, who died on a cross and rose from the dead again, is *truth*. Let us be suspicious when we hear scripture references that don't seem to support the premise being made. Even Satan knows how to quote it, and you can bet your bottom dollar that he isn't supporting a godly truth with it (Mt. 4:1–11 and Lk. 4).

Using all the same verses that these well-meaning preachers use actually give far more information to be extracted so that we can understand a full *truth* that isn't a dead end of a faith-based religion (which isn't understandable).

"Jesus answered, 'I am the way and the truth and the life. No one comes to the Father except through me'" (Jn. 14:6, NIV).

There you have it. Christ is the way and the truth and the life. We come to the Father through belief in our Lord Jesus Christ. There is no argument against this.

"And the Word became flesh and dwelt among us, and we have seen his glory, glory as of the only Son from the Father, full of grace and truth" (Jn. 1:14, ESV).

In addition to salvation through Christ alone, we can see that Jesus came "full of *truth* and grace." This would expand the simplistic definition of the gospel of salvation (as the only meaning for truth) to include everything we know about Jesus and his teachings. Surely, since Jesus is full of truth, everything he did and said while on earth would have emulated *truth*. In addition to understanding what *truth* is, through the life and work of our Savior, it is imperative to see the personal action required of all of us to handle the word of truth. We can only see this valid truth by reading about all that Jesus taught us. We can't gloss over the hard parts, the weird parts, or the inconvenient parts. We can't ignore scriptures that go against popular "doctrine" or other fads. The scriptures are, in and of themselves, complete!

"You shall not add to the word which I am commanding you nor take away from it that you may keep the commandments of the Lord your God which I command you" (Deut. 4:2, NASB).

"Whatever I command you, you shall be careful to do; you shall not add to nor take *anything* away from it" (Deut. 12:32, NASB).

"I testify to everyone who hears the words of the prophecy of this book: if anyone adds to them, God will add to him the plagues that are written in this book" (Rev. 22:18, NASB).

Now that it's been settled that we have to look at all scripture and neither avoid nor skip any parts (Mt. 5:18 and 24:35; Rev. 22:19), let us look further at what is said about *truth*. Paul refers to the word as *truth*.

"Do your best to present yourself to God as one approved, a worker who does not need to be ashamed and who correctly handles the word of truth" (2 Tim. 2:15, NIV).

This scriptural reference commands us to present ourselves *to God* properly with behavior in line with the commandments of Christ.

"So Jesus said to the Jews who had believed him, 'If you abide in my word, you are truly my disciples, and you will know the truth, and the truth will set you free'" (Jn. 8:31–32, ESV).

Bingo! There is a way to know what truth is! This brings us full circle to the fact that we must get into our Bibles (which are true) and learn the ways of Jesus Christ (who is truth), how he lived (by truth), and what he taught us (which is truth). To do this, we can come to know the *truth* and be set free ourselves.

Doesn't this, therefore, beg the question, how do we know the precepts of Jesus Christ to become set free in the knowledge of *truth* if we are supposed to focus on an abstract relationship with Christ and not works? We can't! James, half-brother to Jesus, addressed this very idea in James 2:18–20, ESV "But someone will say, 'You have faith and I have works.' Show me your faith apart from your works, and I will show you my faith by my works. You believe that God is one. You do well. Even the demons believe and shudder! Do you want to be shown, you foolish person, that faith apart from works is useless?"

You see, we have no relationship with our Father without saving faith in Jesus Christ, but we have no saving faith in Christ if we are not driven to obey him. 2 John 1:6, ESV explains this by telling us, "And this is love that we walk according to his commandments. This is the commandment just as you have heard from the beginning so that you should walk in it."

I've ridden horses since I was a kid. They were all broke to ride before I ever met them, but as I got older, I started learning to break horses. I had found a way to go about training that included a form of gentling. It's a technique with many names that I personally call "joining up." I can take a green horse (untrained) into a round pen about 50 or 60 feet in diameter and start moving him around the pen. I have a plastic grocery bag tied to the end of a stick or a stick with a rope string, and I used that stick to drive the animal forward, just by holding it up and using his natural instinct to run from the bag. Round and round the pen he went. There are natural drive lines I can stand in to turn the horse around without any training necessary. He's likely to turn with his rear end swinging in the wrong direction, but he's going to turn, and I can fix that later. Now, depending on the horse, this can take ten minutes or a month of sessions before the "joining up" happens, but when it does, you know! After enough running and turning, the horse starts to realize I'm not such a bad human and turns in toward me. Once we've joined up, the horse will follow me around. If I run straight and cut to the left quickly, so will he. If I walk, he will walk; if I run, he will trot behind me. I can back up, and he will back up. We're joined up, like we trained for a beautiful synchronized dance.

Now, I have his attention, his affection, and most importantly, his trust. I could love on a horse and pet him, groom him, and get him to stand me being around him, but it's not the same as this joining up process. A horse that acts like he likes my petting and loving on him isn't a "joined up" horse. Once a horse is joined up, I can open the gate, and that horse will still follow me rather than leave the pen. One I haven't worked with in this way will leave me in a New-York minute and head for greener pastures. The joined-up horse and I have formed a bond and a relationship though. There have been only two other horses in my lifetime of riding that have built that bond with me outside of joining up, but it took much longer to build that trust and relationship.

This joined-up relationship is like that which we have when we repent and turn to Christ for salvation. When we turn in toward him, trusting him, giving him our attention and our affection, it's like we've joined up with him. We have faith in him and now obey and follow.

You see, when we have a relationship with Christ, we are dedicated to obey and follow him.

There are a dozen verses that declare that the love for God is the obedience of his commandments. Obedience of the commandments are a work, an action that man must actively follow. "My son, if you will receive my words And treasure my commandments within you, Make your ear attentive to wisdom, Incline your heart to understanding; For if you cry for discernment, lift your voice for understanding; If you seek her as silver And search for her as for hidden treasures; Then you will discern the fear of the LORD And discover the knowledge of God. For the LORD gives wisdom; From His mouth *come* knowledge and understanding. He stores up sound wisdom for the upright; *He is* a shield to those who walk in integrity, Guarding the paths of justice, And He preserves the way of His godly ones. Then you will discern righteousness and justice And equity *and* every good course. For wisdom will enter your heart And knowledge will be pleasant to your soul; Discretion will guard you, Understanding will watch over you, To deliver you from the way of evil" (Prov. 2:1–12, NIV).

Christianity isn't a passive religion. Just like the joined-up horse, Christians should be following their master and mimicking his steps. The truth that will set us free is obedience to the laws of Christ. God is full of grace and mercy. We don't do anything to deserve salvation. Jesus died for us when we were still sinners and unable to live in truth, but we have a promise from our Savior that the truth will set us free.

We've discovered what truth is, but what is it that we're free from? What is this freedom in Christ? Heading straight back into the word of God, we can find a very telling verse in Psalms. "I will walk about in freedom, for I have sought out your precepts" (Ps. 119:45, NIV).

I'm seeing a direct connection to the believer seeking out God's will just as we have already found as we pursued truth. Using the same "if-then" logic, "If we seek out God's precepts, then God gives us freedom," it's easy to see how the truth will set us free.

"So Jesus said to the Jews who had believed him, 'If you abide in my word, you are truly my disciples, and you will know the truth, and the truth will set you free'" (Jn. 8:31–32, ESV).

Clearly, our Father in heaven wants us well-acquainted with his Scriptures. There are great benefits in reading and searching. Seeking and obeying God is consistently the "if" part of all the promises and encouraging verses we can find. Let's look a little closer at what freedom is though. We know how to get this freedom, but what is it? Typically, freedom is "the condition or right of being able or allowed to do, say, think, etc. whatever you want to, without being controlled or limited" (https://dictionary.cambridge.org/dictionary/english/freedom).

If we gain freedom once we seek God's precepts, does this mean we are, therefore, free to do as we want? Is this what the era of grace is all about? It seems that seeking God's will, his precepts, and truth lead us to living lives of righteousness. How then are we free? Galatians 5:1 sheds more light on this freedom: "It is for freedom that Christ has set us free. Stand firm, then, and do not let yourselves be burdened again by a yoke of slavery."

Our freedom is from a master of sin in our lives. Our master is Christ when we are believers. We are not controlled by sin. We're changed beings. We will follow our Savior; even when the gate has been left open and the temptation of the world with "greener pastures" tries to lure us away, we stay close to the heels of our Lord. It is a literal change, not a figurative one to call "spiritual."

Christ is in us and saved us from living in darkness. We can rejoice not just because we are automatically free and righteous before our Father, but instead because Christ has made it possible to resist sinning and live righteously.

"So Jesus said to the Jews who had believed him, 'If you abide in my word, you are truly my disciples, and you will know the truth, and the truth will set you free'" (Jn. 8:31–32, ESV).

This verse that we've set out to uncover is set up with an "if" of its own: "If you abide in my word (hold to my teachings)…"

For several years, I battled with the concept of what these verses meant and what I needed to do specifically to comply with them. I printed the Old Testament Law, followed seventh-day Sabbath, dietary law, and all the others that were written for the common Jew to follow. I'm not Jewish, or not very Jewish anyway. I've always considered myself a Gentile, but I wanted to love God, so I felt as though I had to follow the law. I spoke to other pastors and heard many explain that we aren't under the old law, but there were too many verses about following commandments; I couldn't figure out anything else it could have been referring to, so I made sure to have food prepared in a Crock-Pot on the sixth day before sundown, laundry done, and all the household chores so I wasn't working on Sabbath. I did studies in the Bible to find what was suitable for observance and even went so far as to figure out the solar-lunar calendar that some covenant keepers believed was the true calendar to follow for Sabbath keeping, which meant that Sabbath started jumping around. New months had to do with new moons etc.

I did this because I wanted to love God and could not find any way around it though I dared pastors and Bible scholars to prove me wrong so I didn't have to adhere to so many rules no one else around me did. I still wrestle with what to do about Sabbath; however, I do know that "There remains, then, a Sabbath rest for the people of God. For whoever enters God's rest also rests from his own work, just as God did from His. Let us, therefore, make every effort to enter that rest, so that no one will fall by following the same pattern of disobedience" (Heb. 4:9–11, BSB). When Christ told us in in Mark 2:27–28, ESV "…'The Sabbath was made for man, not man for the Sabbath. So the Son of Man is Lord even of the Sabbath," it was not permission to drop the fourth commandment. In fact, when God authored Hebrews, he made sure to include the detail that we are to rest from our own work, just as God did himself. Many want to use this commandment as another attempt to claim following it would mean we are "earning our way to salvation." The logic behind this would mean that we are not to follow Christ and his example then or to love God because loving God is through obedience to his commandments.

One of the ways I'd organize my findings was writing in colored markers on canvas or large pieces of paper with verses all pertaining to the subject so I could see them all together and start putting it together. I have one such word picture I put together a year ago either in defense or to dismantle some idea that I pulled off the wall near my desk. I hung it over my bed so I'd have some quick references to verses as we went through the study for this book. 1 Corinthians 9:21, NLT jumped off the page at me. It was in my own handwriting, but I hadn't seen it like this before now: "When I am with the Gentiles who do not follow the Jewish law, I, too, live apart from that law so I can bring them to Christ. But I do not ignore the law of God. I obey the law of Christ."

The law of Christ is separate from the Jewish law. The verse written below this one on my scripture word picture is in Galatians 6:2, ESV "Bear one another's burdens and so fulfill the law of Christ." Finally, I could see that Jewish law was not the commandments referred to for obedience. It is "the law of Christ." "Not ignoring the law of God" is obedience to the "law of Christ." Now I had to know what the law of Christ was so I could be sure to be obedient to this.

It made me think of the scripture about the Pharisees asking Christ what the most important commandment was. "'Teacher, which is the great commandment in the Law?' And He said to him, '*"You shall love the Lord your God with all your heart, and with all your soul, and with all your mind."* This is the great and foremost commandment. The second is like it, *"You shall love your neighbor as yourself."* On these two commandments depend the whole Law and the Prophets'" (Mt. 22:36–40, BSB).

A greater picture developed in my mind. We must love the Lord God with all our being—to love him is to follow the commandments, and to follow the commandments is to love your neighbor as yourself (the whole law depends on these two commandments). It doesn't mean we love God by singing songs to him, smile at our neighbors when we see them, and do away with all the other requirements given to us by the Creator of the universe. He emphasized the whole law depends on these two commandments to show us that we can't obey any of his commandments without loving God and our neighbor as ourself. To love our neighbor means that serving others is our Christian duty and means of obeying Christ's commandments. Incidentally, I do have another word picture complete with colorful verses about what loving our neighbor means, including Jesus's answer that *everyone*, even the despised Samaritans, are our neighbors (Lk. 10:29–37).

In fact, when I looked this verse up to use here, I found that the three verses leading up to this story of the Samaritan is Luke's version of the previously quoted scripture in Matthew.

"One day an expert in the law stood up to test Him. 'Teacher,' he asked, 'what must I do to inherit eternal life?' 'What is written in the Law?' Jesus replied. 'How do you read it?' He answered, 'Love the Lord your God with all your heart and with all your soul and with all your strength and with all your mind and love your neighbor as yourself.' 'You have answered correctly,' Jesus said. 'Do this and you will live'" (Lk. 10:25–28, BSB).

It isn't actually as challenging a piece to put together as I first thought. It's in black and white in Luke. Jesus's reply, asking "How do you read it?" shows me that he's looking for a different interpretation than was commonly thought. Jesus is telling the Pharisees, whose purpose for existence was to follow the letter of the law, without belief in Christ, and with pride and arrogance and with additional rules and laws added by them for others to follow or be penalized, that a person loving his neighbor as himself will receive eternal life.

A new truth formed in my mind immediately as I progressed from this section of scripture. In Matthew 7:21–23, BSB Jesus makes a strong statement, "Not everyone who says to Me 'Lord, Lord,' will enter the kingdom of heaven, but only he who does the will of My Father in heaven. Many will say to Me on that day, 'Lord, Lord, did we not prophesy in Your name, and in Your name drive out demons and perform many miracles?' Then I will tell them plainly, 'I never knew you; depart from Me, you workers of lawlessness!'"

Notice that Jesus says many will say they "prophesied, drove out demons, and performed miracles." The two greatest commandments are absent here. These people did not follow the law of Christ in obedience to the commandments to love God with their whole heart, soul, or mind, and they didn't bear one another's burdens or love one another as they love themselves.

We have identified the truth to be in Christ, in his teachings, and in our following his teachings and commandments. We know that we can only love God if we follow his commandments and that Paul explained in 1 Corinthians and Galatians that he didn't have to follow Jewish law to be following Christ's law, but it is to love God and to carry our neighbor's burdens that fulfilled the law and commandments.

This isn't the end though. There is another part to this verse we reference that is important not to overlook or skip. It goes as follows: "On these two commandments depend the whole Law and the Prophets" (Mt. 22:40). You see, there are 1,050 teachings in the New Testament. Some are doubles, so that number can shrink to about 800. These teachings, when followed, make us the most burden-sharing, neighbor-loving, following-God-with-our-whole-heart Christians around. Without these, we don't love our neighbors, but without "joining up" with our Savior and becoming saved Christians, we can't carry this burden either, much as the Pharisees found as they tried to follow the Old Testament Law on their own apart from God's saving power. Following the law and man-made requirements were burdensome without the saving grace of Christ. The Ten Commandments are referenced by Christ and must be included for obedience's sake.

> You shall have no other gods before Me.
> You shall not make for yourself an idol in the form of anything in the heavens above, on the earth below, or in the waters beneath. You shall not bow down to them or worship them; for I, the LORD your God, am a jealous God, visiting the iniquity of the fathers on their children to the third and fourth generations of those who hate Me, but showing

loving devotion to a thousand generations of those who love Me and keep My commandments.

You shall not take the name of the Lord your God in vain, for the Lord will not leave anyone unpunished who takes His name in vain.

Remember the Sabbath day by keeping it holy. Six days you shall labor and do all your work, but the seventh day is a Sabbath to the Lord your God, on which you must not do any work—neither you, nor your son or daughter, nor your manservant or maidservant or livestock, nor the foreigner within your gates. For in six days, the Lord made the heavens and the earth and the sea and all that is in them, but on the seventh day He rested. Therefore the Lord blessed the Sabbath day and set it apart as holy.

Honor your father and mother, so that your days may be long in the land that the Lord your God is giving you.

You shall not murder.

You shall not commit adultery.

You shall not steal.

You shall not bear false witness against your neighbor.

You shall not covet your neighbor's house. You shall not covet your neighbor's wife, or his manservant or maidservant, or his ox or donkey, or anything that belongs to your neighbor. (Ex. 20:3–17, BSB)

You see, we can't have false idols or speak of our Lord's name in vain and love him with our whole heart. We can't love everyone else (our neighbor) as ourselves if we don't honor our parents, murder, commit adultery, steal, lie about someone, or wish we had our neighbor's things. This is how it hinges on the whole law; not that these are done away with so we can "love our neighbor" in our own abstract way.

"By this we know that we love the children of God, when we love God and obey his commandments. For this is the love of God, that we keep his commandments. And his commandments are not burdensome. For everyone who has been born of God overcomes the world. And this is the victory that has overcome the world—our faith" (1 Jn. 5:2–4, ESV).

This brings us right back to the point we found earlier. Christianity is not a passive religion. We must live with eternal lives. Righteousness is part of truth. "And put on the new self, which in the likeness of God has been created in righteousness and holiness of the truth" (Eph. 4:24, NASB).

We cannot be sucked into a false religion that stops us from obeying the One who created us and all the plans he made for us to adhere to by claiming the obedience of such is "earning salvation" and, therefore, wrong. God said we are saved through faith in Christ and repentance of our sins, with a result of changed lives and righteousness. God gave us Holy Scriptures to read so that we'd know what to live by and a Holy Spirit within so that we'd have the law written on our hearts. We care about obedience and works because God said to. The Mosaic law can never save us—doing good deeds can't either—but when we love God, we obey his commandments, and it is not burdensome, and good works flow naturally.

One last scripture that seemed to jump right off my colorful page of verse came from Romans chapter 2. It is an overview of the law, of righteousness, of the truth, and of eternal life that seems to be a good summary of our own findings.

> God will repay each one according to his deeds. To those who, by perseverance in doing good, seek glory, honor, and immortality, He will give eternal life. But for those who are self-seeking and who reject the truth and follow wickedness, there will be wrath and anger. There will be trouble and distress for every human being who does

evil, first for the Jew, then for the Greek; but glory, honor, and peace for everyone who does good, first for the Jew, then for the Greek. For God does not show favoritism. All who sin apart from the law will also perish apart from the law, and all who sin under the law will be judged by the law. For it is not the hearers of the law who are righteous before God, but it is the doers of the law who will be declared righteous. Indeed, when Gentiles, who do not have the law, do by nature what the law requires, they are a law to themselves even though they do not have the law. So they show that the work of the law is written on their hearts, their consciences also bearing witness, and their thoughts either accusing or defending them on the day when God will judge men's secrets through Christ Jesus, as proclaimed by my gospel. (Rom. 2:6–16, BSB)

Chapter 3

Who Has Righteousness?

Blessed are those who hunger and thirst for righteousness, for they shall be satisfied.
—Matthew 5:6, NASB

When we fall into the depraved idea that we live in "the era of grace" and God has already forgiven us for our sins of past, present, and future so we don't really have to do anything else but "get saved," we deny the we need to live righteous lives. When we subscribe to the notion that "Jesus cleanses us and makes us as righteous just because we asked for forgiveness but are to still go on living as the sinners we were before we were born again because "only Jesus is perfect," we strip ourselves of the very salvation we thought we had.

"What then shall we say? Shall we continue in sin so that grace may increase? Certainly not! How can we who died to sin live in it any longer?" (Rom. 6:1–2, BSB)

"Although by this time you ought to be teachers, you need someone to reteach you the basic principles of God's word. You need milk, not solid food! For everyone who lives on milk is still an infant, inexperienced in the message of righteousness" (Heb. 5:12–13, BSB). "So let us stop going over the basic teachings about Christ again and again. Let us go on instead and become mature in our understanding. Surely we don't need to start again with the fundamental importance of repenting from evil deeds and placing our faith in God" (Heb. 6:1, NLT).

Ouch. That is some serious toe stomping going on in those verses. Believers who need the elementary truths of God's word to be taught all over again are called babies. The verse in Hebrews specifies that the vital teaching of repenting from evil deeds and placing our faith in God are just the fundamentals of Christianity, the starting place.

Immature Christians are said to *not* be acquainted with the teachings of righteousness. Shouldn't we all want to be mature believers? Matthew 5:6 tells us to hunger and thirst for righteousness. These are action words, not passive, sit-there-and-receive-it type statements.

1 John 1:8–9 (NIV) tells us that "if we claim to be without sin, we deceive ourselves and the truth is not in us. If we confess our sins, he is faithful and just and will forgive us our sins and purify us from all unrighteousness."

Not only will confession of sin purify us from all unrighteousness but "all Scripture is God-breathed and is useful for teaching, rebuking, correcting and training in righteousness" (2 Tim. 3:16, NIV). Therefore, we need to read our Bibles to know what sin is to confess and repent from it as well as for the training in righteousness. This training is key in understanding that righteousness isn't a one-size-fits-all believers covering that falls on us the moment we repent. We are cleansed when we repent. God sees us as believers and free from sin and righteous, but there is a need for training in righteousness to keep us from adding more sins to ourselves simply because God told us to be righteous in our lives as believers. Don't get me wrong; we will still be forgiven for the sins we commit after we become believers. "My little children, I am writing these things to you so that you may not sin. But if anyone does sin, we have an advocate with the Father, Jesus Christ the righteous" (1 Jn. 2:1, ESV). Our Father in heaven remembers our sins no more, but we aren't saved to live like unsaved people. That isn't the point of salvation.

The horses I trained were bonded with me. They didn't automatically know how to tote a rider around for any equestrian discipline though. The difference with these horses and those who were not yet joined up is I had their trust and attention on me. I could easily take them back into the pen and teach them to ride much faster than the old traditional methods of cowboys riding out the buck and wearing them out into submission. I could also go out into a field of horses, and my joined-up horses would come to follow me. They didn't fit in with the other horses in that way. There was a difference, but only a subtle one. We had a relationship, but that was all. I want my horses to come to me, but I'm joining up with them to build a trust needed in foundation to learning so much more.

God wants our trust so that we will seek him and learn so much more. Just as a newly joined-up horse is not disciplined in equestrian training, neither is the believer who doesn't ever go beyond the initial prayer for salvation. I couldn't send a horse straight from the round pen and into the stables for a trail ride or an equestrian event any better than expecting new believers can instantly claim righteousness without doing anything to develop that.

You see, when we are genuinely repentant and make Christ Lord of our lives, we receive eternal life and salvation. Without going into the argument of once saved always saved or one can lose his salvation, we have to realize that the righteousness of our salvation is different than living righteous lives. When we're saved, we want to obey Christ. We have a drive to do the will of our Father in heaven, but we need our Bibles to train us in these ways.

As we saw in the last chapter, there are eight hundred commands listed in the New Testament alone, all of which are there to instruct us, teach us, rebuke us, and correct us. You see, just because we're saved doesn't mean we are automatically living righteous lives unless we actively seek out our Father's will within his word and faithfully walk out the law that he has written on our hearts. "So they show that the work of the law is written on their hearts, their consciences also bearing witness, and their thoughts either accusing or defending them" (Rom. 2:15, BSB). And we can't call our postconversion, sin-stained lives righteous just because we're saved. In other words, being saved is not the act of becoming righteous. Being saved gives us the Holy Spirit in us to help us live righteously. "I say to the Lord, 'You are my Lord; I have no good apart from you'" (Ps. 16:2, ESV).

"I will ask the Father, and He will give you another Helper, that He may be with you forever; that is the Spirit of truth, whom the world cannot receive, because it does not see Him or know Him, but you know Him because He abides with you and will be in you" (Jn. 14:16–17, NASB).

You see, salvation gives us power to live as Christ lived. We get a holy helper, who is the spirit of truth, abiding in us! We can live righteously by the power of God. The Holy Ghost, given by the Father, through the Son, is the missing element in a nonbeliever, who apart from God has no good. We are not apart from God once we believe. When we read that following the commandments are not burdensome, we can be assured that walking in the light with God is not going to be burdensome.

I speak to my tired and burned-out brethren and remind you to drink from the living water. Do not cast away your hope in Christ because you're tired. Are you tired because you've overburdened your lives with what the world says you need to have and do? Christ tells us not to be conformed by this world. Are there things to cut out of your life so that you can live in Christ instead of the world? Being burned out is a warning to you so that you look to God, not forsake him and take the easy road calling it "grace from him."

Our Bibles tell us clearly that when we repent, through faith in Christ that our sins are forgiven and not remembered as far as the east is from the west, they are remembered no more, and we are washed and dressed in white robes. Our Father sees us through "rose-colored glasses" if you will. There is a Jesus filter. He is the one who took the punishment for our sins as though he committed them, and we are free from the sins of our old selves.

Imagine having a credit card and owing lots of money with a high-interest rate on it. It's so high you won't manage to pay it back in full in a lifetime. Then you head to the mailbox and find a letter among your mail with an offer you can't believe! Your balance will be paid in full by someone else. The conditions are that you're not to use credit cards again; you'll be given an app or a manual to instruct you on spending within your budget, and if you put your faith in this method, use the app, and search in the manual to learn how to make good financial choices, you should stay debt-free.

Christ's death for us is very similar to this offer. We get our debts covered by Christ and are no longer held responsible for them in an eternal viewpoint. Some people will still have earthly consequences for their poor choices, but as far as God is concerned, the sins are forgiven eternally.

Like the credit-card debt offer, we have strings attached to Christianity. There are conditions. Our culture has gotten too desperate to convert others to Christianity and boost numbers in churches that no one wants to admit there are any requirements outside of the initial salvation. They like to lure nonbelievers in with promises of salvation as well as a "come as you are and stay as you are" approach to make everyone comfortable. The truth is, these numbers for converts who make no changes dilute the actual numbers. Likewise, teaching new believers that apologizing for sins is all they have to do, period, keeps a person from true conversion.

When we looked at what sin is, we saw many examples listed. We see strong statements that tell us that those who are in these sins will not inherit eternal life. It would be ludicrous to believe that our Savior came to die on the cross to forgive the sins of only those who ask for it but everyone can continue to act just like the nonbelievers who haven't come to this faith and keep sinning. The only difference between saved and non-saved can't possibly be that one has asked forgiveness and the other has not (believers are called to repent, not just apologize).

Paul is the author of thirteen books in the New Testament of the Bible (possibly fourteen if he wrote Hebrews). He was born Saul of Tarsus, of the Tribe of Benjamin, and was a Pharisee. He came from a well-to-do family and was highly educated, and prior to his miraculous conversion on the road to Damascus recorded in Acts 9:1–19, 22:6–21, and 26:12–18, he was a murderer who pledged to imprison all the new Christian believers. As a new believer, his entire character instantly changed. He became an apostle of Christ. Recorded in the books he penned, which were originally letters to various churches of his time, he repeatedly compelled believers to live righteously.

Throughout his teachings, he implores believers to press on, endure, and to follow his example. "Remind them to be submissive to rulers and authorities, to be obedient, to be ready for every good work, to speak evil of no one, to avoid quarreling, to be gentle, and to show perfect courtesy toward all people. For we ourselves were once foolish, disobedient, led astray, slaves to various passions and pleasures, passing our days in malice and envy, hated by others and hating one another. But when the goodness and loving kindness of God our Savior appeared, he saved us, not because of works done by us in righteousness, but according to his own mercy, by the washing of regeneration and renewal of the Holy Spirit, whom he poured out on us richly through Jesus Christ our Savior, so that being justified by his grace we might become heirs according to the hope of eternal life. The saying is trustworthy, and I want you to insist on these things, so that those who have believed in God may be careful to devote themselves to good works" (Titus 3:1–8, ESV).

If we were to read this in an accommodating voice, one might want to skip the first section and heavily emphasize on "But when the goodness and loving kindness of God our Savior appeared, he saved us, not because of works done by us in righteousness, but according to his own mercy, by the washing of regeneration and renewal of the Holy Spirit" (Titus 3:4–5, ESV) and declare that our righteousness is in Christ through Christ and by no part of our own.

In fact, this is not what Paul is stating. He's reiterating that our salvation is purely from Christ. We cannot work hard enough to earn our own salvation. There is nothing we could do to receive eternal life apart from saving faith in Christ Jesus, but the first part of this scripture is full of active participation in our lives thereafter. "Be submissive to rulers and authorities, be obedient, be ready for every good work, speak evil of no one, avoid quarreling, be gentle, and to show perfect courtesy toward all people" are all actions that would be impossible to attain if Paul were saying that Christians are only righteous because they asked God to forgive them.

The very act of repentance is "to turn from sin and dedicate oneself to the amendment of one's life and to feel regret or contrition" (https://www.merriam-webster.com/dictionary/repent).

Amendment means "correction" (https://www.merriam-webster.com/dictionary/amendment).

Therefore, repenting is the action of feeling regret for sin, a brokenness for doing wrong, and the correction of such transgressions. Obviously, repentance requires a lifestyle change or we couldn't repent by mere definition. Without repentance, no one could come to faith in Christ. So anyone claiming to be saved and continuing to live in their sins or preaching such lacks true conversion because they lack "repentance."

By no means is the definition "changing one's mind about the identity and finished work of Jesus" (Andrew Farley, *Twisted Scripture: Untangling 45 Lies Christians Have Been Told*, May 2019. Salem Books, Washington, DC).

When Paul gives instruction for Christian living, he is not speaking in hypotheticals or in riddles. We are saved by faith in Christ who died for our sins and are forgiven our debt, but like the credit-card agreement we spoke of earlier, there are conditions required. If we gratefully took the payment for our cards and did not do away with our credit cards and racked the balance up again, we aren't "repenting" from anything. That is not to say that we can never sin again once we are saved, but look at how John explains it in 1 John 2:1, "My little children, I am writing these things to you so that you may not sin. But if anyone does sin, we have an advocate with the Father, Jesus Christ the righteous."

In fact, John elaborated later in this same book, telling us, "For this is the love of God, that we keep his commandments. And his commandments are not burdensome" (1 Jn. 5:3).

We've looked at what these commandments are through 1 Corinthians 9:21 and Galatians 6:2, but there is also another that expounds on what the commandments are not. 1 Corinthians 7:19 tells us, "For neither circumcision counts for anything nor uncircumcision, but keeping the commandments of God." Circumcision is a Jewish law (Mosaic law). It was a requirement of the Jews prior to the new covenant. Paul is once again telling us to follow the commandments of God. It's important to me because I spent so much time trying to figure out if I had to follow Mosaic law within my salvation in order to love God. Clearly, this is not the case and not because we are such rotten human beings that we can't possibly do anything right and only through our salvation are we washed and, therefore, righteous by this one act in God's divine eyes only, we have been given the Holy Spirit of God to be able to follow his non-burdensome commandments, such as being submissive to rulers and authorities, being obedient, being ready for every good work, speaking evil of no one, avoiding quarreling, being gentle, and showing perfect courtesy toward all people. Take stock in the fact that our Father isn't requiring something that is impossible or theoretical. Hold firmly to your Christian membership card and utilize the perks of salvation from a God who loves us so much, who is all-powerful and able to give us what we need within, to live lives unto him in righteousness.

When you read about Paul telling us to live righteously, remember, you are a child of God and a member of his family who can "do all things through Christ who strengthens (*dunamis*—more on this word/concept in later chapters) us" (Phil. 4:13, BSB). Paul, the man who contends that we must live righteously, also included in his letter to the Philippians a reminder that he can do all things who strengthens him a few short verses prior to another call to believers to live righteously, specifying, "Finally, brothers, whatever is true, whatever is honorable, whatever is right, whatever is pure, whatever is lovely, whatever is admirable—if anything is excellent or praiseworthy—think on these things. Whatever you have learned or received or heard from me, or seen in me, put it into practice. And the God of peace will be with you" (Phil. 4:8–9, BSB).

In the chapter preceding this one, Paul instructs believers to "Join one another in following my example, brothers, and carefully observe those who walk according to the pattern we set for you."

I remember as a young believer, reading and listening to sermons with Paul's epistles quoted that he came across as arrogant. In 1 Corinthians 4:3–4, NLT he said, "As for me, it matters very little how I might be evaluated by you or by any human authority. I don't even trust my own judgment on this point. My conscience is clear, but that doesn't prove I'm right. It is the Lord himself who will examine me and decides." I had to reread this passage several times because it seemed as though Paul was boasting that he had no known sin (post-conversion, obviously not over his entire life). In fact, this is what he is saying. Paul was living a life so righteously that he didn't have any known sin to himself, but he didn't discount the fact that our Father in heaven, who is all-knowing, could know of some unknown sins he was committing that he didn't know of himself. This was including in his letter to the Corinthians to make the point that we are not to waste our time comparing other Christian leaders. "If you pay attention to what I have quoted from the Scriptures, you won't be proud of one of your leaders at the expense of another" (1 Cor. 4:6, NLT).

He's really actually very humble in his letters and asserting to the Corinthians that he and Apollos are "mere servants of Christ who have been put in charge of explaining God's mysteries" (1 Cor. 4:1, NLT) and who are in fact the two leaders he's asking them not to judge or lift one up above the other. However, I'd like to look a little more closely at the fact that his conscience is clear and he knows of no sin in his life at the point of his writing this. It's an important fact I want you to remember when we get to Romans and go through some of Paul's writings from there, but I'd also like to use this now as an argument toward the literal righteous life being lived upon conversion. It's important to note that he gives the credit for this to God: "What do you have that God hasn't given you? And if everything you have is from God, why boast as though it were not a gift?" (1 Cor. 4:7, NLT)

By God, he has the power within him to live so righteously that he isn't committing any obvious sins, even to himself. This, my friends, is a far cry from what we hear from well-meaning Christians who want to sound humble and "admit they're terrible sinners too."

Paul expends a lot of his energy throughout these thirteen or fourteen books, exhorting believers, explaining God's mysteries, and directing Christians to live righteously.

"Therefore I urge you, brothers, on account of God's mercy, to offer your bodies as living sacrifices, holy and pleasing to God, which is your spiritual service of worship. Do not be conformed to this world, but be transformed by the renewing of your mind. Then you will be able to test and approve what is the good, pleasing, and perfect will of God" (Rom. 12:1–2, BSB).

Paul's preaching on righteousness is not always met with eager ears and hearts. Just as there are believers today who want to deny righteous living as part of Christianity, there were people in biblical days who also did not want to hear about it.

"After some days Felix came with his wife Drusilla, who was Jewish, and he sent for Paul and heard him speak about faith in Christ Jesus. And as he reasoned about righteousness and self-control and the coming judgment, Felix was alarmed and said, 'Go away for the present. When I get an opportunity I will summon you'" (Acts 24:24–25, ESV).

In this passage, it is essential to note that righteousness and self-control were spoken of regarding salvation in Christ Jesus. And just like there are so many in today's times, Felix didn't want to know about this part. He wanted the free gift of salvation from hell, but he didn't want the contingency that goes along with it. He sent Paul away and pulled a modern day "don't call me, I'll call you" because he didn't want to offer his body as a living sacrifice. He didn't want to change his worldly ways and be holy and pleasing to God. I guess we can give Felix the credit for not faking it and saying a prayer with Paul for forgiveness with no intention of changing a thing about his fleshly self. He also didn't redefine the doctrine of grace or repentance to claim salvation with *no* good deeds to follow flaunting a false humility in the Savior. Felix didn't give our modern excuse either, "that God knows we are human and are going to stay in our flesh, sinning, but he loves us anyway!"

Paul was a stark advocate for righteousness. He lived in such a way that if he was sinning, it wasn't evident even to himself, let alone others. He gave up his old life of prosperity to spread the whole gospel, which included righteousness and self-control, as well as the future coming judgment. The confidence he has in himself is strong as he holds so powerfully to the rule of God in his life through his salvation. In 1 Corinthians 11:1, he says, "You are to imitate me, just as I imitate Christ." When I was a child, this confidence seemed conceited. As I search and seek my Father's face, instead I see a role model who gave up his own life to serve the Savior, whom he had previously murdered and jailed others for following.

We've spent so much time talking about Paul and getting to know him in this chapter as we work our way through righteousness. There is another portion of Scripture, also written by Paul, that will help to describe how a believer is given a gift or perk that nonbelievers do not share: "What then shall we say in response to these things? If God is for us, who can be against us? He who did not spare His own Son but gave Him up for us all, how will He not also, along with Him, freely give us all things?" (Rom. 8:31–32, NIV)

We have received power from God through our salvation in Christ. We must not only know that God gives this freely, but we must seek after it, ask for it, and receive it.

"Now we have received not the spirit of the world but the Spirit who is from God that we might understand the things freely given us by God. And we impart this in words not taught by human wisdom but taught by the Spirit, interpreting spiritual truths to those who are spiritual. The natural person does not accept the things of the Spirit of God for they are folly to him, and he is not able to understand them because they are spiritually discerned. The spiritual person judges all things but is himself to be judged by no one. "For who has understood the mind of the Lord so as to instruct him? But we have the mind of Christ" (1 Cor. 2:12–16, ESV).

We are members of God's kingdom. We are sons and daughters of the Most High God. He has given us understanding that only believers with the Spirit of God living inside of them could comprehend. Hallelujah, we have the mind of Christ! The truth has set us free. We are free indeed—free to live for God in victoriously righteous lives that will be pleasing to Yahweh—to the One who spoke everything into existence.

Well-meaning ministers with good-intentioned hearts preach about how they mess up so badly and sin all the time. Some talk about their lives and how if we knew how much they sinned, we'd not want them to preach or generally state that they are probably the worst sinner in the bunch. I've heard one preacher talk about how glad he was that he didn't have to be perfect or even try to be and go into a story about "all the years he'd tried but realized that God doesn't want him to be and he's so glad he serves a perfect Savior who was perfect so he doesn't have to be."

Christians are by no means perfect beings upon conversion. They were once sinners in need of a Savior who received grace and truth from the Lord though. Humanity can't be good on its own; this is why we are given the strength and wisdom needed to do so. There needs to be a mindset shift. We need to realize that we don't have to go on sinning. Life is full of grays. Many times, we will have moments when things get tough. Interactions with other people can go sour, we can be part of circumstances, or need to make decisions that we can't pull a specific verse that speaks of our exact issue about. Then what do we do? We pray for God's wisdom. We pray for the Holy Spirit to intercede. When we've been absorbing our minds with scriptures and genuinely prayerful to the Father, we can submit ourselves to him.

I've said many times, "This is hard! I'm not sure how to handle this disagreement or what to decide for the kids. God, help me. Fill me with wisdom that I will speak the words you would have me speak, use the tone you know I should use, and decide the way you want it to be." When we turn our lives over to God and lay it in his hands regularly, dealing with the challenges become easier. This is from our God! This is grace and mercy for people who couldn't follow after God without him explicitly giving us the ability to; all we have to do is ask him.

I hear Paul quoted regularly, "This saying is trustworthy and deserving of full acceptance: 'Christ Jesus came into the world to save sinners,'—and I am the worst of them" (1 Tim. 1:15). The problem with using this is that Paul was jailing Christians and had overseen the murder of Steven before he was on the road to Damascus and saved by God! He was the worst of them as a nonbeliever. He wasn't bragging that as a believer he was the worst sinner yet!

The whole point Paul is trying to make in this scripture is that if the worst of the worst sinners, such as himself, can be saved, so can anyone be saved! It isn't in the Bible so that Christians can quote it from the pulpit or leading small group as their "current" state of being so that everyone can feel better about keeping their sinful natures intact even after conversion or that the speaker can parade his false humility. Inadvertently, by lowering ourselves (as believers) to fleshly beings, sinners of the worst kind, as if it's a contest to admit who is the worst strips the power of Christ away. It makes our God out to be powerless and our salvation only a get-out-of-hell card. This stance creates a doctrine that heralds man's flesh, and his sin nature is too powerful for Christ's death to overcome essentially, stripping the omnipotence of God.

Another verse used incorrectly comes from Romans 7:14–20. Before we dive in, it's important to know that this may be one of the most controversial sections of scripture in the Bible. For over three hundred years after the Romans crucified Christ, the verses in question were accepted and thought to be Paul's description of an unregenerate Christian. Augustine was the first to see this scripture as referring to saved Christians instead, then Luther and Calvin both propelled this perspective forward in their own theological assessments, and few have deviated from it since. It's a tongue twister of sorts that most frequently gets remembered something like this: "I do that which I don't want to do and don't do that which I know I should." It's a pretty good summary, but what is missed is that while Paul is speaking in first person, he can't possibly be talking about himself as a converted believer. We already know that Paul is an anointed apostle of the Lord who exhorted believers to live with self-control and righteousness and warned them that they would not inherit the kingdom of God if they were not. He called believers who were not acquainted with righteousness infants! Paul even listed sins of people who needed to be avoided.

"But understand this, that in the last days there will come times of difficulty. For people will be lovers of self, lovers of money, proud, arrogant, abusive, disobedient to their parents, ungrateful, unholy, heartless, unappeasable, slanderous, without self-control, brutal, not loving good, treacherous, reckless, swollen with conceit, lovers of pleasure rather than lovers of God, having the appearance of godliness, but denying its power. Avoid such people" (2 Tim. 3:1–5, ESV).

Finally, we recall in 1 Corinthians 4:3–4 that Paul lived his life such that he was not conscious of any sin. He didn't discount that he could have unknown sin that the Father, our judge in heaven, would know about, but he, himself, has a clear conscience, which means… if Paul were speaking of himself in Romans chapter 7 as a converted believer in the Lord Jesus Christ, he'd be completely contradicting everything else he's ever preached or said of himself in all the other chapters of this book and the other letters (books) he penned.

You see, Paul is taking this chapter to talk about the law. Paul was a Pharisee from the tribe of Benjamin (Phil. 3:5) who had spent his life following Mosaic law. "The Pharisees were a group of zealous Jews who were contemporaries of Jesus Christ. They believed that the way they would please God and make it to heaven was by meticulously following a long list of religious rules and regulations (Mosaic law)" (https://www.pursuegod.org/rules-pharisees/). When we synthesize this information with the man he describes in Romans 7, he's clearly describing a man who is trying to follow the law, like a Pharisee, to earn himself a place in heaven. He was a Pharisee (past tense). He was trying to (past tense) follow the letter of the law meticulously and was not able to. He, more than any other (non-Pharisee), knows best how impossible it is for the mortal man to follow the law apart from God.

Knowing this helps us understand that when Paul said "For I know that good itself does not dwell in me, that is, in my sinful nature. For I have the desire to do what is good, but I cannot carry it out. For I do not do the good I want to do, but the evil I do not want to do—this I keep on doing" (Rom. 7:18–19) that he was speaking of a nonbeliever, either himself as a Pharisee and remembering what it was like to try to follow the letter of the law without God's helper or hypothetically of a non-regenerate, nonbeliever *but* absolutely not of himself as a converted believer of Christ saved by the blood of the Lamb.

He's making the point that trying to follow the law apart from God is impossible. He finishes this chapter by clarifying the resolution to this: "Thanks be to God, who delivers me through Jesus

Christ our Lord! So then, I myself in my mind am a slave to God's law, but in my sinful nature a slave to the law of sin" (Rom. 7:25).

Paul says, "I myself as a believer am a slave to God, as an unbeliever was a slave to sin." We bury our sinful natures upon conversion and belief. "We know that our old sinful selves were crucified with Christ so that sin might lose its power in our lives. *We are no longer slaves to sin*" (Rom. 6:6, NLV emphasis added).

Paul wrote this verse one chapter ahead of the one many quote to argue that Christians are still fleshly and battling between following the Spirit as well as their own flesh. Either believers are slaves to sin or they are not!

I don't see how it's possible to read thirteen or fourteen books written by a man who is most often thought of as overly confident in his Christianity and elaborating on how our old sinful, fleshly selves were crucified on the cross with Christ and that we ought to aspire to be a mature, spiritual Christian like himself then tell us that it's actually impossible even for the best of us Christians to live righteous lives, who are specifically no longer slaves to sin. And then move into Romans 8 (verses 1–15 specifically) and go back to his very strong stance on living by the Spirit of God, not by the flesh that is dead in Christ who saves us. That is with Christ, all things are possible, and we have his Spirit dwelling in us which saved us from being slaves to our flesh.

> There is therefore now no condemnation for those who are in Christ Jesus. For the law of the Spirit of life has set you free in Christ Jesus from the law of sin and death. For God has done what the law, weakened by the flesh, could not do. By sending his own Son in the likeness of sinful flesh and for sin, he condemned sin in the flesh. (Rom. 8:1–3, ESV)

Paul reiterates that we could not follow the law in our flesh and on our own. He reminds us that Christ condemned sin in the flesh. It's a supernatural power bestowed upon the believer to "go and sin no more." "Come to a sober and right mind, and sin no more; for some people have no knowledge of God. I say this to your shame" (1 Cor. 15:34, NRSV).

> In order that the righteous requirement of the law might be fulfilled in us, who walk not according to the flesh but according to the Spirit. For those who live according to the flesh set their minds on the things of the flesh, but those who live according to the Spirit set their minds on the things of the Spirit. For to set the mind on the flesh is death, but to set the mind on the Spirit is life and peace. (Rom. 8:4–6, ESV)

The requirement for righteousness has been fulfilled by Christ's death. We are no longer slaves to our flesh but are now spiritual. Believers have spiritual minds changed to be sent on spiritual things, not of fleshly sinful things.

> For the mind that is set on the flesh is hostile to God for it does not submit to God's law; indeed, it cannot. Those who are in the flesh cannot please God. You, however, are not in the flesh but in the Spirit, if in fact the Spirit of God dwells in you. Anyone who does not have the Spirit of Christ does not belong to him. (Rom. 8:7–9, ESV)

Paul explains that living in the flesh and living by the spirit are not choices for the believers and nonbelievers. Nonbelievers cannot submit to God's law (also referenced in Romans 7:14–20); likewise, believers cannot live in their flesh. It's one or the other. Either you are of the flesh and are a nonbeliever or you are in the Spirit and are a believer.

> But if Christ is in you, although the body is dead because of sin, the Spirit is life because of

> righteousness. If the Spirit of him who raised Jesus from the dead dwells in you, he who raised Christ Jesus from the dead will also give life to your mortal bodies through his Spirit who dwells in you. So then, brothers, we are debtors, not to the flesh, to live according to the flesh. For if you live according to the flesh you will die, but if by the Spirit you put to death the deeds of the body, you will live. (Rom. 8:10–13, ESV)

The Apostle Paul is pouring out his heart to believers, explaining that if any of them are still stuck in their fleshly lusts of their former lives, they are dead. Anyone still willing to live in their flesh will die and not receive eternal life. They are not believers. Believers cannot live according to the flesh because the Spirit of Christ gives life to mortal bodies who dwells in them. The deeds of the flesh must be put to death in our lives to live and have eternal life.

> For all who are led by the Spirit of God are sons of God. For you did not receive the spirit of slavery to fall back into fear, but you have received the Spirit of adoption as sons, by whom we cry, "Abba! Father!" The Spirit himself bears witness with our spirit that we are children of God, and if children, then heirs—heirs of God and fellow heirs with Christ, provided we suffer with him in order that we may also be glorified with him. (Rom. 8:14–17, ESV)

Paul hasn't implored the believers to follow a faith he cannot follow himself. Paul has not contradicted himself in chapter 7 to go back to his strong stance of the power through Christ who strengthens us to be able to do all things through him. He is explaining how nonbelievers couldn't follow the law apart from God. It's a lead up to the next chapter in which he makes sure to give God the glory for all the power within us to live in the Spirit instead of in the flesh. This is where the true humility lies. *Apart from God*, I would be a terrible sinner, but because of the power of our omnipotent Abba Father, I am no longer a slave to the flesh and to sinning, and he gives me the ability to live without continuing in sin. Anyone who wants to refute this claim by asking "does that mean you never sin again after conversion?" needs to check which spirit drives him.

While Paul is making the claim and explaining that we are no longer bound to the Jewish law, we are called to righteous lives and following the law of Christ. Galatians 6:2, ESV says, "Bear one another's burdens and so fulfill the law of Christ." We're changed creatures in Christ with the power of Christ in us. We're an empowered people now. "No temptation has overtaken you except what is common to mankind. And God is faithful; he will not let you be tempted beyond what you can bear. But when you are tempted, he will also provide a way out so that you can endure it" (1 Cor. 10:13, NIV). John lovingly assures us that we have an advocate should we slip up (1 John 1:7) but by no means does this mean we stay fleshly sinners, slaves to the temptations of this world, or bound to hell either just because of a committed sin in the life of a believer.

Finally, we should remember that Paul instructed us to in 1 Corinthians 11:1, NKJV to "imitate me, just as I imitate Christ." If Paul were struggling so much with his flesh and stuck in his sin nature, he wouldn't have been able to offer himself as anyone to mimic and certainly wouldn't have said he imitates Christ. It would have been blasphemed on his part.

Peter confirms that Paul writes with wisdom that is from God. He clarifies that the letters from Paul can be hard to understand in some parts. "Consider also that our Lord's patience brings salvation, just as our beloved brother Paul also wrote you with the wisdom God gave him. He writes this way in all his letters, speaking in them about such matters. Some parts of his letters are hard to understand, which ignorant and unstable people distort, as they do the rest of the Scriptures, to their own destruction" (2 Pet. 3:15–16, BSB).

Don't fall into the latter category and be ignorant, unstable, and distorting the scriptures. Beware the false teachers who teach that because we are no longer under the Jewish law, that we are not required to do good works either as if they are one in the same thing. Do not fall for the teachers who speak to the "tired and weary," releasing them from striving from any form of righteousness in the name of "grace" as if they've uncovered the meaning of the new covenant to mean freedom from a "gospel plus." We are not saved by our works, but without works, we have no faith. Without faith, what is our salvation in?

"The heart is deceitful above all things and beyond cure. Who can understand it? I, the Lord, search the heart; I examine the mind to reward a man according to his way, by what his deeds deserve" (Jer. 17:9–10, BSB)

The lost man has a deceitful heart. The saved man has the requirements of God written in his heart, with a moral code from the Holy Spirit of God in him to help and direct him. In this way, the saved man can be righteous but isn't righteous just because he's saved, or we wouldn't have scores of verses warning us to endure to the end or about living in the darkness and deceiving ourselves. There really is no way around these verses. We not only have a calling on our lives to live righteously, but God has given us his own Spirit to dwell within us and make it possible. It's like a special membership perk to do that which God wants us to do as Christians. Don't ever fall for the lie that Christians are free from striving for a life in Christ. If a believer is weary, it's not because they're doing wrong in doing good. "And let us not grow weary of doing good, for in due season we will reap, if we do not give up" (Gal. 6:9, ESV).

Righteousness must be sought after. As Christians, we must seek the will of our Father, work toward the laws of Christ, and accept the power of the Holy Spirit in us and the power of God to overcome, especially since our sin natures have been crucified with Christ and we are a new creation. Let us move away from immature teachings that leave us merely hanging onto Christianity as babes. Stark warnings prevail. In James 1:22, BSB it says, "Be doers of the word, and not hearers only. Otherwise, you are deceiving yourselves."

As I sit here today, editing this manuscript a final time before printing, I'm using these very scriptures to walk through difficult times. In two days, there begins a court battle against my abuser. My second husband, the father of my three boys, is waging war and using the children as weapons. There are times I feel helpless. Other times I'm angry and frustrated, but I keep coming back to one thing. My purpose on earth is to bring glory to God. I am here for him, not me. To quench anxiety, fear of the unknown, and to lift the depression associated with the continued battering from a man whom I'd like to forget exists, I remember I am a child of God. I want to love God above all else and go straight to him for his strength. My faith is in the Creator of the universe, and no temptation has overtaken me except what is common to mankind. It is in this that I have assurance that as long as I actively keep my faith in him, seeking the kingdom first and his righteousness, he promises all else will be added unto me. I'm going to hunger and thirst for righteousness all the way through to the end; and I'm going to come back to these scriptures every time I need a reminder to respond in a manner that brings glory to my Father.

Chapter 4

Saved by Faith

Faith is one of those words that we hear all the time. While we hear it, sing about it, and use the word. I'm not sure we still hold onto the value of the true definition any longer.

Someone might ask you what your "faith" is, interchanging the word for "religion." The question is asking if you are Muslim, Jewish, Christian, etc. I'm not so sure that's an accurate use of the word.

Others may conclude that a concept they can't find thorough biblical explanation for is "a faith thing." The Trinity is a hard concept to articulate and find verses to illustrate precisely, so many will conclude after trying to explain it better with an "it's a faith thing, you just have to believe it but not completely understand it."

Even more generically, people will give an encouraging statement to "have faith." Taken at face value, it sounds very scriptural and godly, but I'm not sure I know what it actually means. A person might ask for prayer that their medical tests come back clear. A well-wisher will tell her to have faith. Even after the tests come back with negative results, the same well-intentioned person will tell them to "have faith." None of these statements are bad or even wrong, but they are deeper than a statement. It's important to understand what faith is so that when someone encourages us with a "have faith," we know what it means.

In light of this most recent pandemic, there were bumper stickers, handwritten signs, Facebook posts, etc. that touted "Faith over fear." These people walked around claiming victory over the virus in faith. They didn't want to mask up, socially distance, or change anything about their lives in Christ but fully expected that their "faith over fear" was going to save them.

I suppose on a very surface level of thinking, we could listen to all these encouraging peddlers of faith and be energized with hope. But what exactly is our hope in?

Our hope is in Christ, right? Haven't we heard this throughout our Christian lives when we look at inspirational verses, calendars, etc. "in Christ we have hope"? (1 Cor. 15:19) This is only part of the actual verse though. It literally starts with the word "if," and we know how much I like to find those "if-then statements." Let's look at the whole thing. "If in Christ we have hope in this life only, we are of all people most to be pitied" (1 Cor. 15:19, ESV).

In this chapter, Paul rebuked and admonished the Corinthians for saying that there is no resurrection of the dead. He laid out the gospel again and articulating that without Christ's raising from the dead, we would be believing in vain and our faith would be in nothing. The conclusion would be that if we only have hope in Christ for this life only, then we are so wrong about our salvation and should be pitied for following after a dead man. Instead, we serve a risen Savior, God's only Son, and we have hope in him for eternal life and for the crucifixion of our own flesh. "Wake up from your drunken stupor, as is right, and do not go on sinning. For some have no knowledge of God. I say this to your shame" (1 Cor. 15:34, ESV).

If hope is part of faith and our hope is in Christ, as a risen Savior, we must "rejoice in hope …" (Rom. 12:12).

We can sing and dance around in exuberance that Christ is our salvation and in him we have hope, which is a part of faith, then we have to know what we are rejoicing over. We can rejoice in the fact that we've been saved from the fire of hell, but we've already looked at the fact that salvation is far greater than where we spend eternity. We know we have to live out eternal lives and be righteous through the power of the Spirit of God and the transformation we are granted having our sins forgiven and our flesh crucified with Christ. "So you also must consider yourselves dead to sin and alive to God in Christ Jesus" (Rom. 6:11, ESV).

This is a hope we can rejoice in! It's a faith we can hold onto and live by. "Let love be genuine. Abhor what is evil; hold fast to what is good. Love one another with brotherly affection. Outdo one another in showing honor. Do not be slothful in zeal, be fervent in spirit, serve the Lord. Rejoice in hope, be patient in tribulation, be constant in prayer. Contribute to the needs of the saints and seek to show hospitality" (Rom. 12:9–13, ESV).

"We remember before our God and Father your work produced by faith, your labor prompted by love, and your endurance inspired by hope in our Lord Jesus Christ" (1 Thess. 1:3, NIV).

When an encourager is telling us to have faith in the face of scary medical tests or some other disaster, or situation, we must remember who we are in Christ and what our responsibilities as his follower are. We do our part. We hold onto our faith in spite of what's happening to us or around us and trust in our Father for his part of the promise to be fulfilled. He is our strength. We look to him for strength. We can find peace that passes all understanding when we remain faithful to him.

"But the salvation of the righteous is from the Lord; He is their strength in time of trouble" (Ps. 37:39, KJB).

"What shall we say, then? That Gentiles who did not pursue righteousness have attained it, that is, a righteousness that is by faith; but that Israel who pursued a law that would lead to righteousness did not succeed in reaching that law. Why? Because they did not pursue it by faith, but as if it were based on works. They have stumbled over the stumbling stone, as it is written" (Rom. 9:30–33) and yet "So also faith by itself, if it does not have works, is dead" (Jas. 2:17, ESV).

Faith without works is dead, but works without faith is also useless.

"And without faith it is impossible to please him, for whoever would draw near to God must believe that he exists and that he rewards those who seek him" (Heb. 11:6, ESV).

What then is faith?

"For the Scriptures tell us, 'Abraham believed God, and God counted him as righteous because of his faith'" (Rom. 4:3, NLT).

Believing in God, and putting trust in our Father, is what gave Abraham countenance for his faith. Before the Son of God had been born, crucified, and raised from the dead, Abraham had faith in the Creator, and the coming Savior, so sustaining that, he was counted as righteous.

There is hope in faith and trust in our Lord. If trust is part of faith, there is still more action on our part, beyond lip service in song or in declaration.

Abraham demonstrated this action of strength and trust in his faith, not just by praising God and telling him that he'd follow him (God) anywhere and going on about his own business but by actually following him anywhere. He heard the direction of God to leave his hometown of Ur and head to an unknown land that God was preparing for him. Without knowing even where he was going, he followed God as he was directed. As we think of our lives today, the comforts, the treasures we've stored up in our homes, and the ease of life and following God to another town, another home, we think of the trouble of calling a moving company or boxing up our own things and moving them into a new home, but we're not typically leaving our luxuries behind. To think of biblical days of old and Abraham in Ur, riding a camel to his new home of Canaan, where he'd continue the lifestyle of pitching tents and living the same primitive life, is actually a misnomer.

"Ur had hot and cold running water, a sewer system, multistory buildings, paved roads, major temples, ornate furniture, and a variety of metal instruments" (https://truthonlybible.com/2015/02/13/ur-of-the-chaldees-abrahams-original-home/). While he stayed in Haran, a city in route to major cities temporarily, until Abraham's father-in-law passed, he was moved again by God to the land of Canaan. He uprooted himself and his family from a familiar land to live in another which was inhabited by people whose customs and gods differ from his" (https://amazingbibletimeline.com/blog/abrahams-long-journey-to-canaan-trusting-god/).

As Americans, we live easy lives and take so many of our blessings for granted. Abraham lived in a most prosperous location. He had all the modern conveniences, but he left them behind to follow

God. This is trust! This is living in the hope of a God whom we must be obedient to even when it means stripping the luxuries and comforts of home away. This is what faith looks like. We've lost something that Abraham had. Abraham feared the Lord.

Abraham went on to become the father of Israel. He was promised a son in his old age when he and his wife were well past child-bearing years. In fact, his wife had been barren, and she laughed at the prophecy of the angel who told Abraham of this news, but he believed, and they bore a son. After such a long life without children and finally being blessed with Isaac (his name was later changed to Israel by God), God tested the faith of Abraham and asked him to go to the mountain of Moriah and make an altar to sacrifice Isaac. Without doubt, or murmuring, without bartering or cajoling, Abraham took his son and the needed items for a sacrifice to the mountain God called him to and prepared to do as God asked. I wasn't there and can't know for sure what Abraham was thinking, but I imagine that he was either expecting God to raise his son back to life or provide some other solution for God had already promised that Abraham would be the father of a nation and have more descendants than there are stars in the sky. Abraham had to believe that somehow God was going to resolve the conundrum Isaac's sacrifice and death would cause in fulfillment of his own promise.

Obediently, Abraham laid his child on the altar for sacrifice; trusting his Father's will was more important than his own will and understanding, believing that God would not go back on his promise to make Abraham the father of a nation.

Imagine such faith? Abraham demonstrated this faith and fear of the Lord when he willingly offered his son as a sacrifice. Isaac didn't die that day as the story goes on to tell us that; before the dreaded deed was fulfilled, the Lord provided a perfect ram, in the thicket, perfect for a sacrifice on this altar.

"But the angel of the LORD called to him from heaven and said, 'Abraham, Abraham!' And he said, 'Here I am.' He said, 'Do not lay your hand on the boy or do anything to him, for now I know that you fear God, seeing you have not withheld your son, your only son, from me.' And Abraham lifted up his eyes and looked, and behold, behind him was a ram, caught in a thicket by his horns. And Abraham went and took the ram and offered it up as a burnt offering instead of his son" (Gen. 22:11–13, ESV).

Pay special attention to what the angel of the Lord told Abraham, "For now I know that you fear God."

Faith is hope, trust, and fear in the Lord.

"The fear of the LORD is the beginning of wisdom, and the knowledge of the Holy One is insight" (Prov. 9:10, ESV).

"Praise the LORD! Blessed is the man who fears the LORD, who greatly delights in his commandments!" (Ps. 112:1, ESV)

As we think about what fear of God must be, and how Abraham must have felt, to fear God, we have to go straight back to Scripture to find out what this fear is. "The fear of the Lord is to hate evil; Pride and arrogance and the evil way; and the perverted mouth, I hate" (Prov. 8:13, NASB).

"He who walks in his uprightness fears the Lord, but he who is devious in his ways despises Him" (Prov. 14:2, BSB).

We have come back to the same concept we've already discussed in the previous chapters—that is, our salvation is an action, not a moment in time, and not just the prayer that seals your entry in heaven. To fear the Lord, we must obey him. To live righteous lives, we must obey him. To live in truth and be set free, we must obey him. We know that obedience of the two greatest commandments—to love your God with your whole heart, mind, and soul and to love your neighbor as yourself—are the epitome of following God. Now we know that it is also the fear of the Lord, spoken of countless times throughout the Old and New Testaments and the way that leads to being blessed by our Lord.

"For it is not the hearers of the law who are righteous before God, but the doers of the law who will be justified" (Rom. 2:13, ESV).

Abraham served God above himself! The Scriptures reference him when defining faith: "Now faith is the assurance of things hoped for, the conviction of things not seen. For by it the people of old received their commendation. By faith we understand that the universe was created by the word of God, so that what is seen was not made out of things that are visible" (Heb. 11:3, ESV).

Abraham is a "people of old." "For what does the Scripture say? 'Abraham believed God, and it was credited to him as righteousness'" (Rom. 4:3, NASB).

I believe well-meaning pastors have misled believers into believing that we stay sinners, however, we appear differently before God as though we are sinless, commandment-following lovers of God because we decided to pray once and ask God to forgive us of our sins (oftentimes lead by another and told to just "mean" the words being repeated). There are droves of Christians who will put forth no effort to seek God, follow his commandments, or acknowledge their sins, let alone repent from them but believe that they are justified, righteous, sanctified, propitiated, and deemed righteous because they "got saved" while the Word of God clearly tells us that faith without works is dead and a born-again Christian doesn't continue sinning.

"Little children, let no one deceive you: The one who practices righteousness is righteous, just as Christ is righteous. The one who practices sin is of the devil, because the devil has been sinning from the very start. This is why the Son of God was revealed, to destroy the works of the devil" (1 Jn. 3:7–8, BSB).

Logistically speaking, there must be a difference in the life of a believer. All too often, preachers take this verse and heavily emphasize the word "practice." They say, "No one is perfect, and God knows this. He expects us to keep sinning. What he means by this is practices, keeps doing the sin, like a lifestyle, not just a believer sinning."

Well, that sure sounds good. Right? We're Christians, so we're not practicing sin. It's other people who aren't believers that do that, so...

Is the woman who won't allow anyone to show her a better way because she knows everything already, or this is the way her family has always done it, practicing sin? Yes, pride.

Is the one who wants what she sees others have and is more concerned with getting it and being like them practicing sin? Yes, covetousness or envy.

Is the man overindulgent in eating, drinking, or acquiring tokens that represent wealth practicing sin? Yes, gluttony.

Is the man addicted to pornography or lusting after every well-proportioned body that goes by practicing sin? Yes, lust.

How about the man who won't let anything go? He knows his rights and won't let anyone infringe on them or hell hath no fury? He is angry at everyone who isn't as smart as him, gets in his way, cuts him off, etc. Is that practicing sin or standing up for himself and protecting his own rights? Yes, anger and pride.

How about the believers who have so much money they can easily afford all the luxuries of life but can't spare anything or very little for anyone else? Are they practicing sin? Yes, greed.

What about those who idolize their jobs, families, sports, children, possessions, or put their desires and passions far ahead of God? Yes, idolatry. (Idolatry is not merely worship of a golden calf. It is anything that is more important than serving and worshipping the one true God.)

Are the couple who do not "live together" but are sleeping with each other outside of wedlock practicing sin? Yes, fornication.

How about the man who won't work and avoids exerting himself in any way, he's lazy, and gets by in life doing as little as possible? Yes, slothfulness.

Well, wait, that stepped on too many toes. But the fact of the matter is that Christians are living like this all the time, but as long as they hear pastors splitting hairs over practicing sins versus committing sins—layered in messages that tell them they can keep sinning because their salvation is bathed in a magic potion that makes them sanctified, righteous, justified, and propitiated just because they said they believe in Christ—they will never change. They will live in error and never see themselves as the very ones "practicing sin."

"Now the works of the flesh are obvious. Fornication (sex outside of marriage), impurity (unclean living), licentiousness (extravagance, wastefulness, etc.), idolatry (anything more important than God), sorcery (charming and manipulative), enmities (hatred and hostile), strife (contentious), jealous (covetous and envious), anger (irritable and easily annoyed), quarrels (squabbles over even insignificant things to be right), dissentions (rebellion and discord), factions (setting up cliques), envy (greed), drunkenness, carousing (partying), and things like these, I am warning you as I warned you before, those who *do* such things will *not* inherit the kingdom of God" (Gal. 5:19–21, parenthesis added).

"Anyone born of God refuses to practice sin, because God's seed abides in him; he cannot go on sinning, because he has been born of God. By this the children of God are distinguished from the children of the devil: Anyone who does not practice righteousness is not of God, nor is anyone who does not love his brother" (1 Jn. 3:9–10).

Our Bible is clear. It's not a magical proverbial change that only God sees from above looking through the filter of his crucified Son; it is a difference that is distinguishable from those who do not believe and those who do.

If you recall, I had no huge testimony to share at my young conversion. I could have grown to be a "good" person and lived a fairly good life and not looked any different than any of the scenarios (or others) from above. What would have been the difference? If believers can keep on sinning and be gossips, envious, greedy, hoarders, lustful, etc. with no difference between them and a nonbelieving moral person except that one time they prayed for Jesus into their hearts, then where is the power of God?

That's not what my Bible tells me believers are to behave like.

"For it is not the hearers of the law who are righteous before God, but the doers of the law who will be justified" (Rom. 2:13, ESV).

Our Christianity has become deceptive. We sing at church or along with Christian songs about a mighty God that our chains are broken and we have been set free. We raise our hands and say amen that we have an awesome God, but we lack all the things that mean we have faith in him and truly believe this.

It's one thing to sing about trusting God or giving it lip service, but acting on it, really acting on it, is another thing. There is a clear mandate that we find our faith in hope, trust, belief, and fear of our Lord, all of which hinges on obedience to the Creator of the universe, our Lord, the one true God, which is only possible by his own power in our lives that we must believe and have faith that it is given to us upon conversion and abundantly more upon the asking.

"If any of you lacks wisdom, let him ask God, who gives generously to all without reproach, and it will be given him. But let him ask in faith, with no doubting, for the one who doubts is like a wave of the sea that is driven and tossed by the wind. For that person must not suppose that he will receive anything from the Lord; he is a double-minded man, unstable in all his ways" (Jas. 1:5–8, ESV).

Having faith is a challenge. Without God, I'm convinced we couldn't have faith, but we can see that God has told us that we have to have belief and no doubting, not only to receive wisdom generously, but to avoid being a double-minded man and unstable in all our ways.

There is a constant balance here. Ultimately, it keeps boiling down to one thing: we need God. We need to seek his will, his statutes, his face, and worship the one true God in obedience with belief that he alone is worthy. If we go back to the idea that we looked at in the second chapter about the "if-then statements," we can see that there is a measurement of faith required and sorely lacking in modern Christianity. We can ask God for the gift of faith (1 Corinthians 12:9 and Luke 17:5) and for belief (Mark 9:24).

It seems like there is a chasm between the name-it-and-claim-it group and the "God isn't really going to do that, it's just written that way" in a rhetorical pomposity "to display the power of a God who could do that if we lived in heaven but not here in this fallen, sinful world."

I think we need to breech the chasm and find ground in the middle. Faith is not about naming and claiming what we want; likewise, the promises of God are not ambiguous. When we search for God and strive to find his will by the power he puts inside of us as saved believers, we can come to know God better and get closer to understanding as well as desiring the will of God. "Thy will, not my own, Lord!"

"He said to them, 'Because of your little faith. For truly, I say to you, if you have faith like a grain of mustard seed, you will say to this mountain, "Move from here to there," and it will move, and nothing will be impossible for you'" (Mt. 17:20, BSB).

Faith is the power within us from God alone. When we walk in his will, we will ask him to move the mountains he wills to be moved. When we walk in the knowledge of the power he put inside of us and believe that he is all powerful and a promise keeper, we walk without doubt, we walk with faith.

"So then, those who are of faith are blessed along with Abraham, the man of faith" (Gal. 3:9, ESV).

The most striking thing I've come to learn about faith is that we are to have it. It's spoken of in vague terms in modern Christianity but clearly defined in the Word of God. Faith is a gift from God. It's a belief that our Father is who he says he is and will do what he says he will. It's a trust that no matter what he asks of us (like Abraham), that if we obey, it is going to result in his perfect will. Somehow, we have to find the marriage between having faith to trust God and receiving faith through obedience of God's word by doing what God commanded and not just listening to it and saying we believe.

When we find the perfect blend in that faith, we will march forward as believers living for God by the power of the Lord, through faith in a Savior, with trust and belief that God is in control and will work his will through us. It is accepting that God's will is perfect. It is believing that we are not mere flesh and blood left to wade through life like the sinners we were before we were saved with a membership card to heaven and white robes that cover the fact that we live like we did before we were saved. We are children of God. We are clothed in white, justified of our sins, and free from the bondage of slavery to sin! We don't have to keep on sinning, like our former selves did, because we have the Almighty's Holy Spirit dwelling within us. We're free from the literal bondage of our sinful nature. Is it so hard to have that sort of faith in a God who created the entire world from nothing, who breathed life into dust and created humanity? Is it so hard to believe that we are literally changed and able to follow after Christ like we could not have before we were believers?

Like I told you in the beginning, I am twice divorced and thrice married. My first marriage was made in error as I sought the will of man over God. I listened to countless Christian women from church talk about how important it is to marry the man God had for me rather than any one I'd choose and unintentionally married neither a man whom I liked nor whom God wanted me with. I had no attraction to him, didn't like his mannerisms, and only married because he was a churchgoer who always had a Bible in his hand, and the women in church kept telling me this was to be my husband "from God." I tell you this because Christianity has become a method. You see, I thought I was following God's will. I thought going to church, singing praises to him, living right, and rigorously reading the Bible was the recipe for faith and obedience, but it really wasn't. The word is sharper than a two-edged sword, but I was not using it as such. I was following a formula for Christianity that is not any more pleasing to the Lord than if I'd not been doing any of it at all. I never even asked God if this man was whom he wanted me to marry—I only assumed—and I think most of us have heard the phrase that goes alone with the word "assume."

I know this sounds sacrilegious. I bring this up to you and share the details of my life though because no matter how hard I tried to do the will of God, it's not going to be in line with him until I seek his face. Adhering to a well-scripted Christian plan cannot replace the genuine love, faith, hope, and endurance of salvation in our Lord Jesus Christ that has us personally seeking and not just trying to do what we (and other Christians) think is right.

"We remember before our God and Father your work produced by faith, your labor prompted by love, and your endurance inspired by hope in our Lord Jesus Christ" (1 Thess. 1:3, NIV).

It has to be personal. It has to be a worship by the truest of definitions, a longing to know the Creator. A hunger so deep that we search him out in his Scriptures and look for the pieces of his secrets to put together with his holy power directing us to them.

By the time I was nineteen and married, I'd read my Bible from cover to cover, attended church regularly, and had even been searching for a church of my own to fill the void religion had left. I was a saved believer from the time that I had been thirteen, but I'd been living without the power of Christ in me. I did what I was supposed to do. We had saved ourselves for marriage, and we talked about the Bible all the time, but our lives were not any more Christ-honoring than the next person's.

"And I tell you, ask, and it will be given to you; seek, and you will find; knock, and it will be opened to you" (Lk. 11:9, ESV).

There is *no* formula to following God, no sure-fire method or special list of things to do that will bring you into the will of the Father. It's your action. It's your seeking, your knocking, your *asking*.

The main theme that I keep finding in Scripture is that we need God. We can assume nothing on our own. We can't listen to preachers preach and accept their word without checking the Scriptures for accuracy.

"Beloved, do not believe every spirit, but test the spirits to see whether they are from God, for many false prophets have gone out into the world" (1 Jn. 4:1, ESV).

God wants us hungry for his truth, willing to actively live our lives for him on his terms, not the terms set for us by the majority in modern Christianity. He wants us doing the work ourselves to find his will.

But this is what we do. We go to church, listen to a sermon, forget what we even heard by lunchtime, and live a mediocre life focused on ourselves while we act as though we're good Christians. We sign up for service at our church if we're really good at the formula and pat ourselves on the backs for all the great works we have done. Essentially, we can keep ourselves busy with Christian-looking things that are not anywhere near what God is asking of us.

Our theology is based on what we remember hearing about, what others say, or what we might remember from a sermon and that which is easiest for us to keep doing to keep the most pleasure in life. Scripture-of-the-day apps are our Bible study, and singing empty songs of God accepting us as we are, are our worship. Then because we are not receiving any promises from God (that we read about in our encouraging word of the day), we assume these promises are ambiguous and come up with an abstract theology to say "God is all good, we are all bad. Even Paul said he struggled with sin in that one verse, so I'm set, and God is fulfilling his promises in a God way that I can't understand but accept by faith."

"Was not Abraham our father justified by works when he offered up his son Isaac on the altar? You see that faith was active along with his works, and faith was completed by his works; and the Scripture was fulfilled that says, 'Abraham believed God, and it was counted to him as righteousness'—and he was called a friend of God. You see that a person is justified by works and not by faith alone" (Jas. 2:21–24, ESV).

We can work and do all sorts of things we think God wants of us, but if we haven't sought out his will and are not actively pursuing an obedient lifestyle aligned with the Word of God, our efforts are futile and void in faith. Consider Cain and his offering to God in the beginning of Genesis.

"Now Abel was a keeper of sheep, while Cain was a tiller of the soil. So in the course of time, Cain brought some of the fruit of the soil as an offering to the LORD, while Abel brought the best portions of the firstborn of his flock. And the LORD looked with favor on Abel and his offering, but He had no regard for Cain and his offering. So Cain became very angry, and his countenance fell" (Gen. 4:2b–5, BSB).

Cain had made an offering of fruit from his soil. It was not his first fruit or his best fruit as God had commanded; it was something from his farm. Essentially, he gave to God because he required it, but it was not what God required. It was what Cain felt like he could spare and thought that should be good enough. Self-examine and consider whether you are giving your first and best to God. Are you going through the Christian motions and volunteering for just enough programs to look like you're busy doing Christian work but missing the bar God has set for Christianity? Are you so busy with your own life and doing the things that you've set in motion to keep up with the Joneses that you don't even have time for God, let alone giving him what he desires? Do you still call yourself a faithful believer?

"By faith Abel offered God a better sacrifice than Cain did. By faith he was commended as righteous when God gave approval to his gifts. And by faith he still speaks, even though he is dead" (Heb. 11:4, BSB).

The offering from Abel was the best portions of the first of his flock. God doesn't just desire that we give him our best but requires it from believers; is that too burdensome?

"Everyone who believes that Jesus is the Christ has been born of God, and everyone who loves the Father also loves those born of Him. By this we know that we love the children of God: when we love God and keep His commandments. For this is the love of God, that we keep His commandments. And His commandments are not burdensome, because everyone born of God overcomes the world. And this is the victory that has overcome the world: our faith" (1 Jn. 5:1–4, BSB).

Why would this make a believer upset? Why would this requirement of faith make a believer's countenance change? God asked Cain the same thing.

"'Why are you angry,' said the Lord to Cain, 'and why has your countenance fallen? If you do what is right, will you not be accepted? But if you refuse to do what is right, sin is crouching at your door; it desires you, but you must master it'" (Gen. 4:6–7).

We can see that from the very beginning of mankind, God has admonished us to do that which is right, to be accepted. This would not have been too hard for Cain; Abel was able to do it. This is not too hard for us today; the Holy Spirit of the living breathing God is in us. Sin is crouching at our doors even today; it still desires us, and we must master it or it will master us. Do we want to be sons and daughters of God Most High or sons and daughters of the devil? Don't be deceived. Our fleshly selves were crucified with Christ when he hung on that cross, but the devil is still prowling like a lion, waiting for us to give into his temptation.

"I have been crucified with Christ, and I no longer live, but Christ lives in me. The life I live in the body, I live by faith in the Son of God, who loved me and gave Himself up for me" (Gal. 2:20, BSB).

"Be sober-minded and alert. Your adversary the devil prowls around like a roaring lion, seeking someone to devour" (1 Pet. 5:8, BSB).

"No temptation has seized you except what is common to man. And God is faithful; He will not let you be tempted beyond what you can bear. But when you are tempted, He will also provide an escape, so that you can stand up under it" (1 Cor. 10:13, BSB).

"In addition to all this, take up the shield of faith, with which you can extinguish all the flaming arrows of the evil one" (Eph. 6:16, NIV).

Faith is going to shield us from Satan's attempts to pull us away from God.

My faith could have shielded me from the arrows of my early mistakes. I could have been protected from the evil one by my shield of faith had I known to use it. I mean, of course, I knew of the "Armor of God"; we'd cut out pieces and pasted them to construction paper with that minty-smelling paste when I was little and attending Sunday school. We knew of the parts, we sang of the parts, but we never understood the parts. I never dug deeper to understand until I was allowed to be left in a miserable marriage and had to. I see throughout the Old Testament, the people of God, his children, the Israelites were always going astray. The Lord would allow them to live through their consequences and use them to bring them back to him. I was wrong to marry at nineteen to a man who would later show his evil ways and was never the man whom God had intended for his child to marry. I suffered consequences and made more mistakes in effort to rectify the first mistake, namely in marrying my second husband, who was clearly an evil man from the start. I made choices outside of God's will in the same way that Sarah, Abraham's wife, did.

Remember that Abraham had been promised a son. He'd been shown by God that he would be the father of a multitude, more than there are stars in the heaven. Sarah knew she was old and after a time realized that she was not yet pregnant. Impatiently, she took God's promise into her own hands to make it happen. Instead of having faith that God would provide as God had promised he would provide, she insisted Abraham to sleep with their maidservant, Hagar. Hagar bore Abraham's first true son, however, outside of the will of God. This slip of faith is one that created consequences seen even in today's time and will be seen right up until the end.

Likewise, I saw my daughter being dragged through family court for a custody battle that was supposed to end with her father getting custody because he'd remarried to a woman with children and, therefore, looked to be more "family-like." I lacked faith that God was even helping me, but my doubt was only part of my lack of faith. Recall I felt like I was holding onto him as though he were a speeding car and I was left flapping in the wind. I most certainly was not seeking him and really only read the Bible to find Psalms to pray against her father. I was attending Bible study and looking up the verses I was supposed to read, prayed with these women, but I still wasn't seeking. Looking back, I remember better that God was with me. I was the one working within my own flesh to solve a problem that only a heavenly Father could solve if I would have sought his will and his direction. Instead, like Sarah, I found my Hagar. I married a man whom I wasn't even sure would show up at the wedding and who ignored me unless I did what he wanted and only when he wanted it. Obviously, this was not a match made in heaven, nor was I delusional enough to believe he was going to be a good husband to me? But I married him so that I could have "a family" too and keep custody of my daughter.

Instead of holding onto God and seeking what he would have me do or trusting in him to protect my daughter, I took a husband to make a quick fix; God hadn't fixed yet or maybe wouldn't fix because I was not actively seeking his will, knocking on the door for his fellowship, or acting as the born-again Christian that I was and following his commandments. Man, I know that stings. We believe that there is nothing that we can do to earn our salvation, but this is about loving the God who saved us, not working to gain salvation. Clearly, the Bible tells us that if we seek him...

"But seek first the kingdom of God and his righteousness, and all these things will be added to you" (Mt. 6:33, ESV).

"God's way is perfect. All the Lord's promises prove true. He is a shield for all who look to him for protection" (2 Sam. 22:31, NLT).

I can never stop being so amazed at how God knits scriptures together to provide understanding. Glory be to God! "He is the shield" with a promise for a shield of faith. Faith which is an action of our belief, hope, trust, and fear, which is in living righteously by the power of God because alone, we obviously cannot do any part of it. To have faith in Christ, and to be set free by the truth, is to know that we are justified through our Savior's death and resurrection for our past sins and to be able to live righteously from then forward because God is that big.

Chapter 5

Metamorphic Transformation

"It's not that Christians wanna shove Jesus down your throat, but, man, if *you knew*. If you *knew* how he can transform you, how he can take away all that bitterness, that sorrow, that hurt, that depression, anxiety. We boast about our Lord because he is *mighty!*"

I read this quote on Facebook one afternoon, noticed it had twelve thousand likes and loves, with 490 comments from "She Rises" on February 15, 2021, at 2:57 p.m. The comments were almost entirely made up of mockery, disbelief, and anger.

We boast of a "mighty God" who "takes away all that bitterness, sorrow, hurt, depression, and anxiety," and we say this is why we want to share Jesus with everyone. We claim that we believe God can transform and heal; he's mighty! But do we actually see this? More importantly, do we believe this? All the negative comments were of nonbelievers. They were scoffers, questioning what was so mighty about a God who allowed the Holocaust, children to suffer with leukemia, and many other devastating catastrophes that have or are happening in the world. It's hard to answer this. First, we can discuss the fallen world we live in and the sin that entered in from Adam and Eve with their first sin. We can elaborate on the consequences of our sins and the sinful world we live in. We could talk about how God can tell us "no" when we ask for things and that his ways are higher than ours, so we might not understand this side of heaven why God didn't answer our prayers for healing as we'd asked.

I suppose I'm not saying that any of this is untrue; for certain sure, we live in a sinful world, and we are living within the confounds of consequences from our choices and things that are well beyond our control. Autism, cancers, depression, etc. are all significantly rising in occurrences with no real answers on the horizon. We can guess, speculate, and hypothesize why so many more cases of these illnesses are being diagnosed today, but I tend to look at humanity as the cause. We pollute, use chemicals known to be carcinogenic, modify organisms, and mess around with DNA and RNA in our food and vaccines. There are side effects listed on the pharmaceuticals we consume more and more of as we walk further and further away from a natural diet and lifestyle created by our Father for us to have on Earth; certainly these things take a toll on mankind and increase sickness and disease.

Just look at the story of Daniel, Hananiah, Mishael, and Azariah. In Daniel chapter 1, Daniel asked that he and his friends not eat the choice foods of the king. After the ten-day trial, they looked healthier and better nourished than the others; therefore, being allowed to continue in their healthier diet. This alone should show us that humanity has an impact on its own health even in just the things that we eat.

I digress. "We serve a mighty God." One scoffers mock as we make claims that he transforms believers and "takes away all that bitterness, sorrow, hurt, depression, and anxiety" because we're not seeing these transformations. We pray for healings for loved ones, ourselves, faces that come across our social media feeds who need healing for countless illnesses and injuries and sit in waiting for an answer. Fewer miraculous stories come through than the sad ones in which we read of funeral arrangements or GoFundMe accounts to help families survive during their tragedies. Now, I'm not saying that vegetables are the answer to all these ailments but factoring in the world, the pollution, the poor diets, etc. has to be done.

Another aspect that has to be discussed is that we live with consequences of other people's sins. A drunk can decide to drive himself home and take the lives of others by careening into them in his intoxicated state.

In spite of this though, there are twelve thousand likes and loves on this quote. Do we pay homage to the verbiage without considering the weight of the words? What about the scorners? How can we answer them, who want to disbelieve in God because Christians boast of a mighty God who transforms and heals while we are not seeing this happen in reality?

Then I wonder why we're not seeing this. Is God mighty? Are we promised a transformation? If we're promised a transformation, why then are we not being transformed? Why are we not being healed in larger scales?

I did a Google search for verses about our mighty God. There are scores of verses reminding us of how mighty our Lord is.

"He is wise in heart and mighty in strength—who has hardened himself against him, and succeeded?" (Job 9:4, ESV)

Who is hardened against God? We have to consider the fact that God has also told us that our Father hears the prayers of the righteous and is separate from those with iniquities (sins). The God of the heavens may not be answering the prayers of supposed believers because they are not righteous.

"For the eyes of the Lord are on the righteous, and his ears are open to their prayer. But the face of the Lord is against those who do evil" (1 Pet. 3:12, ESV).

"The Lord is far from the wicked, but he hears the prayer of the righteous" (Prov. 15:29).

"But your iniquities have made a separation between you and your God, and your sins have hidden his face from you so that he does not hear" (Isa. 59:2, ESV).

God has clearly told us that there is one mediator between man and God; that mediator is Jesus Christ. "For there is one God and one mediator between God and men, the man Christ Jesus" (1 Tim. 2:5, BSB).

We cannot live wicked lives without repentance and righteousness or faith, obedience, love for our Father and say a prayer ending with "In Jesus's name" and expect him to hear us just because we ended our prayer "right." We need Christ to be our Savior and not filled "with all wicked deception for those who are perishing, because they refused to love the truth and so be saved" (2 Thess. 2:10, ESV). The one who is hardened against God cannot succeed. My mind started swirling and trying to make sense of this.

I sought out verses about transformations.

"Do not be conformed to this world, but be transformed by the renewal of your mind, that by testing you may discern what is the will of God, what is good and acceptable and perfect" (Rom. 12:2, ESV).

There is an action on the believer's part that is overtly implied. This scripture in Romans is specifically telling us not to be imitators or followers of the world. Secondly, it's telling us to allow the renewal of our mind to transform us, which indicates quite obviously that there has to be a regeneration of the mind upon conversion. The transformation comes by succumbing to, or capitulating to, the change that God has made in our minds to be able to test and discern what the will of God is and what is good, acceptable, and perfect.

Transformation is given freely by the Father upon conversion but is obviously wrapped in the action on our part to accept it, to repel from worldly lives, and use the renewal of our minds to overcome that which we couldn't have without the power of God in us.

I searched for verses with promises of protection and healing.

"He said, 'If you listen carefully to the LORD your God and do what is right in his eyes, if you pay attention to his commands and keep all his decrees, I will not bring on you any of the diseases I brought on the Egyptians, for I am the LORD, who heals you'" (Ex. 15:26, NIV).

I keep finding the same things. No matter the topic, no matter the concept, if we want to build our faith, accept and understand the promises, live with righteousness, fear the Lord, be transformed, or healed, we keep finding the same thing. "Love God with your whole heart mind and soul, and if you love him you will follow his commandments and you will not find them to be burdensome" (Mk. 12:30–31 and 1 Jn. 5:3).

If we seek him, do what is right in God's eyes, keep his commandments, decrees, and precepts, our mighty Father will protect us and heal us in alignment with his will. And we know this because he's told us in his Word.

How can we boast in our mighty God and his transforming power if we are not fulfilling our end of the deal? Is it no wonder that there are scoffers driven further away from salvation and the love of God because they see a group of people, Christians, "shoving Christ down the throats" of nonbelievers with proclamations of transformations and healings from a mighty God that no one witnesses happening?

We serve a mighty God who gives us what we need to succeed but are holding ourselves back from living in this glorious power we speak of and "like" on social media memes by denying the divinely embedded responsibility required by our perfect Lord for the fruition of the transformation and benefits of the mighty Lord God.

The problem is that mainstream Christianity is ripe with those who pay tribute to an "all-powerful God." They speak of their God who is "all-perfect, all-powerful, omniscient, omnipotent, saving, loving, Father who is so powerless he can't transform the believer to turn from sinning because they would rather give more power to the flesh of humanity than the deity of Christ's victory over sin."

God isn't going to change the requirements of his promises that he laid out in perfection. Therefore, the mightiness of God is curtailed and waning within society. It's not the power of God that is weak. It is the consensus of a Christian people that "we are fleshly sinful people who can't be more than a filthy rag on our best day" and, therefore, devoid of fulfilling our part of the promise that quenches God. He's not a liar. He is going to do what he says. Let's look again at the often quoted and sung about verses in 2 Chronicles. "If my people who are called by my name humble themselves and pray and seek my face and turn from their wicked ways, then I will hear from heaven and will forgive their sin and heal their land" (2 Chr. 7:14, ESV).

Let us turn from our wicked ways. Let us not look like the rest of the world. Let's make our lives different than nonbelievers by the power given to us by the holy of holies!

Scriptures inform and instruct us "to put off your old self, which belongs to your former manner of life and is corrupt through deceitful desires, and to be renewed in the spirit of your minds and to put on the new self, created after the likeness of God in true righteousness and holiness" (Eph. 4:22–24 ESV). We are to surrender to a metamorphic change in us. Just as a caterpillar creates a chrysalis and emerges as a different creature—a beautiful butterfly—we, too, are changed by a divine power upon our conversion. Baptism symbolizes the burial of the old self. We rise from the water, leaving our old corrupt, deceitful desires behind, and we come out of the water renewed in the spirit as a new creation. Instead, however, these commandments get ignored and explained away. We hear more and more about how imperfect man is and how impossible it is to battle the flesh. God is all good, and we are all bad. "The heart is deceitfully wicked" (Jer. 17:9, ESV).

But if we were to stop and read the entirety of chapter 17 of the book of Jeremiah, we would see that God is not saying all men are deceitfully wicked. He is imploring his people to seek him and not trust in man or his "flesh" which we were to put off upon our conversion and salvation in Christ.

"Thus says the Lord, 'Cursed is the man who trusts in man and makes flesh his strength, whose heart turns away from the Lord" (Jer. 17:5).

In order for a man to turn away from the Lord, he had to have been turned toward him first. Do not be deceived fellow believers; do not believe we are ruled by our flesh when we have the very living power of God within us when we believe and have faith in our Father.

The Lord searches the heart of man. God wants our trust in him, not the flesh, and believers are to have buried that man with Christ.

"Blessed is the man who trusts in the Lord, whose trust is the Lord. He is like a tree planted by water that sends out its roots by the stream, and does not fear when heat comes, for its leaves remain green, and is not anxious in the year of drought, for it does not cease to bear fruit… 'I the Lord search the heart and test the mind, to give every man according to his ways, according to the fruit of his deeds'" (Jer. 17:7–8, 10).

We have trapped ourselves within a false doctrine, stating that we're too wicked to be any good for God and, therefore, eradicating the covenant agreements God has given us, consequently voiding the power of the mighty Lord God in our lives. We click "like" on the memes that say God is mighty and transforms believers, but we don't live as though he does.

We say that our God is mighty, but we quickly call our best day as filthy rags before God and call our lives righteous only through Christ by virtue of our salvation instead of our own actions. Even though we see verse after verse from our God, instructing us to love him by following his commandments, decrees, and precepts and that he searches our hearts and judges according to the fruit of our deeds, we eradicate our part by claiming human ineptness. Humanity is incompetent.

We *are* born deceitfully wicked. Our best days are as filthy rags before God, but then that changes when we find salvation through the Son of the living God.

We say "we can't." God says "with me, *you can*." "Submit yourselves therefore to God. Resist the devil and he will flee from you. Draw near to God, and he will draw near to you. Cleanse your hands, you sinners, and purify your hearts, you double-minded. *Lament and mourn and weep*. Let your laughter be turned into mourning and your joy into dejection. Humble yourselves before the Lord, and he will exalt you" (Jas. 4:7–10, NRSV, emphasis added).

But if we aren't, if we refuse to believe that the Creator of the universe is powerful enough to change us from fleshly beings to spiritual beings, then there is no change, and we only accomplish nothing. We walk around with our own form of humility, labeling ourselves as unable to please God—and merely righteous because Jesus took our sins upon himself—not that the Spirit of God works through us, and we can live righteously with good works, the very good works that our Father in heaven both requires of us and empowers us to accomplish and our salvation stays infantile at best.

We quote that "our best day is as filthy rags unto the Lord." And deny any responsibility or participation in the promises of God. Then we go out claiming promises that don't come to fruition and making a mockery of Christ, opening disdainers up to lash out and question whether God is truly mighty or not.

Just like the verse we looked at a few paragraphs back, "He is wise in heart and mighty in strength—who has hardened himself against him, and succeeded?" (Job 9:4, ESV)

We will not succeed or show off the mightiness of God if we live believing that we can't do anything good. We wait in vain for God to move while we tie his hands.

"Are any among you suffering? They should pray. Are any cheerful? They should sing songs of praise. Are any among you sick? They should call for the elders of the church and have them pray over them, anointing them with oil in the name of the Lord. *They prayer of faith will save the sick, and the Lord will raise them up; and anyone who has committed sins will be forgiven. Therefore confess your sins to one another*, and pray for one another, so that you may be healed. *The prayer of the righteous is powerful and effective.* Elijah was a human being like us, and he prayed fervently that it might not rain, and for three years and six months it did not rain on the earth. Then he prayed again, and the heaven gave rain and the earth yielded its harvest" (Jas. 5:13–18, NRSV, emphasis added).

We can be bringing our own illness and death upon ourselves or discipline from the Lord (1 Cor. 11:28–32) and fail to realize the self-examination, humility, confession, and repentance needed to live healthy lives. By God we have the same power Elijah had. Are we willing to live in such a way that God grants our powerful effective prayers as his righteous ones?

Several weeks ago, I had a prospective buyer looking at a horse of mine. She came to me claiming she could ride. She most certainly looked incredibly familiar with horses as I watched her work around this gelding. She came with her own saddle and bridle and looked like she was ready to ride.

When it was time to get on, she asked me to ride first, which I did, weaving in and out of cones, picking up speed and gaiting him, stopping him, etc. so she could see what he was capable of. When it was her turn to ride the same horse, she didn't know how to move him. He kept bringing her back to the horse paddock with his other buddies. She'd traipse through my new flower bed and all the new flowers I'd just planted because while she thought she knew what horsemanship was all about, she obviously didn't know her part to do. Without doing her part, he couldn't do his part. She didn't know how to steer him.

A week or so later, another young girl came by to test ride my gelding. She used her legs and seat as well as her hands to steer this horse and rode beautifully. She gaited him smoothly and moved him through obstacles the other girl couldn't get him nearby.

When we work with horses and know the fundamentals of riding and horsemanship, we are successful in our riding endeavors. She went on to buy him and ride him with far more ease than the other girl who believed she already knew what to do and it was just the horses fault she couldn't get what she wanted from him. The horse needed her to do her part so he could do his. Likewise, we have to be sure we know what we're doing in Christianity.

God requires us to live righteously after his own heart. He lays out the methods and actions we must employ. We can look like we know what we're doing, carry our Bibles around appropriately, and look as though we are very familiar with the Word. The problem is when we aren't reading the Word for truth and seeking God for both his character and our ordained responsibilities, like the first girl, we can look like we know what we're doing but deny the power of God with our ignorance. Then we have to come up with a good sounding story to explain why things didn't go as we thought they should or why God said "no."

On the contrary, we can live our lives in the manner God requires and show the world that we serve a mighty God. We won't even have to "shove God down anyone's throats!"

Back in the book of Daniel (chapter 3), Hananiah, Mishael, and Azariah, whose names were changed to Shadrach, Meshach, and Abednego, find themselves being forced to worship Nebuchadnezzar's golden statues and gods. These men were not "conformed to the world" and would not bow down as the king required. With faith, obedience, and trust in God, they served the one true God in action and deed. As the Scripture tells, Nebuchadnezzar required his servants to make the fire of the furnace seven times hotter than usual and to throw these three men into this fire as punishment for their refusal to worship his gods. The fire was so hot that the servants pushing these three men into the furnace burned up and died from the heat.

Our mighty Lord God went into the furnace with these three men and kept them from burning. Nebuchadnezzar saw four men in the fire and that one was like the "son of the gods." He called the three men out who didn't even smell like smoke, let alone have a singed hair on their bodies and Nebuchadnezzar declared, "Blessed be the God of Shadrach, Meshach, and Abednego, who has sent His angel and delivered His servants who trusted in Him. They violated the king's command and risked their lives rather than serve or worship any god except their own God. Therefore I decree that the people of any nation or language who say anything offensive against the God of Shadrach, Meshach, and Abednego will be cut into pieces and their houses reduced to rubble. For there is no other god who can deliver in this way" (Dan. 3:28–29, BSB).

Let us live so that everyone knows we serve a mighty God without doubt.

If we turn to the book of Isaiah, chapter 64, verse 6b, you can see where the idea of "our righteous acts are like filthy rags." By taking that piece of one verse and quoting it just like that, we not only miss the context but deny the warning that our Lord is giving in this passage, which clearly tells us to gladly do right and remember (God's) ways and not become unclean.

"You welcome those who gladly do right, who remember Your ways. Surely You were angry, for we sinned. How can we be saved if we remain in our sins? Each of us has become like something unclean, and all our righteous acts are like filthy rags; we all wither like a leaf, and our iniquities carry us away like the wind. No one calls on Your name or strives to take hold of You. For You have hidden Your face from us and delivered us into the hand of our iniquity" (Isa. 64:5–7, BSB).

Shadrach, Meshach, and Abednego clearly had not become like something unclean. God did not hide his face from them or deliver them into the hands of iniquity. The God of Shadrach, Meshach, and Abednego fulfilled his promise upon their fulfillment of his required responsibility. They served a mighty God. We serve the same God!

We don't have to live as though are best day is as filthy rags and must never declare such a falsehood again.

There is a disconnect with what the Bible is clearly telling us and how we live our lives. Our Bibles tell us God welcomes those who love him, who obey his commandments, and "gladly do right." Our faith in our Savior gives us the power needed to actually comply with God's requirements for us. We can't keep sinning, or we will be turned over to our iniquities and be carried away like the wind, living with the consequences thereof. If God is so mighty, why is it so hard for his people to believe that he can change us and draw us to him to actually live out righteous lives literally, not fleshly "I walked the aisle to get saved so God sees me as a child of God in white and my sins are forgotten, forgiven, and not seen kind of way."

"By his divine power, God has given us everything we need for living a godly life. We have received all of this by coming to know him, the one who called us to himself by means of his marvelous glory and excellence" (2 Pet. 1:3, NLT).

You see, we do not need to walk around crying out to God or telling other believers that our best day is as filthy rags if we are living within the divine power our salvation has awarded us. We do not need to feign humility or excuse a sinful life with misquotes from either Paul or Peter to say that we stay in sin and are only looked upon by God as righteous; nothing actually changes in us or our lives. I want to love God! I want righteous, powerful change in my life that brings righteous, powerful, and effective prayers.

"For this is the love of God, that we keep His commandments. And His commandments are not burdensome" (1 Jn. 5:3, BSB).

If his commandments are not burdensome but we boast of being the worst sinner of all or a filthy rag in God's eyes, how do we ever acknowledge the power of our Savior and the Spirit of the living God within us? How do we ever please our God or love him if we are so wrapped up in a false doctrine that says we can't? When our own Bibles tell us that we must live righteously, having good works, for without works, faith is dead, and that all this is not difficult if you're truly saved?

Now, if we lived with that sort of godly power, if we believed and feared the Lord God most High, We would know that our God is mighty! Not just in words but in actuality.

The sadness I felt as I read twelve thousand people liked a quote that we serve a mighty Lord is laced with a knowledge that Christians lack in belief. It's not just Christians of today, even in biblical times, there were prayers going up and disbelief that God would actually answer them.

In the book of Acts, it's recorded that disciple, Peter, was taken to prison. "So Peter was kept in prison, but the church was fervently praying to God for him" (Acts 12:5, BSB).

The church was fervently praying to God for Peter's deliverance. An angel of the Lord came to Peter. He woke him, loosed his chains, opened gates divinely, and set Peter free and on his way.

"Then Peter came to himself and said, 'Now I know for sure that the Lord has sent His angel and rescued me from Herod's grasp and from everything the Jewish people were anticipating.' And when he had realized this, he went to the house of Mary the mother of John, also called Mark, where many people had gathered together and were praying. He knocked at the outer gate, and a servant girl named Rhoda came to answer it. When she recognized Peter's voice, she was so overjoyed that she forgot to open the gate, but ran inside and announced, 'Peter is standing at the gate!'" (Acts 12:11–14, BSB)

God answered the zealous prayers of the church…but watch what happens once Rhoda announced Peter's arrival and answer to their prayers. "'You are out of your mind,' they told her. But when she kept insisting it was so, they said, 'It must be his angel'" (Acts 12:15, BSB).

We pray all the time and do not expect an answer from God. When it knocks on our very door, we often don't recognize it as answered prayers, but we say we believe when we actually do not. We serve a mighty God, let us live with faith and belief like we know he is.

> O, those who through the righteousness of our
> God and Savior Jesus Christ have received a faith

as precious as ours: Grace and peace be multiplied to you through the knowledge of God and of Jesus our Lord. His divine power has given us everything we need for life and godliness through the knowledge of Him who called us by His own glory and excellence. Through these He has given us His precious and magnificent promises, so that through them you may become partakers of the divine nature, now that you have escaped the corruption in the world caused by evil desires. For this very reason, make every effort to add to your faith virtue; and to virtue, knowledge; and to knowledge, self-control; and to self-control, perseverance; and to perseverance, godliness; and to godliness, brotherly kindness; and to brotherly kindness, love. For if you possess these qualities and continue to grow in them, they will keep you from being ineffective and unproductive in your knowledge of our Lord Jesus Christ. But whoever lacks these traits is nearsighted to the point of blindness, having forgotten that he has been cleansed from his past sins. Therefore, brothers, strive to make your calling and election sure. For if you practice these things you will never stumble, and you will receive a lavish reception into the eternal kingdom of our Lord and Savior Jesus Christ. Therefore I will always remind you of these things, even though you know them and are established in the truth you now have. I think it is right to refresh your memory as long as I live in the tent of my body, because I know that this tent will soon be laid aside, as our Lord Jesus Christ has made clear to me. And I will make every effort to ensure that after my departure, you will be able to recall these things at all times. (2 Pet. 1:1–15, BSB)

Chapter 6

Enemy of God

We've spent a considerable amount of time looking at what the promise of God is, how the truth sets us free, who is righteous, and what that looks like, as well as how to have faith. All this has centered around a concept that we've only loosely spoken of, that is sin.

We listed a few sins earlier in the first chapter as we contemplated how to be saved and that we needed to be saved because we are sinners, but what is it that makes us sinners? Why is there such a battle between flesh and the spirit that we can't please God apart from him and can't have fellowship with him because of our sins, which led our Father to his own Son's crucifixion to save us?

The answer to these complex questions all boils down to "the enemy." We can read from Genesis to Revelation about the enemy. Satan is usually the first we think of in context of an enemy of God, but there are many others. "You adulteresses, do you not know that friendship with the world is hostility toward God? Therefore whoever wishes to be a friend of the world makes himself an enemy of God" (Jas. 4:4). If I were texting this bit of information, I'd insert a shock faced emoji. Wow, this wasn't where I thought I was headed when I started this next chapter about the enemy. The enemy of God is humanity, or at least those who are worldly and desire the things of this world.

The idea that humankind can be the enemy of God is rather farfetched in today's Christian thinking. In fact, I recently encountered a woman who summed up the full embodiment of just how implausible the concept is in today's belief system: "I have never cared what people think of me. Less stress that way. When it's all said and done, I am only going to answer to one person, and he knows what I am going to do before I think it or do it! And the great thing about it is he loves me anyway, and for that I am thankful."

You see, there is a belief system in play today that not only are "we dirty rotten sinners but God loves us anyway." If we create and believe a logic that "he already knows what we're going to do before we think it or do it," we incorrectly assert that we have no responsibility for our own actions and that God, who loved the world so much that he gave his only begotten Son, is going to love us no matter what we do. But is this true? The simple answer is no.

"Whoever has my commandments and keeps them, he it is who loves me. And he who loves me will be loved by my Father, and I will love him and manifest myself to him" (Jn. 14:21, ESV). Our God reveals himself to those who love him through obedience to his commandments, so to seek him and receive his revelation is to obey him. One is impossible without the other.

I know this is starting to sound like a broken record, but all things keep pointing back to the inherent responsibility of humanity to literally change after they've become believers. This is only possible by the power of God but must be actively sought after. Christianity isn't supposed to be a passive religion. We aren't supposed to say a one-time prayer and then expect God to work in us as though we have no participation. We are called to seek, knock, and pursue the Father. We are called to keep his commandments. Christianity is not based on a God who knows what we are going to do but loves us anyway. The love that God has for us is provision for sinners who need a savior. He loves us so much that he gave his only son for our ransom that we might be saved from the slavery of sin, worldliness, and eternal damnation that we may live for him and his glory.

We can't just say we love God and go on as though there is no divine power in our lives. James 4:4 tells us that whoever loves the world is an enemy of God. 1 John 2:15 (ESV) explicitly says, "Do not love the world or the things in the world. If anyone loves the world, the love of the Father is not in him." We literally, cannot be of this world and love God at the same time.

"'No one can serve two masters, for either he will hate the one and love the other, or he will be devoted to the one and despise the other. You cannot serve God and money" (Mt. 6:24, ESV).

To put this into perspective, we have to define worldliness. "For all that is in the world—the desires of the flesh and the desires of the eyes and pride in possessions—is not from the Father but is from the world" (1 Jn. 2:16, ESV). Additionally, we can see that the love of money is also a worldly characteristic. "Keep your life free from love of money, and be content with what you have, for he has said, 'I will never leave you nor forsake you'" (Heb. 13:5, ESV).

Interestingly enough, we find a solution in James that describes how to stay unpolluted from the world. "Religion that is pure and undefiled before God the Father is this: to visit orphans and widows in their affliction, and to keep oneself unstained from the world" (Jas. 1:27, ESV).

Worldliness has crept into our faith though. Our religion is based on a worldly notion that the simple act of asking Jesus into our hearts not only spares us from hell but judgment and any condemnation. We have come to create a religion around gratitude to a god who requires one single prayer, and that is all.

Why did Christianity become a walk down the aisle, the "sinner's prayer," singing songs about how happy we are to be free in Christ accompanied sometimes by a euphoric feeling that we equate to being in God's presence?

When did the words of the Bible fade away and become obsolete?

How did salvation become "the moment our names were sealed in the Lamb's Book of Life" *and* "the first day of our lives in *freedom* from *accountability* for our sins"?

What is the difference between an unbeliever and a believer, except that one said a prayer and the other didn't, if they keep on living lives that look the same?

"Anyone born of God refuses to practice sin, because God's seed abides in him; he cannot go on sinning, because he has been born of God. By this the children of God are distinguished from the children of the devil: Anyone who does not practice righteousness is not of God, nor is anyone who does not love his brother" (1 Jn. 3:9–10, BSB). So if you think you're a saved Christian but are not distinguishable from the children of the devil because you go on sinning, you need to question if "God's seed abides in you."

John explicitly tells us that the children of God are distinguishable from the children of the devil. Believers cannot go around boasting of a god who saved them from accountability of the sins they continue to practice…

Jesus did not come to Earth just so he could die and forgive all our sins…no! His life and death was so much more than that.

"And everyone who has this hope in Him purifies himself, just as Christ is pure. Everyone who practices sin practices lawlessness as well. Indeed, sin is lawlessness. But you know that Christ appeared to take away sins, and in Him there is no sin. No one who remains in Him keeps on sinning. No one who continues to sin has seen Him or known Him" (1 Jn. 3:3–6, BSB). Taking away our sins isn't only about forgiving those we repented from at that moment of conversion but also taking away sin from our lives as we walk in the power of the Holy Spirit and live as slaves to Christ instead of sin.

While believers go around boasting of their salvation, freedom in Christ, and singing their praises to a god who accepts them as they are, they fail to receive the true freedom Christ died to give. That is, freedom from our flesh, worldliness, sin, and the fruit of our former father, Satan.

"Little children, let no one deceive you: The one who practices righteousness is righteous, just as Christ is righteous. The one who practices sin is of the devil, because the devil has been sinning from the very start. This is why the Son of God was revealed, to destroy the works of the devil" (1 Jn. 3:7–8, BSB). Christ didn't come just to forgive sins; he came to destroy the power of sin within the believer.

The books of Corinthians were written as letters from Paul to the Corinthians. He uses these letters to exhort, instruct, and to praise these new believers whom he'd preached the good news to. Near the end of his second letter, he writes, "For I am afraid that when I come, I may not find you as I wish, and you may not find me as you wish. I fear that there may be *quarreling, jealousy, rage, rivalry, slander, gossip, arrogance*, and *disorder*. I am afraid that when I come again, my God will humble me before you, and I will be grieved over many who have sinned earlier and have not repented of their *acts of impurity, sexual immorality*, and *debauchery*" (2 Cor. 12:20–21, BSB).

Those are not sins these new Corinthian believers are being coddled for having. Paul is not telling these believers to praise God because they are already forgiven for these sins and God expects nothing less of them. If we look in the previous letter he sent to the same believers of Corinth, Paul had already warned them not to be deceived.

"Do you not know that the wicked will not inherit the kingdom of God? Do not be deceived: Neither the *sexually immoral*, nor *idolaters*, nor *adulterers*, nor *men who submit to* or *perform homosexual acts*, nor *thieves*, nor the *greedy*, nor *drunkards*, nor *verbal abusers*, nor *swindlers*, will inherit the kingdom of God" (1 Cor. 6:9–10, BSB).

We might be inclined to say that Paul wasn't talking to the believers but maybe those who hadn't been converted yet, but the next verse of that chapter shows us it is in fact the believers who have fallen back into these sins. "And that is what some of you were. But you were washed, you were sanctified, you were justified, in the name of the Lord Jesus Christ and by the Spirit of our God" (1 Cor. 6:11).

"For this people's heart has grown dull, and with their ears they can barely hear, and their eyes they have closed, lest they should see with their eyes and hear with their ears and understand with their heart and turn, and I would heal them" (Mt. 13:15, ESV).

"Do not harden your hearts as in the rebellion, on the day of testing in the wilderness… Take care, brothers, lest there be in any of you an evil, unbelieving heart, leading you to fall away from the living God" (Heb. 3:8, 12, ESV).

God requires changed hearts and lives. We can't simply pay homage, verbally, to God's mercy and grace and live in such a way that could lead to a hardened heart. Christ didn't come to forgive our sins just so that we could avoid punishment for them. He came to heal us, transform us, make us new creatures in him, not slaves to sinning but slaves to God with righteousness that produces godly lives.

We are called to "Pursue peace with everyone, as well as holiness, without which no one will see the Lord. See to it that no one falls short of the grace of God, and that no root of bitterness springs up to cause trouble and defile many" (Heb. 12:14–15, BSB).

If grace is merely forgiveness from God when we don't deserve it, and our salvation is hinged on accepting this through faith, why then are we called to see to it that no one falls short of the grace of God?

The modern Christian sings songs about once being dead in their sins, being forgiven by grace and made new by the loving mercy of God, then contrast old lives as being lost, and new lives as being found but go straight to a refrain or chorus, shouting a thank you for freedom from punishment. There are cheers and excitement at the parts about not being slaves to sin and chains being broken, but no one wants to address the obvious obvious—we should be cheering for the fact that we are no longer slaves to sin. This is what our freedom is from.

I grieve for those who are so deceived. They are first to exclaim, "No one is perfect. Jesus is the only perfect one, and Christianity is about grace covering our sins and mercy where we don't deserve it. Jesus paid for our sins so we don't have to. God knows we can't stop sinning, that's why he sent his Savior." They tell us that they are so glad that there is nothing we have to do because Christ did it all, and they believe that they are preaching on the doctrine of salvation. Their eyes are closed, their ears can barely hear, and their hearts have grown dull, or they never received the message at all.

This doctrine essentially allows "believers" to continue living in their sins, looking no differently than the nonbeliever next door. We've created and support a religion that worships a God with songs that speak of a proverbial freedom from sin, only in regard to our own punishment; we attend church to hear sermons that are neither intended to move us nor convict us of anything but rather to encourage us so we feel good and keep coming back. We read the parts of Scriptures that promise us protection and goodwill from God and skip the rest, calling it "faith in God's grace" and expect God's mercy in our lives.

"But He said to me, 'My grace is sufficient for you, for My power is perfected in weakness.' Therefore I will boast all the more gladly in my weaknesses, so that the power of Christ may rest on me. That is why, for the sake of Christ, I delight in weaknesses, in insults, in hardships, in persecutions, in difficulties. For when I am weak, then I am strong" (2 Cor. 12:9–10, BSB).

"He saved us, not by the righteous deeds we had done, but according to His mercy, through the washing of new birth and renewal by the Holy Spirit. This is the Spirit He poured out on us abundantly through Jesus Christ our Savior, so that, having been justified by His grace, we would become heirs with the hope of eternal life. This saying is trustworthy. And I want you to emphasize these things, so that those who have believed God will take care to devote themselves to good deeds. These things are excellent and profitable for the people" (Titus 3:5–8, ESV).

Verse upon verse, precept upon precept, the Holy Scriptures tell us to stay true to the Lord. Acts 11:23 tells us that there is "evidence of God's blessing," and when Barnabas saw this in the church at Jerusalem, "he encouraged the believers to stay true to the Lord." If there was nothing to stay true to, because of our own ineptness as humans, what is the point of this encouragement?

"Now we command you, brothers, in the name of our Lord Jesus Christ, to keep away from any brother who leads an undisciplined life that is not in keeping with the tradition you received from us. For you yourselves know how you ought to imitate us, because we were not undisciplined among you" (2 Thess. 3:6–7, BSB).

The truth is that we are required to live disciplined lives; we are to live out righteous lives. There is nothing figurative about it. Christ died so that we would not be slaves to the flesh of undisciplined lives; we must live out our lives with that truth. We must imitate Christ and Paul who imitated Christ and sacrificed his life to do so. Remember, this man was imprisoned, suffered, and beheaded for following after Christ. (According to many secular sources, the Apostle Paul died by beheading by order of Nero, the Roman Emperor at the time of the early Christian church. How did Paul die in the Bible? | Study.com.)

"I appeal to you therefore, brothers, by the mercies of God, to present your bodies as a living sacrifice, holy and acceptable to God, which is your spiritual worship. Do not be conformed to this world, but be transformed by the renewal of your mind, that by testing you may discern what is the will of God, what is good and acceptable and perfect" (Rom. 12:1–2, ESV). We must note that our spiritual worship isn't about singing an emotional song but living with bodies sacrificed, holy, and acceptable to God. In the Old Covenant, God's people had to sacrifice spotless animals and spill their blood for atonement. Under the new covenant, Christ's blood atones. But Paul still appeals to believers to actively present their bodies as spotless sacrifices, living though because Christ was the final sacrificial lamb but holy and acceptable to God because of our active role in living righteously for the love of God.

I see here that there are "mercies of God"—but not like the mercies that we hear spoken of in the modern doctrine of Christianity—mercies that give us the ability to present our bodies as living sacrifices, holy and acceptable to God. Don't you see, by God's power in us, upon conversion and salvation, given only from our Savior, Jesus Christ, we can live holy and acceptable lives unto God! We are commanded to do so, lest we become enemies of God. There is also "grace from God," but it is not an abstract forgiveness for being human. Hebrews 12:15 tells us that "we are to see to it that no one falls short of the grace of God." Titus 2:11–13 (NRSV) clearly defines *grace* for us: "For the grace of God has appeared, bringing salvation to all, training us to renounce impiety and worldly passions, and in the present age, to live lives that are self-controlled, upright, and godly, while we wait for the blessed hope and the manifestation of the glory of our great God and Savior Jesus Christ." In the present age! Now not once we die or Christ returns and we live in heaven. God's grace doesn't give us permission to stay in our sin; it trains us to renounce sinfulness, wickedness, irreverence, and worldly passions so that we will be self-controlled, upright, and godly in our lives as we wait for death or the return of Christ.

"For the grace of God has appeared, bringing salvation to everyone. It instructs us to renounce ungodliness and worldly passions, and to live sensible, upright, and godly lives in the present age, as we await the blessed hope and glorious appearance of our great God and Savior Jesus Christ. He gave Himself for us to redeem us from all lawlessness and to purify for Himself a people for His own possession, zealous for good deeds. Speak these things as you encourage and rebuke with all authority. Let no one despise you" (Titus 2:11–15, BSB).

God is gracious indeed, but obviously, the biblical form of grace that God has isn't the same that we keep singing about all the time. "The grace of God has appeared"; grammatically speaking, the following sentence that begins with "it" is referring to "grace." Therefore, grace instructs us to renounce ungodliness and worldly passions and live sensible, upright, and godly lives in the present age as we await the blessed hope and glorious appearance of our great God and Savior Jesus Christ.

The "grace abounds" doctrines are part of the truth of God. It encompasses the promise of salvation and eternal life, but it expands beyond the simplistic definition of "getting something we don't deserve." Grace is found in the believer who renounces ungodliness. Renouncing ungodliness is an action, a responsibility on our parts, only possible by the power of God in our saved selves.

"Beloved, although I made every effort to write to you about the salvation we share, I felt it necessary to write and urge you to contend earnestly for the faith entrusted once for all to the saints. For certain men have crept in among you unnoticed—ungodly ones who were designated long ago for condemnation. They turn the grace of our God into a license for immorality, and they deny our only Master and Lord, Jesus Christ… These men are discontented grumblers, following after their own lusts; their mouths spew arrogance; they flatter others for their own advantage" (Jude 1:3–4, 16, BSB).

Jude calls this false doctrine of "living under grace" out! He warns us of "ungodly ones who turn grace into a license for immorality!" Is this not the same idea that we are hearing about in our supposed praise and worship songs and from the pulpits of modern American Christianity today? Isn't the "doctrine of grace" merely permission to live as sinners in our flesh? Do we not hear pastors praying to God and thanking him that he saved us so that we can stay human? When we hear the false humility in broken voices of praise declaring we serve a god who doesn't want us to keep trying to live righteously "because our Savior is the only one who could and he died to save us from having to do the same," we should mourn.

You see, if we only articulate that mercy is "*not* getting what we deserve (in punishment form)" and grace is "getting what we do *not* deserve," then we risk turning our religious experience into just that, a religious experience. We simplify salvation to such a point that we jeopardize our own salvation by "turning the grace of our God into a license for immorality" (Jude 1:4) and defying the very definition God has given us that "we renounce ungodliness and worldly passions, living sensible, upright, and godly lives." (Titus 2:12).

Today's gospel message has become a desperate attempt to create a religion that everyone will want to partake in. The faith has been described as grace and mercy, salvation for all who ask Jesus into their hearts. We see signs that say to come as you are and hear talks about accepting everyone…but we mostly fail to go beyond that and say, "Now that we're saved, we must change."

Consider the parable Jesus shares, "And he told them many things in parables, saying, 'A farmer went out to sow his seed. And as he was sowing, some seed fell along the path, and the birds came and devoured it. Some fell on rocky ground, where it did not have much soil. It sprang up quickly because the soil was shallow. But when the sun rose, the seedlings were scorched, and they withered because they had no root. Other seed fell among thorns, which grew up and choked the seedlings. Still other seed fell on good soil and produced a crop—a hundredfold, sixtyfold, or thirtyfold. He who has ears, let him hear'" (Mt. 13:3–9, BSB).

As "farmers," it's important to consider the soil we're planting in. When I say "consider," I mean that we better not be fixing the soil to be rocky ground where we have "believers" spring up quickly, only to get scorched quickly by the elements of the world.

Consider, then, the parable of the sower. "The seed sown on rocky ground is the one who hears the word and at once receives it with joy. But since he has no root, he remains for only a season.

When trouble or persecution comes because of the word, he quickly falls away" (Mt. 13:20–21, BSB).

It may look good in our numbers or make us feel like we're going and being fishers of men by getting nonbelievers hyped up and excited to believe, but creating a gospel message that is so appealing through worldly standards that it equates to a seed falling on rocky ground will help no one. Certainly not the man "believing" who will either go away with a false security that he is saved because of that joyful "experience" and set for life to live as he wants regardless of what God's word tells us otherwise, or an entirely different scenario can occur. This once joyful and excited new believer can be so sure that salvation is a guarantee for an easy life (wrongly promised by many) and become bitter and scornful the moment trouble or persecution comes and, therefore, falls away with a malice toward a God they never actually served. Or worse, they stay dead in Christ and continue attending church, "getting involved" with the purpose of convincing themselves and others that they are actually godly and worthy of praise for being "good Christians." They are self-righteous and errantly believe they are saved because they said that prayer and go to church, actively participating in all the programs for their own glory. They sing all the churchy songs about what God is supposed to do for them, with a refrain repeated a dozen times about how they are enough just as they are because God loves them anyway. They sing their own praises as they worship themselves all the while looking for the feelies to confirm a nonexistent relationship with the Savior. These are the so-called Christians who busy themselves with following the social mores of a Christianity that lacks true conversion and worship of God. Their pride and selfishness are laced with greed, swindling others into believing they are worthy of special church positions, idolaters of themselves, and all the other desires they have of this world, perhaps verbal abusers or even drunkards; and Paul told us not to associate with or even eat with anyone who claims to be a brother or sister in Christ with such attributes in 1 Corinthians 5:10–11. Perhaps these are the people falling prey to the new "gospel plus nothing" message. They are weary from the busyness of looking like they are good Christians and eagerly grasp onto the "Jesus did it all so we don't have to gospel," which only feeds their ego further as they look at the others striving for godly and holy lives as described biblically and cast them down fallaciously as self-righteous instead of themselves. They bask in their new gospel beliefs that "to strive is to deny Christ's finished work." And they walk forward with their heads held high, denying Christ's commandments, holding fast to their fleshly desires, pride in possessions and in themselves, and living hypocritically.

Jesus declared a curse in Matthew 23:13 on the hypocrites because they shut off the kingdom of heaven from people. He warned them that they will not enter themselves, nor do they allow those who are entering to go in either.

In fact, if we read through the first four Gospels of Christ, we find that our Savior spent time with sinners. He loved them and told them to repent and turn from their wicked ways. He didn't hang out with them and tolerate their sin, but he wasn't afraid to be seen with those who would have been considered the most vial. It is the hypocrites that he did not have patience for. He called them sons of Satan and called them out on their fake religion. He acknowledged that they followed the law and did their duty to look like they were religious, but they had no love. They were consumed with doing to get others to look up to them and see them as wonderful while they had no love for those who were beneath them. Christ didn't say that following the commandments was wrong; instead, he told his followers, "So practice and observe everything they tell you. But do not do what they do, for they do not practice what they preach. They tie up heavy, burdensome loads and lay them on men's shoulders, but they themselves are not willing to lift a finger to move them. All their deeds are done for men to see… They love the places of honor at banquets, and chief seats in the [churches] synagogues, the greetings in the market places and the title of [leader, teacher, etc.] 'Rabbi' by which they are addressed" (Mt. 23:3–7 BSB).

We need to look at the sin of hypocrisy, especially carefully to be sure that we do not fall into this sin. We must always be turning to God to fill us with his love so that our motives are pure, and we do the "religious things" for the right reasons. Then we will find ourselves doing even above and beyond and not simply waiting for the next list to pop up for volunteers at church. We will be looking for ways to love our neighbors when no one is looking because our motive is not to fake Christianity but to love God and others, remembering, "The greatest among you shall be your servant. For whoever exalts himself will be humbled, and whoever humbles himself will be exalted" (Mt. 23:11–12 BSB).

The second part of the Savior's parable is also just as relevant in today's lifestyle. We must be careful not to sow the seeds of the gospel among thorns. "The seed sown among the thorns is the one who hears the word, but the worries of this life and the deceitfulness of wealth choke the word, and it becomes unfruitful" (Mt. 13:22, BSB).

An unfruitful Christian is not following the commandments of the Father. He who is unfruitful, isn't carrying the burden of his neighbors, brothers, or sisters. There is no time "to visit orphans and widows in their affliction, and to keep themselves unstained from the world" (Jas. 1:27, ESV) because they are so obsessed with themselves, their own families, and maintaining the means to keep this lifestyle going. When life is so busy and full, we don't necessarily think of it as a bad thing; oftentimes, we hear encouragement in the form of "free passes." They tell us that some of us are in seasons of our lives that keep us busier than others and not to feel bad about that. While there are times in our lives that we are busier than others, and can't help it, we must be careful not to measure our success as wives, husbands, businessmen and women, mothers, and fathers by what we are providing and affording for our lives, children, and our families. If such lifestyles become all consuming, we leave no time for the gospel or God's will in our lives. We can't bear fruit by bearing the burdens of others when we have packed our schedules to tightly that we haven't got time or money for anyone else but ourselves.

We must be very wary not to create a gospel around a lifestyle that is neither fruitful nor godly and call it Christianity. Believers have been told we'll be judged by our fruit. In fact, we're told good trees produce good fruit and bad trees produce bad fruit. When Jesus warns us that the seeds sown among thorns become unfruitful, we must take heed and prepare the soil for planting well. "But the seed sown on good soil is the one who hears the word and understands it. He indeed bears fruit and produces a crop—a hundredfold, sixtyfold, or thirtyfold" (Mt. 13:23, BSB).

Fellow farmers, it is time to sow; cultivate the soil by setting the right example, presenting the whole true gospel, and holding ourselves and others accountable. Our Father promises us that seeds grown on good soil will produce crops a hundredfold, sixtyfold, or thirtyfold. The math is obvious! We will have true kingdom-minded converts who love the Lord God with all their hearts, souls, and minds and who love others as themselves *times* thirty, sixty, or one hundred if we take the time to prepare the soil.

Last year, I decided to start a garden. It was a last-minute idea. I bought seedlings, and I was ready to put them into the ground as soon as I got home. I didn't want to prepare the soil though. I didn't feel like hand-turning the soil, pulling the weeds, or anything else that needed to be prepared for a good garden spot. Instead, I went into the pasture with a pitchfork and pulled hay out of the horse's round bale and put it on top of the grass. It seemed like it was going to be so much easier than pulling weeds and tilling soil. I covered my little rectangle space and expected the grass to die under the weight of the hay. I immediately set out to dig a few shallow holes to put my new plants in and called it a garden. Within a week, I knew I'd made a huge mistake. The weeds were growing more prolifically than before. The hay was lifting off the ground with large clumps of weeds pushing it up. It was as if I'd planted more grass instead of killing it, which is in fact what I did if you consider that hay is tall grass, gone to seed, and I put it in by the pitchfork loads. I wanted an easy garden. I didn't want to prepare the soil but for some reason expected that my garden plants would be the only thing to grow in my little patch. Instead, it was mostly weeds with a few plants struggling to live or straight up dying.

Before long, I had to create a real garden. I took a spade shovel and started digging out the sod, one scoop at a time. I put the sod in low spots in the yard, thereby accomplishing two tasks at once. It took time, work, muscle, and a lot of effort. My boys all helped, and eventually, we had all the grass and weeds out. Carefully, we laid black gardener's plastic over the prepared earth to keep weeds from growing (and not accidentally seeding it with weeds like the first garden) and transplanted the first seedlings that hadn't already died. We had created a larger space to grow in than the first patch, so I planted more seeds to grow. These plants flourished. They didn't have the competition of the other weeds crowding them out. We had peppers, carrots, tomatoes, etc. all growing and bearing fruit now because we had taken the time to plant in the right soil.

As believers, we need to be sure that we aren't ourselves, seedlings being choked out by the things of this world. Christianity isn't as easy as we want to make it. No matter how well-intentioned we are, changing the gospel isn't going to lead more people to eternal life, and it isn't going to secure our own ticket if we're so callous about our salvation that we lean on the idea that God is going to accept our sinful selves no matter what we do. We can never forget that we are sinners saved by a gracious God who shows mercy and forgives us of our sins, writing our names into the Lamb's Book of Life, but we must also realize that every time our Savior spoke of this salvation, he told us to turn from sin, go and sin no more, or to repent from our sins. Never did he tell us to ask him into our hearts and continue on as we are. In fact, and clearly articulated in the parable of the soils just mentioned, he warns us not to plant where we will be choked out or scalded by the sun. If salvation were easy and as simple as saying a "sinner's prayer," there would be no reason to warn us with such a parable.

"Jesus put before them another parable: 'The kingdom of heaven is like a man who sowed good seed in his field. But while everyone was asleep, his enemy came and sowed weeds among the wheat, and slipped away. When the wheat sprouted and bore grain, then the weeds also appeared. The owner's servants came to him and said, "Sir, didn't you sow good seed in your field? Where then did the weeds come from?" "An enemy did this," he replied. So the servants asked him, "Do you want us to go and pull them up?" "No," he said, "if you pull the weeds now, you might uproot the wheat with them. Let both grow together until the harvest. At that time, I will tell the harvesters: First collect the weeds and tie them in bundles to be burned; then gather the wheat into my barn"'" (Mt. 13:24–30, BSB).

This parable was explained a little further along in Matthew. "He replied, 'The One who sows the good seed is the Son of Man. The field is the world, and the good seed represents the sons of the kingdom. The weeds are the sons of the evil one, and the enemy who sows them is the devil. The harvest is the end of the age, and the harvesters are angels. As the weeds are collected and burned in the fire, so will it be at the end of the age. The Son of Man will send out His angels, and they will weed out of His kingdom every cause of sin and all who practice lawlessness. And they will throw them into the fiery furnace, where there will be weeping and gnashing of teeth. Then the righteous will shine like the sun in the kingdom of their Father. He who has ears, let him hear'" (Mt. 13:37–43, BSB).

In this world, be the wheat. Grow strong and true, bearing grain and fruit. Be careful that you are not a weed growing among the wheat, hiding in plain sight, because God knows who his children are and knows those who belongs to the father of lies. Inspect your fruit. Are you a wheat with a strong tassel of grain, or are you a weed hanging out with the wheat? It's important that you inspect your own fruit. Live as though you are a child of God. Live obediently and in accordance with the commandments of our Father in heaven. Go out into the nations and spread the gospel to others with the full inconvenient truth of the promise. Cultivate the soil so that the seeds will grow and produce good fruit.

"Likewise, every good tree bears good fruit, but a bad tree bears bad fruit. A good tree cannot bear bad fruit, and a bad tree cannot bear good fruit. Every tree that does not bear good fruit is cut down and thrown into the fire. So then, by their fruit you will recognize them. Not everyone who says to Me 'Lord, Lord,' will enter the kingdom of heaven, but only he who does the will of My Father in heaven. Many will say to Me on that day, 'Lord, Lord, did we not prophesy in Your name, and in Your name drive out demons and perform many miracles?' Then I will tell them plainly, 'I never knew you; depart from Me, you workers of lawlessness!'" (Mt. 7:17–23, BSB).

We began this chapter expecting to discuss Satan and his demons, instead we found that man can be an enemy of God. In fact, man cannot only be an enemy of God, but he can erroneously believe he is a child of God and later be turned away by the Savior himself. We've looked at this last verse several chapters earlier. At that time, it was pointed out that the ones being turned away had prophesied in Christ's name, driven out demons, and performed many miracles, but they had not apparently been obedient to the commandments of our Father. These people are workers of lawlessness, sinners, obviously, "having a form of godliness but denying its power" (2 Tim. 3:5, BSB).

The problem with today's culture and modern Christianity is that we say this isn't us. Some believers walk around claiming salvation from the one true God, by the only begotten Son, but are "lovers of themselves, lovers of money, boastful, arrogant, abusive, disobedient to their parents, ungrateful, unholy, unloving, unforgiving, slanderous, without self-control, brutal, without love of good, traitorous, reckless, conceited, lovers of pleasure rather than lovers of God, having a form of godliness but denying its power. Turn away from such as these! They are the kind who worm their way into households and captivate vulnerable women who are weighed down with sins and led astray by various passions, who are always learning but never able to come to a knowledge of the truth" (2 Tim. 3:2–7, BSB).

Be careful that you don't get so wrapped up in a "forgiving, gracious, merciful God" that you forget he requires repentance and instead live life "weighed down with sins and led astray by various passions." You could be the one with your daily devotional every morning and in church every time the doors are open, but if you are more concerned with what pleases you, getting your own way, making sure to have all the possessions you want, conceited, and bragging about how you're better or even just thinking you're better than others, haughty and entitled as though you deserve everything you want and expect others to serve you, unappreciative for the things you have been given or had done for you, worldly, and so concerned with yourself that you can't help others or even have empathy for someone else' trials, pains, or challenges, bitter, and unforgiving, then you are the one Timothy is talking about and an enemy of God. If these are your characteristics, when you stand before the Son of the living God and remind him that you said the "sinner's prayer," spent hours reading your Bible, and declaring how many times you were in church, he will still deny knowing you. We have been warned and instructed. Let us not waste our lives serving the wrong gods.

In the last book of our Bibles, John warns the Christian churches, "'I know your works: you are neither cold nor hot. Would that you were either cold or hot! So, because you are lukewarm, and neither hot nor cold, I will spit you out of my mouth. For you say, I am rich, I have prospered, and I need nothing, not realizing that you are wretched, pitiable, poor, blind, and naked. I counsel you to buy from me gold refined by fire, so that you may be rich, and white garments so that you may clothe yourself and the shame of your nakedness may not be seen, and salve to anoint your eyes, so that you may see. Those whom I love, I reprove and discipline, so be zealous and repent. Behold, I stand at the door and knock. If anyone hears my voice and opens the door, I will come in to him and eat with him and he with me. The one who conquers, I will grant him to sit with me on my throne, as I also conquered and sat down with my Father on his throne" (Rev. 3:15–21, ESV).

Right into the last book of the Bible, we are given instruction on how to be a child of God. Put yourself in this verse and inspect your own lives. Do you look at your life, see possessions and a job that makes it easy to afford these things? Do you attest to your salvation through this prosperity and consider it a sign that God is happy with you? Jesus was asked by a young rich man what good he must do to inherit eternal life.

> "Why do you ask Me about what is good?" Jesus replied. "There is only One who is good. If you want to enter life, keep the commandments." "Which ones?" the man asked. Jesus answered, "'Do not murder, do not commit adultery, do not steal, do not bear false witness, honor your father and mother, and love your neighbor as

yourself.'" "All these I have kept," said the young man. "What do I still lack?" Jesus told him, "If you want to be perfect, go, sell your possessions and give to the poor, and you will have treasure in heaven. Then come, follow Me." When the young man heard this, he went away in sorrow, because he had great wealth. Then Jesus said to His disciples, "Truly I tell you, it is hard for a rich man to enter the kingdom of heaven. Again I tell you, it is easier for a camel to pass through the eye of a needle than for a rich man to enter the kingdom of God." When the disciples heard this, they were greatly astonished and asked, "Who then can be saved?" Jesus looked at them and said, "With man this is impossible, but with God all things are possible." (Mt. 19:17–26, BSB)

Chapter 7

Camping Out

I found a quaint little campground and park a couple months ago while looking for a place to let my boys ride their bikes. As we drove through, looking for a good spot to park and unload the bikes we'd packed, I noticed the campground was divided into two sections. There were the RV spots with full hookups and bathrooms nearby. Most of the spots were taken up with few left to occupy. On the other side of the park were the tent spots. They were the more primitive spots for those who wanted to rough it. We saw three tents with a couple campfires, folding chairs, and clotheslines set up for towels to dry. The thing that struck me is that there was no in between. It was either full-service RV parking with all the amenities of home or straight-up roughing it in a tent and hoofing it to the bathroom for water with a need for battery-operated flashlights come dark.

Christianity has gotten to be a lot like this campground. It seems that most of what I hear preached is about God's grace. I see signs in front of churches, on social media memes, and even in the bathroom stalls of this campground that we visited that God loves us unconditionally and we are saved by grace. Over the last couple of decades as I read my own Bible and found many of the verses and concepts that we've discussed thus far, the same folks etching messages about God's unconditional love into bathroom stalls were the first to correct me for thinking there was anything I could do for God that he might find favor in and, therefore, accused me of lacking in faith and being a straight-up blasphemer. It seems that those in the grace camp believe that they are entitled to the amenities of God simply because they asked Jesus into their hearts, and anyone trying to do good by God have missed their calling for salvation and are trying to earn salvation.

I hear a reverence and a sincerity in the cries from these same people that "they are undeserving but God loved them and everyone so much he gave his only Son that we might have salvation and not get the punishment we deserve," as well as a mantra that "we are covered by his grace and since we are human, there is nothing we can do to please God." "We are clothed in white only by the admission of our sins, forgiven for past, present, and future sins, and we deserve the good life because we're saved."

While I can't walk away from this side of the camp and say that it's entirely wrong because we are unable to earn our way to saving faith, what I can say is that my God didn't give us his Word that we would accept this free gift of salvation and go on sinning as well as living worldly lives. We are saved by Christ alone.

On the other side of the camp are those who feel like they're not camping unless they're sleeping on the ground with a thin piece of fabric between them and the outside world. This side puts forth so much effort to prove they can do it. They turn their noses up toward the other side and fail to count RV camping as actually camping.

Likewise, there seems to be a sense of pride in these RV campers as they look on toward the tent campers. They truly seem to feel sorry for the poor people who think they have something to prove by tent camping and roughing it.

When it comes to camping, preference really does take precedence. It doesn't matter one way of the other whether it's a tent or a fully furnished RV. Both are considered camping and neither way is superior, except in the mind of the man camping who is most definitely entitled to his own opinion. The problem is when we establish two entirely different camps based on Christianity and refuse to see the biblical value in each stance or that it has to be that both are right in order to actually be right.

Those in the "grace and mercy for all" camp really need to move their campers a little closer to the good-works tent campers just as the good-works tent campers need to move their tents a little closer to the grace-and-mercy-for-all RV campers. We need to find the middle ground, not only for unity as believers, but because our Bible is full of instruction on both doctrines. We've spoken at length about the need to actually be active in our faiths. We know that we have to live in obedience to God and have seen that continuing in a life of sin, with worldly behaviors, is the antithesis of Christianity, so the simple terms of "grace and mercy" are by no means a complete representation of the gospel. On the other hand, we've seen that without God's grace and mercy poured out for us as sinners, in the provision of the sacrifice of Christ, God's only Son, we could not have saving faith either. It's both.

As we delved into the Scripture up to this point and looked at the commandments of the Lord being heavily rooted in doing for others, I've thought of many philanthropists who have given to the poor, needy, suffering, etc. They have raised money to help those in third-world nations and even adopted children into their own families from such nations to give them life and hope. You see, without Christ as our savior, it is possible to do good things. Doing good things is not the marker of Christianity. It is belief in Christ and repentance of our sins that saves us, but it must drive us to produce good fruit. It should be sobering to see famous actors and actresses or other renowned professed nonbelievers donating millions collectively to suffering neighbors without the assistance of the Holy Spirit and know that believers ought to be exceeding that. That's not to say that there aren't Christians who have done the same or are loving their neighbors as themselves, but how much more should we believers be supporting, coming along side, and helping widows, orphans, and neighbors in their afflictions, as a whole, if nonbelievers are able to?

This may be one of the leading reasons Christianity is so rejected! While we tout a free gift of salvation from a God who loves us unconditionally, we, as a body of believers, fail to match the nonbelievers in their humanitarian efforts. When the Lord of heaven and Earth told us that the two greatest commandments are to love the Lord God with our whole heart, mind, and soul, and our neighbors as ourselves, he mandated humanitarian efforts. Our salvation is rooted in faith in a Savior who came to earth to save *all* of us if we would believe and repent. We've been instructed to spread the gospel. "So also the Lord directed those who proclaim the gospel to get their living from the gospel" (1 Cor. 9:14, NASB).

Our lives are to be deep-seated in the gospel, which is about righteous living and loving our neighbors as ourselves. When we limit the gospel to salvation alone, we limit ourselves to an elementary teaching. "Therefore, let us leave the elementary teachings about Christ and go on to maturity, not laying again the foundation of repentance from dead works and of faith in God" (Heb. 6:1, ESV). We are babes in Christ if we refuse to receive more than milk. "I fed you with milk, not solid food, for you were not ready for it. And even now you are not yet ready" (1 Cor. 3:2, ESV).

The fact of the matter is that being babes in Christ is not the place we should desire to stay, and no one should want to use this as an excuse for their stance in being saved by grace alone and works are not necessary. "We have much to say about this, but it is hard to explain, because you are dull of hearing. Although by this time you ought to be teachers, you need someone to reteach you the basic principles of God's word. You need milk, not solid food! For everyone who lives on milk is still an infant, inexperienced in the message of righteousness. But solid food is for the mature, who by constant use have trained their senses to distinguish good from evil" (Heb. 5:11–14, BSB).

The Church of Laodicea keeps coming to my mind as we go through this part of our study. "To the angel of the church in Laodicea write: 'These are the words of this verse the faithful and true Witness, the Originator of God's creation. I know your deeds; you are neither cold nor hot. How I wish you were one or the other! So because you are lukewarm—neither hot nor cold—I am about to vomit you out of My mouth!'" (Rev. 3:14–16, NIV).

This passage of the Scripture can be debated whether it's historical or prophetic. I tend to think of it both ways. Colossians 2:8 is a letter from Paul to the Laodiceans in which he reminds them to "see to it that no one takes you captive by philosophy and empty deceit, according to human tradition, according to the elemental spirits of the world, and not according to Christ." You see, there was a literal historical Church of Laodicea. The entire chapter reminds them of their faith in Christ and warns them not to go back to their worldly living. "If with Christ you died to the elemental spirits of the world, why, as if you were still alive in the world, do you submit to regulations—'Do not handle, Do not taste, Do not touch' (referring to things that all perish as they are used)—according to human precepts and teachings? These have indeed an appearance of wisdom in promoting self-made religion and asceticism and severity to the body, but they are of no value in stopping the indulgence of the flesh" (Col. 2:20–23, ESV).

We can also extrapolate from this message that the Laodiceans were going back to the safety and familiarity of what they knew to be religious and acceptable. Paul referred to this as having an appearance of wisdom in promoting self-made religion and asceticism. In other words, Paul rebuked this church for going through motions that looked religious but carried no more merit than a nonbeliever performing the same religious tasks (such as the Pharisees). In fact, it is written, "Woe to you, teachers of the law and Pharisees, you hypocrites! You shut the door of the kingdom of heaven in people's faces. You yourselves do not enter, nor will you let those enter who are trying to" (Mt. 23:13, NIV).

"And anyone who believes in God's Son has eternal life. Anyone who doesn't obey the Son will never experience eternal life but remains under God's angry judgment" (Jn. 3:36, NLT).

To obey the Son, we must remember that Galatians 6:2 elaborated that we are "to carry one another's burdens and in this way (we) will fulfill the law of Christ."

If we come back to the book of Revelation and look at the rest of chapter 3 verse 17–19, we see that the Church of Laodicea was missing the mark. "You say I am rich. I have grown wealthy and need nothing. But you do not realize that you are wretched, pitiful, poor, blind, and naked. I counsel you to buy from me gold refined by fire so that you may become rich, white garments so that you may be clothed and your shameful nakedness not exposed, and salve to anoint your eyes so that you may see. Those I love, I rebuke and discipline. Therefore, be earnest and repent."

Historically, we can see that the Laodiceans were not obeying the law of Christ. They were religious in their deeds perhaps but unable to see that they were actually wretched, pitiful, poor, blind, and naked. Prophetically, we must look at this as a warning. Remember how we've talked about the humility of Christians acknowledging "their wretchedness and their best day's as filthy rags before God." I went so far as to call that a false humility. Take heed, look at how the Creator of the universe looks at the Church of Laodicea; whether of old or prophetically, we can learn how our Father wants us to know him. To these people, he tells them that they are neither hot nor cold and he will spit them out of his mouth. He calls them wretched, blind, poor, etc. and does not afford them favor for believing in his Son and remaining as such wretches. He spits them out! Regard his warning now! "Those I love, I rebuke and discipline. Therefore, be earnest and repent."

Do not be like the Laodiceans who have a form of religion, following the customs and going through the motions of modern Christianity. Do not mock God and stay in a wretched state of humanity feigning humility, believing that because you've asked for forgiveness from God through his Son and cried over your sins that you are saved but too human to be anything but wretched you'll be spat out!

Apart from God, we are nothing! "I am the vine; you are the branches. Whoever abides in me and I in him, he it is that bears much fruit, for apart from me you can do nothing" (Jn. 15:5, ESV).

Oh, but with our God! With our Father who loves us so much he sent his only begotten Son that he would be sure to give us his Word so that we can know. "Everyone who practices sin also practices lawlessness; and sin is lawlessness. You know that He appeared in order to take away sins; and in Him there is no sin. No one who abides in Him sins; no one who sins has seen Him, or knows Him. Little children, make sure no one deceives you. The one who practices righteousness is righteous, just as He is righteous, the one who practices sin is of the devil; for the devil has sinned from the beginning. The Son of God appeared for this purpose, to destroy the works of the devil. No one who is born of God practices sin, because His seed abides in Him, and he cannot sin, because he is born of God. By this the children of God and the children of the devil are obvious. Anyone who does not practice righteousness is not of God, nor the one who does not love his brother" (1 Jn. 3:4–10, NASB).

Take note to the key word "abide"; it's a verb and means to remain, continue, or stay (dictionary.com).

Abiding in God is a mandate in order for us to be anything, do anything, or accomplish anything good. It's an action, a perpetual act, that must be practiced so that we can bear good fruit. It's also an act that will keep us practicing righteousness and avoid sinning. It is an action that our Father told us to do, not just read about, talk about, or to deny!

"Behold, I stand at the door and knock. If anyone hears My voice and opens the door, I will come in and dine with him, and he with Me. To the one who overcomes, I will grant the right to sit with Me on My throne, just as I overcame and sat down with My Father on His throne. He who has an ear, let him hear what the Spirit says to the churches" (Rev. 3:20–22, BSB).

In order to be clothed in righteousness, wearing white garments, that we may not be clothed in shameful nakedness, we must answer the voice of Christ and open the door to him. We can't be like the demons who know of Christ but do not *know him*. "But someone will say, 'You have faith and I have works.' Show me your faith apart from your works, and I will show you my faith by my works. You believe that God is one; you do well. Even the demons believe—and shudder!" (Jas. 2:18–19, ESV).

"I counsel you to buy from Me gold refined by fire so that you may become rich, white garments so that you may be clothed and your shameful nakedness not exposed, and salve to anoint your eyes so that you may see. Those I love, I rebuke and discipline. Therefore be earnest and repent" (Rev. 3:18–19, BSB).

"For God so loved the world that he gave his one and only Son, that whoever believes in him shall not perish but have eternal life"

(Jn. 3:16, NIV). We can't throw our chance for a relationship with the Father away because we succumbed to a false doctrine stating that we are undeserving yet entitled believers.

Let us repent from our sins and know that through faith in Christ, by the power of the Holy Spirit, we can go forth and fulfill the commandments of Christ and of the Father by loving him with our whole heart and with all our souls and with all our minds and that we will love our neighbors as ourselves. Let us buy refined gold from the Father and become rich in faith wearing white garments as it is written not as we'd like it to be and campout in our faith knowing that we are saved by grace, forgiven with mercy, and expected to live righteously, loving our God with our whole selves, our neighbors like ourselves, and supporting, helping, and protecting the afflicted.

CHAPTER 8

Armor of God

"Put on the full armor of God, so that you will be able to stand firm against the schemes of the devil. For our struggle is not against flesh and blood, but against the rulers, against the powers, against the world forces of this darkness, against the spiritual *forces* of wickedness in the heavenly *places*. Therefore, take up the full armor of God, so that you will be able to resist in the evil day, and having done everything, to stand firm. Stand firm therefore, having girded your loins with truth, and having put on the breastplate of righteousness, and having shod your feet with the preparation of the gospel of peace; in addition to all, taking up the shield of faith with which you will be able to extinguish all the flaming arrows of the evil *one*. And take the helmet of salvation and the sword of the Spirit, which is the word of God. With all prayer and petition, pray at all times in the Spirit, and with this in view, be on the alert with all perseverance and petition for all the saints" (Eph. 6:11–18, NASB).

This infamous section of the Scripture has been the theme of many Sunday-School lessons and Vacation Bible School curricula. There are children's books, toys, and craft supplies in catalogs, online stores, and Bible bookstores depicting these verses in "easy to understand" materials. I wonder though if we actually comprehend it.

The book of Ephesians was written as a letter from Paul to the Gentiles of Ephesus. These Ephesians were new believers of Jesus Christ and were being instructed by Paul to put on the armor of

God. It's important to note that the purpose of this armor is to protect against the schemes of the devil. "For our struggle is not against flesh and blood but against the rulers, against the powers, against the world forces of this darkness, against the spiritual forces of wickedness in the heavenly places."

I can only remember ever being taught that Christians were automatically safe from the demons. They told me that there is only space for one spirit. Since believers are filled with the Holy Spirit, there is, therefore, no room for a demon or any such sort. I spent thirty-something years thinking I was safe, but when I open my Bible and read for myself, it's clearly written in there that we believers have to be prepared and protected from Satan and his demons, rulers, powers, world forces of this darkness, and spiritual forces of wickedness. "Be sober-minded; be watchful. Your adversary the devil prowls around like a roaring lion, seeking someone to devour" (1 Pet. 5:8, ESV).

As we make our way through these lives holding onto faith and truly seeking to follow after God, we can't forget to shield our lives with the full armor of God. "Stand firm therefore, having girded your loins with truth" (Eph. 6:14a).

In order to protect our most sensitive and vulnerable areas of our lives, we've got to be girded up with truth. This is the first piece of armor listed.

Merriam-Webster defines "girded" as "to prepare oneself for action or muster up one's resources" (https://www.merriam-webster.com/dictionary/gird).

We already know that our resource is the Bible, the Holy Scriptures. We can't draw on our resources if we don't know what they are. Imagine being given an arsenal of weaponry without knowing how to use it. A life preserver can't save our lives unless we have it on correctly! Consider how it wouldn't matter if we had a security system in place but are unaware of how to arm it or what features it even had. No, the only way a security system is helpful is if we know the powers we get from it and know how to use it.

"Girding our loins with truth" is very much the same. We have a protection plan from God, but we have to arm ourselves with it.

Further, there is a reason God instructs us to gird our loins with truth first. Without the truth of Scripture and salvation in Christ, we couldn't possibly put on any other piece of armor. Let us arm ourselves, fellow believers, and start reading the instruction manual regularly!

The second piece of armor we've been given is a breastplate of righteousness: "And having put on the breastplate of righteousness" (Eph. 6:14b).

The breastplate has to go on after the loins are girded or your armor will not be correctly aligned for safety. We can't live righteously without having the truth first. This piece of armor protects our vital organ; it's placed here to save our spiritual lives. Consider for a moment what righteousness is. Merriam-Webster defines "righteousness" as "acting in accord with divine or moral law or free from guilt or sin" (https://www.merriam-webster.com/dictionary/gird).

"Do you not know that when you present yourselves to someone *as* slaves for obedience, you are slaves of the one whom you obey, either of sin resulting in death, or of obedience resulting in righteousness?" (Rom. 6:16, NASB)

Without righteousness, we will die spiritually.

1 John 1:8–9 (NIV) tells us that "If we say we have no sin, we deceive ourselves, and the truth is not in us. If we confess our sins, he is faithful and just to forgive us our sins and to cleanse us from all unrighteousness."

See how it's all connected? We've been looking at scriptures and studying the details closely. We know without a doubt that the believer is to be righteous. Putting on this breastplate protects our lives in Christ as well as from the schemes of the devil. If we fail to find the value in righteous living and instead lay claim to a proverbial righteousness, abstractly provided through the belief in Christ but with no action on our part to literally live righteously, we leave our souls bare and open to the oppressors, demons, and powers of darkness. Ephesians 4:27 warns us, "and do not give the devil a foothold."

According to the Cambridge Dictionary, a foothold is a noun meaning "a situation in which someone has obtained the power or influence needed to get what is wanted" (Cambridge English Dictionary).

Forgoing the use of the breastplate of righteousness is not only contrary to God's instructions for us believers but leaves a gaping hole for the devil to gain access, power, and influence over our lives.

Paul lists shoes as our third piece of the armor. "And as shoes for your feet, having put on the readiness given by the gospel of peace" (Eph. 6:15, NIV).

Shoes are going to make going the distance much easier. We tend to look down at where we are going when we are barefooted so that we don't step on anything.

A few years ago, I saw a loose pony being chased after by his owner. Flip-flop clad but eager to help get this pony to safety, I went running through a harvested soybean field. Even though I was careful where I was going and had a form of shoe on, it wasn't sturdy like this fitted sandal, and I made one wrong step that left a small hole in the bottom of my foot and a nice trail of blood. If I'd been looking down and watching my steps, I could have avoided it, but I couldn't have helped catch this pony if I was not looking up to see which way he was going. This was just some pony catching. I can hardly imagine what my feet might have looked like if I were engaged in a battle without the proper footwear.

Going to war with well-fitting shoes on will mean we can look ahead at our adversary and keep our attention on the battle at hand, but we need to consider further what the "gospel of peace" must be. We're in a war "against rulers, against the authorities, against the powers of this dark world and against the spiritual forces of evil in the heavenly realms" (Eph. 6:12a). When would we ever think about peace and war mixing? I'm quite sure we're not talking about any "peacemaking" with the demons, so what might have been meant by "gospel of peace"?

"And how are they to preach unless they are sent? As it is written, 'How beautiful are the feet of those who preach the good news!'" (Rom. 10:15, ESV). "How lovely on the mountains are the feet of him who brings good news, who announces peace and brings good news of happiness, who announces salvation, *and* says to Zion, 'Your God reigns!' (Isa. 52:7, NASB). If we take these verses representing what the gospel of peace is, we can see that an important, protecting part of our armor, which will keep us looking ahead and from being slowed down in our battle, is preaching the good news! We can have beautiful, shoe-clad feet by praising and proclaiming the entire gospel of the saving grace of God through his Son, Jesus Christ.

The fourth piece of armor is listed as a shield. "In addition to all this, take up the shield of faith, with which you can extinguish all the flaming arrows of the evil one" (Eph. 6:16).

Here again we are looking at why we are putting the armor on—to extinguish the evil one! Did you know that Roman shields (the ones that would have been used during the time of this analogy) were leather? Dry leather would burn though. So the Roman shield would only be able to extinguish flaming arrows if it were water-soaked.

The only way a shield could be water-soaked is to be completely immersed in water. Believers are to be completely immersed in water for baptism (which is the symbol of burying the old self). So this shield could very well be an analogy for believers being water-baptized.

"Baptism, which corresponds to this, now saves you, not as a removal of dirt from the body but as an appeal to God for a good conscience, through the resurrection of Jesus Christ" (1 Pet. 3:21, ESV). Like a butterfly emerging from a chrysalis, unable to return back to being a caterpillar, we emerge from the baptismal water metamorphically transformed into a new creation.

If this shield is to represent baptism, then the shield of faith is about having a clear conscience toward God. A clear conscience brought on from obedience in water baptism will deflect the fiery attacks of the evil one. A clear conscience comes from confessing our sins and repenting to the Holy God, not just that "one time" when we repeated a sinner's prayer or even that one time we genuinely cried out to God for salvation through repentance and belief in Christ. Nonetheless, baptism is a biblical requirement, symbolic of this act of repentance and promise to live righteously as the old self stays buried under the water. A new person, slave to Christ, free from the flesh emerges instead. "For we died and were buried with Christ by baptism. And just as Christ was raised from the dead by the glorious power of the Father, now we also may live new lives" (Rom. 6:4 NLT).

"Now why do you delay? Get up and be baptized, and wash away your sins, calling on His name" (Acts 22:16, NASB).

"Having been buried with Him in baptism, in which you were also raised up with Him through faith in the working of God, who raised Him from the dead" (Col. 2:12, NASB).

We rise up out of the water with him through faith in the working of God. The shield of faith may very well be all about the act of baptism, our transformation, and the active faith we have in God.

"Repent, and each of you be baptized in the name of Jesus Christ for the forgiveness of your sins; and you will receive the gift of the Holy Spirit. For the promise is for you and your children and for all who are far off, as many as the Lord our God will call to Himself" (Acts 2:38–39, NASB).

"God's way is perfect. All the Lord's promises prove true. He is a shield for all who look to him for protection" (2 Sam. 22:31, NLT).

Fifth in the list of armor Paul gives is the helmet of salvation. "And take the helmet of salvation…" (Eph. 6:17, ESV).

A helmet protects our heads. Our heads house our minds, so this helmet of salvation is a protection of our minds.

"For though we walk in the flesh, we do not war according to the flesh, for the weapons of our warfare are not of the flesh, but divinely powerful for the destruction of fortresses. *We are* destroying speculations and every lofty thing raised up against the knowledge of God, and *we are* taking every thought captive to the obedience of Christ" (2 Cor. 10:3–5, NASB).

I believe this scripture is in direct correlation to the "armor of God." It seems to me that the helmet of salvation is a call to action that we "take *every* thought captive to the obedience of Christ." Obviously, this can only be done through salvation from Christ, power from the Holy Spirit, and in obedience to our Lord. This is the same power of God we've been talking about in how it assists us in our lives that we do not have to sin. As believers, we can come boldly to our Father through Christ who saved us and ask for his will to be done within us. We can surrender our lives to him and claim his power in our lives through the blood of his Son. "Submit yourselves therefore to God. Resist the devil, and he will flee from you" (Jas. 4:7, ESV).

The final piece of armor listed is the sword of the Spirit. "…And the sword of the Spirit, which is the word of God, praying at all times in the Spirit, with all prayer and supplication…" (Eph. 6:17–18, ESV).

The ESV version punctuates this passage differently than the other mainstream translations. There is a comma in this translation that seems to define that the sword of the Spirit is the word of God, and another comma indicating a connection with praying at all times in the Spirit.

The BSB version and many others not only finish the sentence in verse 17 with a period but begin a new paragraph with the eighteenth verse as shown below.

"And take the helmet of salvation and the sword of the Spirit, which is the word of God. Pray in the Spirit at all times, with every kind of *prayer* and petition. To this end, stay alert with all perseverance in your *prayers* for all the saints. *Pray* also for me, that whenever I open my mouth, words may be given me so that I will boldly make known the mystery of the gospel, for which I am an ambassador in chains. *Pray* that I may proclaim it fearlessly, as I should" (Eph. 6: 17–20, BSB).

The sword of the Spirit is no doubt the word of God. We can read it literally and derive the concept that the sword of the Spirit is the Bible. I'm not going to denounce that as truth; the Bible is our truth, full of knowledge, wisdom, and commandments for believers to use, but I rather consider the ESV translation which is based on "a literal word-for-word translation philosophy" (What is the English Standard Version (ESV)? | GotQuestions.org).

"…And the sword of the Spirit, which is the word of God, praying at all times in the Spirit, with all prayer and supplication…" (Eph. 6:17–18, ESV).

So what is "praying in the spirit" then that is referenced in "the whole armor of God" (Eph. 6:18), and is it related to speaking in tongues or not? It's not only a controversial topic but largely disputed among Protestant and Charismatic denominations. Some believe all the gifts of the Spirit have passed away. They are called cessationists. There are other denominations who believe that speaking in tongues is *the* evidence of a baptism of the Holy Spirit. I personally agree with neither. While we can look at the stories of Acts and see that the listing of the spiritual gifts being given to believers include tongues in each of the three stories, it doesn't ever say that it is the evidence.

In fact, Paul does actually list the evidence of those who live by the Spirit in Galatians 5:22–26 (NRSV), "By contrast, the fruit of the Spirit is love, joy, peace, patience, kindness, generosity, faithfulness, gentleness, and self-control. There is no law against such things. And those who belong to Christ Jesus have crucified the flesh with its passions and desires. If we live by the Spirit, let us also be guided by the Spirit. Let us not become conceited, competing against one another, envying one another."

"Pursue love, yet desire earnestly spiritual *gifts*, but especially that you may prophesy. For one who speaks in a tongue does not speak to men but to God; for no one understands, but in *his* spirit he speaks mysteries" (1 Cor. 14:1–2, NASB).

"But you, beloved, by building yourselves up in your most holy faith and praying in the Holy Spirit, keep yourselves in the love of God as you await the mercy of our Lord Jesus Christ to bring you eternal life" (Jude 1:20–21, BSB). "For through (Christ) we both have access to the Father by one Spirit" (Eph. 2:18, BSB).

We can use Scriptures to support the fact that the Holy Spirit gives us access to the Father and that we must build ourselves up in our most holy faith praying in the Holy Spirit, which has been argued to have nothing to do with tongues, but there is a section in 1 Corinthians that speaks also of a conversation or prayer with God that is self-edifying and also for building ourselves up and worth looking at to connect the dots to.

"The one who speaks in a tongue edifies himself, but the one who prophesies edifies the church… Therefore, the one who speaks in a tongue should pray that he may interpret. For if I pray in a tongue, my spirit prays, but my mind is unfruitful. What then shall I do? I will pray with my spirit, but I will also pray with my mind. I will sing with my spirit, but I will also sing with my mind. Otherwise, if you speak a blessing in spirit, how can someone who is uninstructed say "Amen" to your thanksgiving, since he does not know what you are saying? You may be giving thanks well enough, but the other one is not edified. I thank God that I speak in tongues more than all of you. But in the church, I would rather speak five coherent words to instruct others than ten thousand words in a tongue" (1 Cor. 14:4, 13–19, BSB).

Paul seems to be very clear in explaining that speaking, singing, and praying in tongues is for personal (spiritual) edification. In fact, with regard to the church, he tells the one speaking in tongues to pray for interpretation so that others might be edified. But if we look at this for the purpose of how to build oneself up, then praying in the spirit is the epitome of building ourselves up in our most holy faith, just as we saw in Jude 1:20–21, BSB: "But you, beloved, by building yourselves up in your most holy faith and praying in the Holy Spirit, keep yourselves in the love of God as you await the mercy of our Lord Jesus Christ to bring you eternal life."

Paul thanks God that he speaks in tongues more than all the others. Just like in everything else about our faith in God, we only need to go before him and ask him to give us a gift that would be self-edifying, to build ourselves in faith in his glory, and, therefore, fully armed with the armor that God has provided for us to wear, that we might be insulated from the schemes of the devil and the demons.

"This is the confidence which we have before Him, that, if we ask anything according to His will, He hears us" (1 Jn. 5:14, NASB).

If praying in the spirit means we must pray in tongues, then all we need to do is ask that God grant us that spiritual gift. We can go before the Father with sincerity that we are seeking after his heart. We see that Paul spoke of edifying oneself is by "praying in the spirit," and we can pray for the faith we need to accept God's will, even if what that will is, surprises us.

If praying in the spirit has nothing to do with tongues, it most certainly has to be about being in a mental state of spirituality and reverence within God's will that we're not really in what we think of as the normal human consciousness. Not that it means we're in a trance or other state of mind but to be so hyper-focused on communing with the one true God, whom you are righteously and obediently living for. Like being drunk on God and giving control over to the Spirit. True committed humility and submission to the Father. We must die to our own pride and understanding. We cannot denounce the Holy Spirit in our lives and confine him to a minor ambiguous role of the Trinity or within our lives. He's not just a feeling we use to decide what we want to do. We can absolutely be led by the Spirit in our daily decisions and trust him to give utterance to both God and man, but when we are not living in submission to God and are not slaves to Christ Jesus, and we are fornicating, practicing idolatry, selfish, greedy, loving self over all others, we are living in the flesh and kid ourselves if we think we are being spirit-lead. There is a personal action required, belief. Not belief only paying tribute to words without actions, a belief that we are dead to self and living for Christ. We are listening to the Spirit for conviction and acting upon his wisdom in repentance and changes that are obvious in our fruit.

These are the parts traditionally given as the armor of God: the belt of truth, the breastplate of righteousness, the shoes to proclaim the gospel, the shield of faith, the helmet of salvation, and the sword of the Spirit. Go back to the section of Scripture in Ephesians 6 that speaks of the entire armor of God. Let us note that the last four verses of this section are about prayer. It is listed and instructed upon seven times. Paul is calling believers to prayer. He's proclaiming the imperative need for believers to pray, pray, pray, pray, pray, pray, and pray some more.

In the gospels of Matthew, Mark, Luke, and John, we see more evidence of the power of prayer and the repercussions of the lack of prayer. Peter was warned by Jesus himself that he would deny him three times before the rooster crowed. A few verses later, we find, "Then he returned to his disciples and found them sleeping. 'Simon, are you asleep? Could you not watch one hour? Watch and pray that you may not enter into temptation. The spirit indeed is willing, but the flesh is weak'" (Mk. 14:37–38, ESV).

Notice that our Savior was both disappointed and warning Peter to pray that he will not fall into temptation… Peter did not prepare himself in prayer.

Then about thirty verses later, "seeing Peter warming himself, she looked at him and said, 'You also were with Jesus the Nazarene.' But he denied *it*, saying, 'I neither know nor understand what you are talking about.' And he went out onto the porch. The servant girl saw him, and began once more to say to the bystanders, 'This is *one* of them!' But again, he denied it. And after a little while the bystanders were again saying to Peter, 'Surely you are *one* of them, for you are a Galilean too.' But he began to curse and swear, 'I do not know this man you are talking about!' Immediately a rooster crowed a second time. And Peter remembered how Jesus had made the remark to him, 'Before a rooster crows twice, you will deny Me three times.' And he began to weep" (Mk. 14:67–72, NASB).

The parallel here is uncanny. Without praying, Peter was ill prepared to defeat the enemy and gave into the very temptation he had even been forewarned of. We've been taught to "rejoice always, pray without ceasing, give thanks in all circumstances; for this is the will of God in Christ Jesus for you" (1 Thess. 5:16–18, ESV).

Prayer is conversation with our Father. It's praising him, thanking him, talking to him, being still and listening for him, as well as bringing forth our petitions to him. He knows everything before we talk to him, but he desires that intimacy with us. "Devote yourselves to prayer, keeping alert in it with *an attitude of* thanksgiving" (Col. 4:2, NASB).

In the book of Mark, there is an account of a boy who is possessed by an evil spirit. We are told that he has had this spirit from childhood and the disciples were not able to deliver him from this spirit. Jesus does so and is later asked by his disciples why they were unable to deliver the boy themselves. "Jesus answered, 'This kind cannot come out except by prayer.'"

Remembering to pray regularly can be a struggle, but knowing what to say while we pray is even harder for a lot of people. Jesus tells us, "And when you are praying, do not use thoughtless repetition as the Gentiles do, for they think that they will be heard because of their many words" (Mt. 6:7, NASB). Christ is telling us to have a relationship with our Father through prayer and in the way that we pray. There should an intimacy between a believer and our Lord. When we pray, we are to speak to him, not at him. He wants us to talk to him as his loving sons and daughters. Christianity is about loving God. We love him in our obedience, just as we lovingly want to talk with him, tell him about our day, what we're happy about, and what we're struggling with. It is a time to praise him and pay honor to him. Worship is an act of showing our Lord that we value him most; prayer is the way to talk to the most revered one of our lives.

Christ gives us insight into praying and gives us what is now known as "The Lord's Prayer." Since he has forewarned us not to use thoughtless repetition, I don't think he meant for us to repeat this prayer mindlessly. I don't think it's a bad thing to use this prayer and to repeat it or memorize it, but we do need to take care not to mindlessly repeat it with no meaning behind it. "But when you pray, go into your room and shut the door and pray to your Father who is in secret. And your Father who sees in secret will reward you… Pray then like this, 'Our Father in heaven, hallowed be your name. Your kingdom come, your will be done, on earth as it is in heaven. Give us this day our daily bread, and forgive us our debts, as we also have forgiven our debtors. And lead us not into temptation, but deliver us from evil'" (Mt. 6:6, 9–13, ESV).

The beginning of this prayer is in reverence of our Father in heaven, communicating to our God that he is holy and we know it. The second line is a statement that announces to our God that we want his kingdom on Earth; it's a statement that acknowledges in prayer that there will be a new heaven and Earth to come (Christ and many prophets spoke of this) and that we want that. Third, we pray that God's will be done. When we are in his Word, seeking after him and not just to fulfill our time with the Bible open for the day, we come to know him and think more in accord with him. We want his will to be done on Earth as it is in heaven, moving away from prayers that are motivated by selfish gains. The fourth line askes for our daily needs to be met. I think of the manna provided for the Israelites for forty years and how they were told not to store up extra except on Fridays so that they did not need to gather manna on the Sabbath. About twenty-three verses from this statement, Christ says, "Therefore do not worry about tomorrow, for tomorrow will worry about itself. Today has enough trouble of its own" (Mt. 6:34, ESV) and I realize that this has been a theme of Christ's. Do not worry about the future. Pray daily for sustenance and worry not about the days to come.

The next line of this prayer Christ taught us goes to asking God for forgiveness. We have forgiveness through Christ. We do not need to go to the priests and Give sacrifices for forgiveness from God, but we do need to realize that our Savior is speaking to believers and communicating to us that we need to ask for forgiveness of our sins even after that moment of our conversion. "My dear children, I am writing this to you so that you will not sin. But if anyone does sin, we have an advocate who pleads our case before the Father. He is Jesus Christ, the one who is truly righteous" (1 Jn. 2:1, NLT). We are not to sin again after conversion, but if we do, Jesus is still our savior. The emphasis in our lives must be on sinning less and not using this part of the Lord's Prayer as permission or validation to continue in the same sin we were in. Because "Dear friends, if we deliberately continue sinning after we have received knowledge of the truth, there is no longer any sacrifice that will cover these sins" (Heb. 10:26, NLT).

There is also a homage given to the fact that we need to forgive others of their sins against us, and right after Christ finishes this prayer, he elaborates, "For if you forgive others their trespasses, your heavenly Father will also forgive you, but if you do not forgive others their trespasses, neither will your Father forgive your trespasses" (Mt. 6:14–15, ESV).

Finally, this lesson in prayer instructs us to ask God not to let us be tempted as well as delivered from evil. I grew up reciting this prayer. I knew it from a very young age as I came up in church and attended Sunday school, but there is something striking about this line. While I knew this to be the last line of the prayer before Amen and could recite it without thinking, I'm carried back in time, in my mind, about four years ago.

I was coming down the pike of a fourteen-year-long marriage to a man who had done nothing but destroy me from the inside out. I'd been miserable, beaten down, sick, and desperate for him to change for almost all those years. As I think back though, there are two things that stick out as different and possibly the reason God provided a way to escape this treacherous life. You see, I began seeking God's Word. Instead of reading the Bible and finding scriptures and verses that seemed to go against what I was learning in church and feeling frustrated, I began searching them with hunger and justification that these are the words of God that hold the very depth of his saving grace, regardless of what others say and preach. The other thing I began to do differently was specifically pray for God to "deliver me from evil." Demonic influence had been illuminated for me. Passages and scriptures about how believers need to be weary of Satan and his demons began jumping off the pages at me...there was no single verse I'd read or been reminded of that lead me to pray for deliverance specifically while this popular prayer laid dormant and unthought of in my mind. I felt an urgency and had been given this very phrase in prayer by someone I could only identify as the Holy Spirit.

"Lord, deliver me," and after fourteen years of abuse and pleading, begging, and frustration with unanswered prayers, God heard me and delivered me. No one will convince me that it was coincidental as I'm sure that it was divine. I don't believe it was a lesson I was learning through this marriage or something I had to endure for a certain number of years for a certain deific growth but rather I believe God was patiently waiting for me to come to know him, do as he has spelled out for us in the holy living Word of God that I'd often put down because it didn't match the doctrines or sermons I'd been hearing, and I didn't want to fight or deal with the turmoil that grew within me because of it. I believe God let me get to my bottom, the place where I'd contemplated suicide and dreamed up ways to fulfill it because I had to need him. He let the Israelites fall victim to their adversaries as he waited for them to turn back to him (as a people) countless times. True, authentic relationships are what our Father craves. Prayers that are meaningful, thoughtful, and derived from his Word and his will are the elements of a purposeful prayer life.

After Jesus instructed us on how to pray, he told us about fasting. "And when you fast, do not look gloomy like the hypocrites, for they disfigure their faces that their fasting may be seen by others. Truly, I say to you, they have received their reward. But when you fast, anoint your head and wash your face that your fasting may not be seen by others but by your Father who is in secret. And your Father who sees in secret will reward you" (Mt. 6:16–18, ESV).

Fasting and praying go hand in hand at times.

"When they reached the crowd, a man approached and knelt down before Him. 'Lord,' he said, 'have mercy on my son because he has seizures and suffers severely. He often falls into the fire and often into the water. I brought him to your disciples, but they couldn't heal him.' Jesus replied, 'You unbelieving and rebellious generation! How long will I be with you? How long must I put up with you? Bring him here to be.' Then Jesus rebuked the demon, and it came out of him, and from that moment, the boy was healed. Then the disciples approached Jesus privately and said, 'Why couldn't we drive it out?' 'Because of your little faith,' he told them. 'For I assure you. If you have faith the size of a mustard seed, you will tell this mountain. "Move from here to there," and it will move. Nothing will be impossible for you.' However, this kind does not come out except by prayer and fasting" (Mt. 7:14–21, Holman Christian Standard Bible).

"So we fasted and petitioned our God about this, and he answered our prayer" (Ezra 8:23, NIV).

The following section of Scripture in the book of Isaiah comes as a response from God to (most likely) Isaiah.

Previously, Isaiah came before God and asked, "Why have we fasted and You do not see? Why have we humbled ourselves and You do not notice?" (Isa. 58:3, NASB)

God answers Isaiah by showing him that they were not humble as they fasted.

The verses to follow (6–7) are a response from God explaining to Isaiah (and we readers) that fasting is to loosen bonds of wickedness, yokes of oppression, to give to the hungry, homeless, and poor, to cover the naked, and to let the oppressed go free.

The Lord goes on to elaborate that fasting is an effort to overcome your own flesh. It is symbolic as we withhold food from our hungry selves, that we, too, are denying the desires of our flesh. In verses 8–12, God explains that through proper, humble fasting, our lights will break through the darkness, and our righteousness will shine before us. The glory of our Lord will be our protector, watcher of our backs, and then we will be heard by the Lord. There is a reiteration of our yoke of slavery to sin and wicked accusations being removed as we fast in truth and humility and the fulfillment of our duty as believers to give to the hungry and help the afflicted, that our lights will rise in darkness and our gloom will vanish. The Lord will guide us and provide us even in the scorched places and give us strength as we rise up without fail to live lives for our Lord.

Fasting is a powerful tool in prayer and coming closer to our Lord in our Christian walks.

> Is this not the fast which I choose to loosen the bonds of wickedness, to undo the bands of the yoke, and to let the oppressed go free and break every yoke? Is it not to divide your bread with the hungry and bring the homeless poor into the house; When you see the naked, to cover him; and not to hide yourself from your own flesh? Then your light will break out like the dawn, and your recovery will speedily spring forth; and your righteousness will go before you; The glory of the Lord will be your rear guard.
>
> Then you will call, and the Lord will answer; You will cry, and He will say, 'Here I am.' If you remove the yoke from your midst, the pointing of the finger and speaking wickedness, and if you give yourself to the hungry and satisfy the desire of the afflicted, then your light will rise in darkness and your gloom will become like midday.

> And the Lord will continually guide you, and satisfy your desire in scorched places, and give strength to your bones; and you will be like a watered garden, and like a spring of water whose waters do not fail. Those from among you will rebuild the ancient ruins; You will raise up the age-old foundations; and you will be called the repairer of the breach, the restorer of the streets in which to dwell. (Isa. 58:6–12)

Prayer is pivotal in our preparedness and walk with the Lord. As we put on the whole armor of God, there will be times when we don't know what to even pray. There have been times in my own life when I felt as though all I ever said to him was the same thing. Then there were other parts of my life when I had no words to say. I knew I needed him and that prayer was my direct link to the Creator of the universe, but I did not know what to say. "In the same way, the Spirit helps us in our weakness. For we do not know how we ought to pray, but the Spirit Himself intercedes for us with groans too deep for words" (Rom. 8:26, BSB).

I'm quite certain that this is how I knew to pray for deliverance. Nearly fourteen years of repetitive pleadings went unanswered until I sought God. I moved past the feelings of inadequacy and dependence on what I'd been hearing taught and the contrast of what I was reading for myself, and I finally wholeheartedly sought after truth. This seeking was the "If you will" part necessary for the "then" promised by God, "You will call upon Me and come and pray to Me, and I will listen to you. "You will seek Me and find Me when you search for Me with all your heart. I will be found by you, declares the Lord, and I will restore you from captivity…" (Jer. 29:12–14).

God provides everything for us. We must be willing and seeking after, but through him, by him, and in him, "we can do all things through Christ who strengthens us" (Phil. 4:13) and even have intercession of prayer by the Holy Spirit of God when we ourselves have no words.

"And Peter said to them, 'Repent and be baptized every one of you in the name of Jesus Christ for the forgiveness of your sins, and you will receive the gift of the Holy Spirit'" (Acts 2:38, ESV).

The armor is completely protective as a whole. Without one piece, we're not only left vulnerable but missing the support for the other protective pieces to stay in place. Notice here that Peter is telling believers to repent and then be baptized, to receive the Holy Spirit. Knowing that Jesus sent the Holy Spirit to us after his death to be our helper and that by his death he defeated the rulers and authorities, "When He had disarmed the rulers and authorities, He made a public display of them, having triumphed over them through Him" (Col. 2:15), we can expand this definition of the "sword of the Spirit, which is the Word," to the authority we have in Christ to expel the demons in the name of Jesus by the power of his Holy Spirit, given to us by Father God. "Jesus called his twelve disciples to him and gave them authority to drive out impure spirits and to heal every disease and sickness" (Mt. 10:1, NIV).

There are many accounts of the disciples and apostles doing just that, driving out impure spirits (as well as diseases and sickness). If we put on all the pieces of armor, we're ready to slay demons. While Paul emphasized praying, the sword of the Spirit "is the word of God praying at all times in the Spirit."

"Truly, truly, I say to you, whoever believes in me will also do the works that I do; and greater works than these will he do, because I am going to the Father. Whatever you ask in my name, this I will do, that the Father may be glorified in the Son. If you ask me anything in my name, I will do it. If you love me, you will keep my commandments. And I will ask the Father, and he will give you another Helper, to be with you forever, even the Spirit of truth, whom the world cannot receive, because it neither sees him nor knows him. You know him, for he dwells with you and will be in you" (Jn. 14:12–17, ESV).

The Holy Spirit of God is the Spirit of truth. He is often the most forgotten, misunderstood, ill-used, and neglected of the three, but without him, we are lost. "These things I have spoken to you while I (Jesus) am still with you. But the Helper, the Holy Spirit, whom the Father will send in my name, he will teach you all things and bring to your remembrance all that I have said to you" (Jn. 14:25–26, ESV).

As a teen, I sensed something was missing in my life. I was a born-again, baptized believer, but I knew little of the Holy Spirit. He was merely described as "a helper," and while I didn't imagine him as the little angel on my shoulder, he was likened to that within my own belief system. This very same Spirit was speaking to me though and opening my eyes to the truth about him. In Acts 2:38 (NRSV), it says, "Peter said to them, 'Repent, and be baptized, every one of you, in the name of Jesus Christ so that your sins may be forgiven and you will receive the gift of the Holy Spirit.'" This much I knew, but what I needed to understand was that the indwelling or filling of the Holy Spirit was to be more than a minor role. Just as we've looked at righteousness and the fact that it isn't an abstract concept with ambiguous meaning, being a spirit-filled believer is not either.

With all due respect, I tread lightly through this topic but with confidence that we're using the scriptures to find answers. We know that we need to pray in the Spirit in order to use the fullness of the security God has given to all his believing children and to defeat the prowling devil and the powers of darkness, but being a spirit-filled believer doesn't mean we set our sword on a special shelf only to be taken down to slay dragons. The book of Acts describes "the coming of the Holy Spirit" while we can find many verses prior to this account of the Holy Spirit's presence in various different people's lives before this, the outpouring of the Spirit came upon the ascension of Christ after his crucifixion. "Nevertheless I tell you the truth: it is to your advantage that I go away, for if I do not go away, the Advocate (or helper) will not come to you; but if I go, I will send him to you… When the Spirit of truth comes, he will guide you into all the truth; for he will not speak on his own, but will speak whatever he hears, and he will declare to you the things that are to come. He will glorify me (Christ), because he will take what is mind and declare it to you" (Jn. 16:7, 13–14, NRSV).

To be indwelled with the Holy Spirit and live by him is to give control to him. We must be committed to submission. In the book of

Acts, the twelve disciples illustrate the fact that being a believer does not guarantee a spirit-filled life. In fact, when they set out to choose seven men to serve the Hebrew widows, they specified, "Therefore, friends, select from among yourselves seven men of good standing, full of the Spirit and of wisdom, whom we may appoint to this task" (Acts 6:3, NRSV).

Paul commands us to "live by the Spirit, I say, and do not gratify the desires of the flesh... Now the works of the flesh are obvious: fornication, impurity, licentiousness, idolatry, sorcery, enmities, strife, jealousy, anger, quarrels, dissensions, factions, envy, drunkenness, carousing, and things like these. I am warning you, as I warned you before: those who do such things will not inherit the kingdom of God" (Gal. 5:17, 19–21, NRSV).

In fact, Ephesians 5:18 (NRSV) contrasts being drunk with wine and being filled with the spirit: "Do not get drunk with wine, for that is a debauchery; but be filled with the Spirit."

To be drunk with spirits, or alcohol, control is lost. To be filled with the Holy Spirit, control is given up to the holy godhead. The third person of the Holy Trinity is the Holy Spirit. He is God just as much as Christ is the "*I am*" (John 14:6).

Earlier in Acts, when the Holy Spirit first came "and suddenly from heaven there came a sound like a rush of violent wind, and it filled the entire house where they were sitting. Dividing tongues, as of fire, appeared among them, and a tongue rested on each of them. All of them were filled with the Holy Spirit and began speaking in other languages, as the Spirit gave them the ability... And at this sound the crowd gathered was bewildered, because each one heard them speaking in the native language of each... And how is it each of us hears in our native language? Parthians, Medes, Elamites, and residents of Mesopotamia, Judea and Cappadocia, Pontus and Asia, Phrygia and Pamphylia, Egypt and the parts of Libya belonging to Cyrene, and visitors from Rome, both Jews and proselytes, Cretans and Arabs—in their own languages we hear them speaking about God's deeds of power. All were amazed and perplexed, saying to one another, 'What does this mean?' But others sneered and said, 'They are filled with new wine'" (Acts 2:2–4, 6, 8–13, NRSV).

Peter addressed the crowd, assuring them that it was too early for them to be drunk and declares this outpouring of the Holy Spirit is fulfillment of the prophet Joel. Notice that these men had given complete control to the Holy Spirit, like a drunkard loses himself to alcohol. The main parts to take away from this section of Scripture is that there were at least seventeen different languages present at this day of Pentecost. Many like to assume that tongues is in a known language, but here it says that while the Holy Spirit was poured out on these believers, they spoke tongues that "in they heard, each in their own language." Have you ever been in a large crowd where the people were all speaking the same language? Could you understand them? Now imagine there were at least seventeen different languages being spoken at once. Do you think you'd be able to pick out your native tongue and identify the content of what was spoken? No, these men were not speaking known languages of the earth. They were speaking in the Spirit, unknown languages that were heard by each person there in their own tongue (language), clearly enough that they knew they were speaking of the powerful deeds of God. This is the mystery of the Spirit. He gives us gifts of power in wisdom, knowledge, faith, healing, miracles, prophecy, discernment of Spirits, revelation, apostles, prophets, teachers, deeds of power, gifts of healing, forms of assistance, forms of leadership, tongues of various kinds, and interpretation of tongues (1 Cor. 12 and 14).

Those who heard the tongues spoken were given the gift of interpretation that our Lord be glorified. The second point to take from this is that those who sneered "they were full of new wine" made a strong comparison to drunkenness of wine with drunkenness of the spirit. 1 Samuel 10:6 (NRSV) gives a similar description, "Then the spirit of the Lord will possess you, and you will be in a prophetic frenzy along with them and be turned into a different person."

To be filled with the Holy Spirit is to give over control. Paul was speaking to believers who had been filled with the Holy Spirit already when he told them in Ephesians 5:18 not to get drunk with wine but to be filled with the Spirit. He was (as in all his letters) encouraging believers to stay strong in their faith and abandon themselves and to be controlled by the Spirit of God. Realizing that this command comes one chapter before the infamous "whole armor of God" section in chapter 6, verse 10–20, we've got to feel the urgency Paul was feeling.

We've talked a lot about grace so far. We've looked at the debauchery others have turned this word into and what the Word of God says about this concept. Let us look at another letter from Paul. In 1 Corinthians 1:4–9 (NRSV), it says, "I give thanks to my God always for you because of the *grace* of God that has been given you in Christ Jesus, for in every way you have been enriched in him, in speech and in knowledge of every kind—just as the testimony of Christ has been strengthened among you—so that you are not lacking in any spiritual gift as you wait for the revealing of your Lord Jesus Christ."

My fellow believers, this grace that we have from God is not merely an idea that we are saved from damnation that we deserve. This grace of God enriches us in speech, knowledge, the testimony of Christ, and in our receiving spiritual gifts from the Holy Spirit.

Let me warn you, however, "Those who are unspiritual do not receive the gifts of God's Spirit, for they are foolish to them, and they are unable to understand them because they are spiritually discerned. Those who are spiritual discern all things, and they are themselves subject to no one else's scrutiny. 'For who has known the mind of the Lord so as to instruct him?' But we have the mind of Christ" (1 Cor. 2:14–16, NRSV). "As for you, the anointing that you received from him abides in you, and so you do not need anyone to teach you. But as his anointing teaches you about all things, and is true and is not a lie, and just as it has taught you, abide in him" (1 Jn. 2:27, NRSV).

I fear oftentimes we kid ourselves upon conviction from the Holy Spirit, and instead of heeding the loving guidance of our Holy Spirit, we go through a form of the stages of grief. Grief over the loss of our pride, arrogance, and unrighteousness or misunderstanding. We hear the call. We feel the conviction, but humanity is so good at justifying themselves to stay in the wrong.

Instead of moving forward in a godly fashion, we convince ourselves that we were already doing it correctly or we go into denial.

Many turn to anger. They don't want to be convicted of wrongdoing, so it's easier to get mad at the one who brought it to attention or some project their anger onto others, all in effort to avoid acceptance of the content of the conviction. Some go straight to the bargaining stage and start offering God other parts of their lives or change after this one more time of doing something wrong. I remember listening to an abusive husband talk about going on a mission's trip, and in exchange for "his service to God," he was forgiven of the abuse he bestowed upon his wife and then continued doing.

Then there are those who get to the fourth stage. They become depressed at the fact that they had been doing something wrong, but they stay there in depression and reassign the catalyst of this deep sadness by reverting back to blame. They portray themselves as victims and look for comfort in as many people as they can get to listen to the slander about the one they blame. They stay there in this depression as if it's somehow a godly emotion and fail to make the change the Spirit was revealing needed to be changed. They go down such a road of blame that their entire existence becomes that of validation.

Instead of focusing on the life the Holy Spirit is prodding for, they become bitter and hateful at the person or "caused" their depression and find solace in slander and comradery with all those who will validate them as they walk further from God and his calling. They form a sense of self-righteousness, and instead of the repentance required by the Holy Spirit, they make religion their god. Their time is focused on looking a part and telling others of their godliness while knocking others down to feel higher and yet still claim to be led and guided by the Holy Spirit in their own selfish pursuits. They feel "godly" because they are going to church, Bible study, or pinning scripture up on social media. They play a part so well that they become numb to the gentle nudge of the Holy Spirit and settle down into a religion full of devotionals that validate the "feelies" they felt when singing a song about "having scars that God loves anyway" and fail to ever live by the Spirit.

Their true fruit, when no one is looking, is mushy and rotten. The fruit they put on display is a false fruit, like the plastic fruit popularly displayed on tables in the fifties. Their true selves are lacking in love, joy, peace, patience, kindness, generosity, faithfulness, gentleness, and self-control.

Passionate believers in Christ know the voice of the Holy Spirit and more often than not go straight to acceptance. They skip the first four stages of grief as the only thing that grieves them is the grief they've caused God. They see the verse, or the sin in their lives, and they adjust by the power of the Holy Spirit. They know that "the greatest commandment is to love God with our whole heart, mind, and soul." To love God is to obey him. To obey him is to be full of love.

"If I speak in the tongues of men and of angels, but have not love, I am only a ringing gong or a clanging cymbal. If I have the gift of prophecy and can fathom all mysteries and all knowledge, and if I have absolute faith so as to move mountains, but have not love, I am nothing. If I give all I possess to the poor and exult in the surrender of my body, but have not love, I gain nothing" (1 Cor. 13:1–3, BSB).

When we avidly desire to spend time with the Creator and come into his presence with no outside distractions, loving him, seeking him, marveling at the glory of God, submissive to him and all that he requires, realizing that we are here to serve him and not to be served by God, then we pray in the Spirit.

Paul speaks of the individual members of the body and points out that not all believers are given the same gifts. He asks in 1 Corinthians 12:30, "Do all speak in tongues?" He finishes his thought with verse 31, "But strive for the greater gifts. And I will show you a still more excellent way." With this verse, we can see that not all people filled with the Holy Spirit will speak in tongues, and, therefore, if praying in the spirit is speaking in tongues, then those who do not receive the gift cannot pray in the Spirit, and this seems unlikely.

Some suggest that speaking in tongues and praying in tongues are two different things. There is nothing definitive within scripture that says whether this is true or not to my knowledge. If you believe you must pray in tongues to pray in the Spirit, avoid divisions within the body by holding your opinion to yourself. If you desire to pray in tongues and do not, we serve a Father who says to ask in the name of his Son and he will give you the Holy Spirit (Lk. 11:13). Live your life in such submission to the glory of God that all fleshly desires are gone. Believe in the power of an Almighty God that he not only saved you from hell and punishment for your sins but for you to be slaves of righteousness, believe and ask that God help in your unbelief (Mk. 9:24). "Well then, does God supply you with the Spirit and work miracles among you by your doing the works of the law, or by your believing what you heard?" (Gal. 3:5, NRSV)

There is one last thing to consider as we learn to live by the Spirit and what that means. Matthew 12:31–32 (ESV) says, "Therefore I tell you, every sin and blasphemy will be forgiven people, but the blasphemy against the Spirit will not be forgiven. And whoever speaks a word against the Son of Man will be forgiven, but whoever speaks against the Holy Spirit will not be forgiven, either in this age or in the age to come."

The concept of what "blasphemy of the Holy Spirit" is tends to be controversial. Grammatically, it seems to be whoever speaks against the Holy Spirit. Hebrews addresses the Holy Spirit this way: "For in the case of those who have once been enlightened and have tasted of the heavenly gift and have been made partakers of the Holy Spirit, and have tasted the good word of God and the powers of the age to come, and *then* have fallen away, it is impossible to renew them again to repentance since they again crucify to themselves the Son of God and put Him to open shame" (Heb. 6:4–6, BSB).

Notice that being "once enlightened and partakers (participants) of the Holy Spirit" and then falling away results in the impossibility to be renewed through repentance again. This is the same unforgiveable sin Christ spoke of in Matthew 12:32. Blasphemy of the Holy Spirit is falling away, denying the power, and quenching the spirit. 1 Thessalonians 5:19 (ESV) tells us, "Do not quench the Spirit." Do not smother, reduce, or snuff out the Spirit.

When we walk within a religion that pays homage to the fact that there is a Holy Spirit, who is part of the Holy Trinity, but do not properly honor and revere or worship and submit ourselves to the Holy Spirit, we walk into a territory of the possibility of blaspheme of him and will reap the consequences promised.

Go, therefore, and put on the full armor of God every piece and on every day so that we are shored up against the enemy and our own demise.

Chapter 9

Love

Beloved, let us love one another because love comes from God. Everyone who loves has been born of God and knows God. Whoever does not love does not know God, because God is love.

—1 John 4:7–8

Love is such an overused word in today's culture. We say we love fried chicken, French fries, chocolate, and a myriad of other foods, things, animals, and people. This isn't the kind of love our Savior was referring to or what John was explaining when he wrote these verses. Paul, in fact, defines this term in a letter to the Corinthians: "Love is patient, love is kind. It does not envy, it does not boast, it is not proud. It is not rude, it is not self-seeking, it is not easily angered, it keeps no account of wrongs. Love takes no pleasure in evil, but rejoices in the truth. It bears all things, believes all things, hopes all things, endures all things. Love never fails" (1 Cor. 13:4–8, BSB).

"If anyone says 'I love God' but hates his brother, he is a liar. For anyone who does not love his brother, whom he has seen, cannot love God, whom he has not seen. And we have this commandment from him. Whoever loves God must love his brother as well."

The Scriptures make it clear that we can get all the "godly" things right, but if we do not have love, then it is all worthless. In fact, without love, we are without God. It's that simply put. Over the years, I've been accused of lacking in love. My former husband left us without food, a leaking roof, the ramifications of his lifetime addiction to porn, and the rage and anger often associated with such addictions, etc., but he held me captive with one single accusation. If I didn't love him, then I didn't love God. He'd quote 1 John 4:20–21 at me with a finger and spittle spraying across my face.

This verse was a cause for spiritual paralysis in my life. Even after I finally left him, he'd come to my door or leave messages on my phone telling me that I didn't love God because I didn't love him. It made my faith quake but caused me to seek deeper. Before I left him, I had to find a way to reconcile my divorcing him, hatred for his crimes against us, and whether God could ever love me in spite of it. When I prayed, I'd remind God who I was and question if he even heard my voice anymore. For a time, I believed God couldn't love me and that I was unlovable by anyone. The view of who I was in Christ had been skewed by a man. The love that my Father has for me overpowered that darkness and gently called me back to himself. I found myself with a new paradigm. I had to learn what love looked like, how God saw me, and what he wanted from me for our relationship to grow.

"This is how God's love was revealed among us: God sent His one and only Son into the world so that we might live through Him. And love consists in this: not that we loved God, but that He loved us and sent His Son as the atoning sacrifice for our sins. Beloved, if God so loved us, we also ought to love one another. No one has ever seen God; but if we love one another, God remains in us, and His love is perfected in us. By this we know that we remain in Him, and He in us: He has given us of His Spirit. And we have seen and testify that the Father has sent His Son to be the Savior of the world. If anyone confesses that Jesus is the Son of God, God abides in him, and he in God. And we have come to know and believe the love that God has for us. God is love; whoever abides in love abides in God, and God in him. In this way, love has been perfected among us, so that we may have confidence on the day of judgment; for in this world we are just like Him" (1 Jn. 4:9–17, BSB).

By the Holy Spirit of God, when we love one another, God remains in us and his love is perfected in us. As our relationship with God grows, through prayer, obedience, and righteous living, we can be assured that we're living within his will as our love for others grows. I regularly hear the same response to any notion of doing anything "for God." There is this fallacious idea that to love God and to accept his grace is to live in freedom of doing nothing. The result of this thinking leads to church members who are first to sign up for "church services." They feel convinced that if they are attending church regularly, serving in the "churches" ministries and programs set up there, they are loving God. The rest of the list might include those little handy devotionals that often read like horoscopes with a verse attached to the end, being done daily, and the really spiritual will commit to reading their Bibles in a year. The boxes get checked off, they look around, pat themselves on the back, or get pat on the back by their church peers and even lifted up on some fashion of a pedestal because of their good works, but the first moment they hear of another who wants to commit to striving for biblical obedience because their love is so great for Abba that they would do anything he wants, there is immediate judgment. They want to condemn any such person of legalism and hatred for the church.

A true follower of Christ who loves the Creator of the universe will do more than laboriously read the Bible but will delight in the scriptures searching to find the truth so that they can fulfill God's desires and really getting to know their Abba so deeply. When Jesus is known, really sought after to love Him, we don't sign up for "ministries" to fill Easter eggs with candy and call that serving God. We don't sing Christian tunes looking for a fleeting feeling that we can convince ourselves is evidence of being in the "presence of God." No, we sing from our soul to bless the Lord. We long to give him praise, and our purpose is to make God feel the blessing. We thank God for all his blessings, not to take our minds off the things we still don't have, but because from a guttural place, we have nothing but gratitude for the provisions of the Lord. When we want to know who God is, we seek him. When we love God, we want to do what makes him pleased and the fruit of the spirit pours out of us. We become filled with the jubilation, love, grace, and faith like Zacchaeus (Lk. 19:1–10) instead of the rich man who followed the rules (Mt. 19:16–23) but didn't have the heart to give his life to God.

You see, when the love of God is at the core of your faith, you'd stand on your head and sing the alphabet backward if that is what he asked. Obedience to the commandments and precepts of the Bible is essential, but the love of the Lord is where that obedience has to come from, and a desire to know how to please God as he requires is the essential aspect to love. In fact, a good litmus test of our faith is if we love others.

A young believer once said to me, "I thought being saved would be easier…" He didn't want to have to think of others or change things in his life. While he'd been moved to see himself as a sinner during a revival and went forward for forgiveness, but his faith was shallow and without love for the Lord of the heavens, he stepped away from the service unwilling to change anything about his life to align with God and his standards for Christian lives. "For this is the love of God, that we keep His commandments. And His commandments are not burdensome" (1 Jn. 5:3, BSB).

While there are those who don't want to put forth effort, there are also those who put forth a ton of effort but without love and essentially are noisy gongs. There is a tendency within humanity to get lazy. I hear my students say things like, "Let's just put this answer so we can get it done." I've had other students turn in elaborate projects that missed the point of the assignment argue with me that they don't need to make corrections or have tutoring during their study hall period because they were fine with the grade that they got. Some Christians have the tendency to do the same thing. There's an informal list of "service" or "ministries" that people can sign up for or programs of things to do from home to tick off boxes as done, but their heart is not based on love.

It's habitual, tedious, sacrificial work that they do because they know "good Christians" do this. They may carve out a time each day to read and highlight in their Bibles or do a Bible study published by a favorite evangelist or Christian publisher. They may respond to those asking for prayers by telling them that they are praying and even go to church a couple times a week, but this is not the perfect formula for Christianity. In fact, if we are doing the right things for the wrong reasons, we are accomplishing nothing for the glory of God and may in fact be treading on thin ice with a false sense of security for a salvation that might be missed.

The new covenant isn't a list or set of laws to follow diligently, like the Jews did with the law of Moses. While there are absolutely rights and wrongs, and things we need to do as believers, we must be motivated by *love*. Love for our Father, if doing what he told us to do, in such a way that is not burdensome. It's not a checklist to be marked off accordingly for each Christian looking feat we've accomplished. We don't need to build a résumé to prove to God that we had love for others and his Word by following a rigid daily agenda of what we think looks like Christian deeds. We need to be so filled with the Holy Spirit of God that love pours out of us to do his work almost naturally. We've also got to realize that loving God in the way that he set up is greater than looking like good Christians because we are doing the things that modern Christianity has created to look "Christianly."

Today's mantra is "you do you, I'll do me." There is an overwhelming sense of selfishness: "Accept me as I am, I won't change." "Take me or leave me." "You can't please everyone, so please yourself." With these notions is the concept that we don't need to work on relationships. We don't have to care how other people feel about our behavior, opinions, or actions…as well as the more subtle idea that we can love everyone well on our own terms. They are screaming loud and clear with this mentality that if you don't feel loved by the way they want to love you, then it's your own fault.

If I approached my own husband with this sort of mentality and cared nothing to learn of what makes him feel loved and appreciated and rather handed him my own version of what I was willing to do, my husband would fail to feel loved. Gary Chapman wrote *The 5 Love Languages* book, breaking down the types of ways that people might feel love and makes an analogy using love tanks that need filling. When one or both spouses refuse to consider how the other receives love, Gary explains that love tanks do not get filled. If a wife's dominant love language is quality time and a husband refuses to make time for her, her love tank remains unfilled. He could buy her flowers, bring home gifts, and lavish her with jewelry, but if she doesn't feel loved by this type of language, she's not going to feel loved!

Our Father in heaven is the same way. The Old Testament is laced with a multitude of stories of both the righteous and the unrighteous. Those whom God found worthy were the ones who loved him so much that they were loyal to him. He rebuked the Israelites for allowing pagan ritual to infiltrate in their faith toward God. The New Testament is exactly the same. Paul rebukes the Corinthians because they keep going back to add their pagan practices to their new faith in God. God does not want lip service. He doesn't want any of us to say we love him but refuse to love him in his "love language." We can't tell God we don't like his commandments, precepts, and teachings so we're going to do something different for him and call that love. Today's Christianity wants to look at God and say, "I love you but on my terms." The Bible says this, but I don't feel like doing that (or worse, I don't even read the Bible to know what you like or who you are and get my theology from Facebook memes and devotionals).

Relationships require work. We can't "rest in Christ" and "dwell in relationship" with him if we won't work on our relationship with him on his terms. There is a rise of Christian speakers and Christian books that speak of "being in relationship with him" by "resting in Christ." The phrases are ambiguous at best but probably more dangerous. It's a false religion that puts Christianity on our own terms. It undermines the authority and accuracy of Scripture and strips us of the very love we say we want to have for our Father. A focus on this philosophy with a healthy dose of looking "Christian" by posting your verse of the day, a "pic" of your daily devotional, or the fulfillment of being able to say that you read your Bible in a year is the way to go about breaking relationship with God and lacking the love he so desires.

Likewise, I can't expect to build a strong relationship with my husband if I insist on loving him on my terms with no consideration of him and his own desires or love languages. My love for my husband is so strong that it isn't burdensome to do the things that I know makes him know I love him, consider him above myself, and want to make his life happy. My love for God is even greater. "For this is the love of God, that we keep his commandments. And his commandments are not burdensome" (1 Jn. 5:10, ESV). With this genuine love outflows the fruits of Christianity. Generosity, patience, love, and kindness to others, just like he told us, the greatest commandments are to love our God with our whole heart, mind, and soul and to love our neighbor as ourselves (Mk. 12:28–31).

As a type-A personality, I have lists of things to do today, to get done soon, and things I don't want to forget about doing within the next few months. If I have orders coming through the mail or a delivery service, I have lists of the items to check off as they come in. I used to keep a large calendar in my purse at all times and couldn't understand how anyone functioned without one. The thing I've learned about God though is that he wants our hearts. He wants us to desire him so much that we aren't checking off lists and doing what we think looks Christian. He wants us to be so enmeshed with his ways through consistence in the Word, reading scriptures with the purpose of seeking the Lord, praying, and fellowshipping with other believers that we naturally love others, caring not just for their spiritual well-being but their physical needs as well.

"When the Son of Man comes in His glory, and all the angels with Him, He will sit on His glorious throne. All the nations will be gathered before Him, and He will separate the people one from another, as a shepherd separates the sheep from the goats. He will place the sheep on His right and the goats on His left. Then the King will say to those on His right, 'Come, you who are blessed by My Father, inherit the kingdom prepared for you from the foundation of the world. For I was hungry and you gave Me something to eat, I was thirsty and you gave Me something to drink, I was a stranger and you took Me in, I was naked and you clothed Me, I was sick and you looked after Me, I was in prison and you visited Me.' Then the righteous will answer Him, 'Lord, when did we see You hungry and feed You, or thirsty and give You something to drink? When did we see You a stranger and take You in, or naked and clothe You? When did we see You sick or in prison and visit You?' And the King will reply, 'Truly I tell you, whatever you did for one of the least of these brothers of Mine, you did for Me'" (Mt. 25:31–40).

Christ isn't going to look at those before him on judgment day and say that "he saw us read our daily devotional each day, highlight a bunch of verses, and sing to our favorite Christian radio station, well done my good and faithful servant." No, in fact, he is separating the goats from the sheep by the acts of love and kindness that they did for others. "So the last will be first, and the first will be last" (Mt. 20:16).

When we are giving to others and doing for them with love, we are not in danger of becoming self-centered. Such a state of being will no doubt put us last but has also been warned of in many of the New Testament scriptures.

"Do nothing from rivalry or conceit, but in humility count others more significant than yourselves. Let each of you look not only to his own interests, but also to the interests of others" (Phil. 2:3–4, ESV).

"But if you have bitter jealousy and selfish ambition in your hearts, do not boast and be false to the truth. This is not the wisdom that comes down from above, but is earthly, unspiritual, demonic. For where jealousy and selfish ambition exist, there will be disorder and every vile practice" (Jas. 3:14–16, ESV).

God isn't playing around. He's not a lax God who makes statements that have no real merit. We are so used to living within a Christianity that doesn't attest to the demonic world, and yet the brother of Jesus himself warned us that jealousy and selfish ambition are earthly, unspiritual, and demonic. He didn't mince words. Where these practices are, there will be disorder and every vile practice; quite frankly, it is why there is such a heavy calling for righteousness and exhortation within the Word because God wants unity among the brethren. Our current practices and toleration have left us in disharmony with our Creator just as much as we are with our fellow brethren.

"What good is it, my brothers, if someone says he has faith but does not have works? Can that faith save him? If a brother or sister is poorly clothed and lacking in daily food, and one of you says to them, 'Go in peace, be warmed and filled,' without giving them the things needed for the body, what good is that? So also faith by itself, if it does not have works, is dead" (Jas. 2:14–17, ESV).

After Jesus described the deeds of the sheep in Matthew 25:31–40, he went on to describe those he classified as goats. "Then He will say to those on His left, 'Depart from Me, you who are cursed, into the eternal fire prepared for the devil and his angels. For I was hungry and you gave Me nothing to eat, I was thirsty and you gave Me nothing to drink, I was a stranger and you did not take Me in, I was naked and you did not clothe Me, I was sick and in prison and you did not visit Me.' And they too will reply, 'Lord, when did we see You hungry or thirsty or a stranger or naked or sick or in prison, and did not minister to You?' Then the King will answer, 'Truly I tell you, whatever you did not do for one of the least of these, you did not do for Me.' And they will go away into eternal punishment but the righteous into eternal life" (Mt. 25:41–46, NIV).

We cannot serve God from home behind stacks of Bibles or from our church pew, making sure to do the Christian-looking things. Salvation isn't about going to heaven and avoiding hell; it's about living a life that serves God, living righteously, seeking after him, and being the hands and feet of a body of believers who serve others' needs with a heart motivated by love. Christians who are motivated for self-recognition or notoriety really need to self-examine and readjust their thinking. "Beware of practicing your righteousness before other people in order to be seen by them, for then you will have no reward from your Father who is in heaven. Thus, when you give to the needy, sound no trumpet before you, as the hypocrites do in the synagogues and in the streets, that they may be praised by others. Truly, I say to you, they have received their reward. But when you give to the needy, do not let your left hand know what your right hand is doing, so that your giving may be in secret. And your Father who sees in secret will reward you" (Mt. 6:1–4, ESV).

"Love is patient and kind; love does not envy or boast; it is not arrogant or rude. It does not insist on its own way; it is not irritable or resentful; it does not rejoice at wrongdoing, but rejoices with the truth. Love bears all things, believes all things, hopes all things, endures all things. Love never ends" (1 Cor. 13:4–8, ESV).

> Let love and faithfulness never leave you; bind them around your neck, write them on the tablet of your heart. Then you will win favor and a good name in the sight of God and man. (Prov. 3:3–4, NIV)

Chapter 10

Forgiveness and Judgment

Do not judge by appearances, but judge with right judgment.
—John 7:24, ESV

Merriam-Webster defines judgment as "the process of forming an opinion or evaluation by discerning and comparing" (https://www.merriam-webster.com/dictionary/judgment).

It's a word that gets used often, usually by people telling us "Don't judge me!" "Walk a mile in my shoes, see what I see, hear what I hear, feel what I feel, then maybe you'll understand why I do what I do. Until then, don't judge me." "Judge lest ye be judged." Or "God is my only judge."

There is a movement of "nonjudgmentalness." Essentially, no one wants accountability and have heard scriptures get misquoted or other believers say "Don't judge" so many times that they think it's a godly thing. The problem with this logic is that it means we can all just go on sinning. Is this what God intended when he authored scriptures? Are Christians called to be nonjudgmental? Look at this passage in 1 Corinthians.

"I wrote to you in my letter not to associate with sexually immoral people—not at all meaning the sexually immoral of this world, or the greedy and swindlers, or idolaters, since then you would need to go out of the world. But now I am writing to you not to associate with anyone who bears the name of brother if he is guilty of sexual immorality or greed, or is an idolater, reviler, drunkard, or swindler—not even to eat with such a one. For what have I to do with judging outsiders? Is it not those inside the church whom you are to judge? God judges those outside. 'Purge the evil person from among you'" (1 Cor. 5:9–13, ESV).

This section of Scripture goes against years of conditioning and instructions to believers not to judge. In fact, this passage reminds us to judge those inside the church.

We can see this (seemingly extreme) mandate again in Matthew. "If your brother sins against you, go and tell him his fault, between you and him alone. If he listens to you, you have gained your brother. But if he does not listen, take one or two others along with you, that every charge may be established by the evidence of two or three witnesses. If he refuses to listen to them, tell it to the church. And if he refuses to listen even to the church, let him be to you as a Gentile and a tax collector" (Mt. 18:15–17, ESV).

Anyone calling him or herself brother or sister is supposed to live righteously. We are called to judge those within the church for the purpose of restoring them to faith and sanctification in righteousness.

"If any of you has a dispute with another, do you dare to take it before the ungodly for judgment instead of before the Lord's people? Or do you not know that the Lord's people will judge the world? And if you are to judge the world, are you not competent to judge trivial cases? Do you not know that we will judge angels? How much more the things of this life!" (1 Cor. 6:1–3, NIV).

"However, if you have warned the righteous man that the righteous should not sin and he does not sin, he shall surely live because he took warning; and you have delivered yourself" (Ezek. 3:21, NASB).

For the sake of our brothers and our sisters in Christ, and for our own sake, we must judge ourselves and our brethren. Rebuke, exhort, and encourage our fellow believers to live righteously.

The second part of the "don't judge me" doctrine is an overemphasis of the word "conviction" and the shirking of accountability back to God. We talk about this idea that "God convicted me" of such and such, but I can't tell this other brother in Christ about his same sin because God will be the one to convict him. There is usually an elaborate explanation associated with this claim that "only God" can convict people, change people, etc. and that they are on their own walk with God. They say that just because they themselves have been convicted, another is not at the same place in their journey and, therefore, it's not their place to judge. "Leave it to God." "God has perfect timing." "Don't be the Holy Spirit for someone else." But I cannot find any scripture to verify this debauchery.

When Paul spoke of believers who were weaker in faith, he spoke of not doing something that would cause them to sin. "So if what I eat causes another believer to sin, I will never eat meat again as long as I live—for I don't want to cause another believer to stumble" (1 Cor. 8:13, NLT). Paul's reference to a weaker Christian is entirely bound up in not causing them to stumble. This is the antithesis of how Christians have come to misuse this verse in an attempt to let everyone walk their own path and stay in sin. Two short chapters ago, Paul reminded us that we are to judge our fellow believers on earth (1 Cor. 6:3).

Seeing another brother or sister in Christ sin and calling them out on it is hard for me and probably many others. No doubt part of it is from this conditioning which is unbiblical, but it's hard to tell someone they're wrong. We don't want to hurt their feelings. I know I don't. This becomes our own form of sin. In the book of Ezekiel, we read, "If I say to the wicked man, 'You will surely die,' but you do not warn him or speak out to warn him from his wicked way to save his life, that wicked man will die in his iniquity, and I will hold you responsible for his blood" (Ezek. 3:18, BSB).

We can't take this as a license to go bashing people over the head about their sins as we have looked at how imperative love is, but we are called to exhort in love, with love, and with a motive to restore a person back to faith or to faith. When Paul spoke of his conscience being clear in 1 Corinthians 4:4, he clarified God "will bring to light what is hidden in darkness and will expose the motives of men's hearts" (verse 5). Just as we are called to exhort fellow believers, we must prayerfully consider our motives. Ezekiel 3:19 (NLT) clarifies, "If you warn them and they refuse to repent and keep on sinning, they will die in their sins. But you will have saved yourself because you obeyed me." Keeping this in mind is key. It is not our job to convince them. We need not be angry in our rebuke or push our brother until he sees the truth. It is our job to tell them, in love, and then pray for them that they will see and not fall away or be lost.

    A few years back, I went to a church where I knew a young husband and wife. We watched their little family begin to grow with the birth of a little girl. A year later, the wife left her husband for another man she'd met at the gym and had been having an affair with. She left the church and went to another. This church focused on love. They proclaim they are nonjudgmental and want to love on all the parishioners with the love of God. The adulteress couple lived together and sat together in church on the back row for over a year. They were given serving positions within the church so they felt welcome and needed. Eventually, they married and seemed to be living happily ever after. She openly spoke of her past sin and her repentance in the women's Bible study she attended weekly, discussed the lesson, prayed with the other ladies, and looked like a changed woman. She had never been exhorted or held accountable in any way. Less than a year after marrying again, she was pregnant…by another man. She ended up divorced from her second husband, who grieved for months. While she does not attend church regularly any longer, she still shows up to church sporadically. She has not been called out on her sin. This church has taken the same stance with her that they did the first time. "They are just going to hug her and love her every time she shows up."

    The idea is lovely. Their hearts are to love her and to make her feel welcome and not shamed, but can you see how this sort of practice from a Christian church has not followed any part our biblical passages have instructed? Our society has pushed an agenda of softness, "no judging," "welcome all as they are," and "no shame" that our churches have eagerly adopted. The church is obviously not the ones who set her up with her next adulteress affair, but did their all-accepting love and refusal to biblically rebuke or to hold her accountable make it easier for her to go out and do it again? Will their "love" keep her from doing it again? This is a professing believer, a supposed sister in Christ who is committing sexual sins. Paul speaks of something just like this in 1 Corinthians.

"It is actually reported that there is sexual immorality among you, and of a kind that is intolerable even among pagans: A man has his father's wife. And you are proud! Shouldn't you rather have been stricken with grief and have removed from your fellowship the man who did this? Although I am absent from you in body, I am present with you in spirit, and I have already pronounced judgment on the one who did this, just as if I were present. When you are assembled in the name of our Lord Jesus and I am with you in spirit, along with the power of the Lord Jesus, hand this man over to Satan for the destruction of the flesh so that his spirit may be saved on the Day of the Lord. Your boasting is not good. Do you not know that a little leaven works through the whole batch of dough? Get rid of the old leaven, that you may be a new unleavened batch, as you really are. For Christ, our Passover lamb, has been sacrificed. Therefore, let us keep the feast, not with the old bread, leavened with malice and wickedness, but with the unleavened bread of sincerity and of truth" (1 Cor. 5:1–8, BSB).

Biblically, she should have been rebuked after the first affair. Certainly, someone should be at least exhorting this woman, but according to Paul, she should be removed from fellowship within the church. It's such a foreign concept that no one wants to even consider such a strong response, but it is really for her sake as well as the other members of the church.

"When you are assembled in the name of our Lord Jesus and I am with you in spirit, along with the power of the Lord Jesus, hand this man over to Satan for the destruction of the flesh, so that his spirit may be saved on the Day of the Lord" (1 Cor. 5:5, BSB).

Our dictionary definition says that "judgment is the process of forming an opinion or evaluation by discerning and comparing."

If a law established what is right and what is wrong, would an officer of the law be guilty of "judging" for giving a citation to the person found breaking the law? Likewise, if God is the author of what is right and wrong, are we really judging when we name a sin a sin?

Think about it carefully. God gave us the rules. He named the sins. Did he call us to be blind to other's sins? Did he call us to be blind to our own sins? These are important questions for Christians to consider as they grow in their faiths if they are going to grow in their faiths. They are important questions to consider as they repeat mantras and behave based on teachings that go against Scripture itself rather than the conduct of Christianity God laid out for us.

If we hide behind a misquoted verse and refuse to judge others or command others not to judge us and we claim that God is the only one who can do the convicting so we aren't supposed to tell another believer of their sins, are we not in fact just saying we want to stay in our sin and letting others stay in there's?

Modern child psychology and good parenting books tell us that we aren't supposed to tell children that "they are bad." We are supposed to call their behavior bad. Likewise, there are others who have said "Hate the sin, love the sinner." There is value in this quote. We have been called to "love our enemy" (Mt. 5:44).

However, we have also been called to righteousness, accountability, and even rebuke because we love our brothers, sisters, and enemies. So "hate the sin, love the sinner" takes on a completely new connotation in a very biblical way.

"Judge not, that you be not judged. For with the judgment you pronounce you will be judged, and with the measure you use it will be measured to you. Why do you see the speck that is in your brother's eye, but do not notice the log that is in your own eye? Or how can you say to your brother, 'Let me take the speck out of your eye,' when there is the log in your own eye? You hypocrite, first take the log out of your own eye, and then you will see clearly to take the speck out of your brother's eye" (Mt. 7:1–5, ESV).

Notice the second verse of this chapter. Pair this with verses that speak of forgiveness and notice the pattern. "For with the judgment you pronounce, you will be judged, and with the measure you use, it will be measured to you."

"For if you forgive other people when they sin against you, your heavenly Father will also forgive you. But if you do not forgive others their sins, your Father will not forgive your sins" (Mt. 6:14–15, NIV).

"Bear with each other and forgive one another if any of you has a grievance against someone. Forgive as the Lord forgave you" (Col. 3:13, NIV).

When we look at the forgiveness spoken of in these two verses, there is a judgment of sin that needs to be forgiven. We can't hold a grudge or treat another who sins against us as if their sin is unforgivable or ours will be unforgivable to God. It's important to note that God has made it clear that he will not forgive us our sins if we do not forgive others who trespass against us (Mt. 6:12). Likewise, we can look at "judgment" in the same manner. If we condemn a person for his sin, we will be judged and condemned with the same measure for our own (of the same kind). This does not mean at all that we are not to take the speck out of our brother's eye.

When we look further, the latter half of this section of Scripture is also extremely telling. Notice the judgment is referenced as a speck in the eye of a brother. The analogy then continues with usage of a hyperbole: "Or how can you say to your brother, 'Let me take the speck out of your eye,' when there is the log in your own eye?" (Mt. 7:4)

It's important to realize that we are talking about people who are in the same sin but more so we are talking about a "judge" who is in greater bondage of the same sin. In this case, it would be correct to say "Who am I to judge?" if and only if I am guilty of the same sin too!

Quite frankly, imagine someone who steals cars telling you not to steal the pen you used at the bank. We'd look at the guy like he was crazy and even negate the severity of our own sin comparing it to his seemingly worse one. Phrases such as "that is the pot calling the kettle black" come to mind as a fantastic illustration of just what Jesus is trying to tell us in this portion of Scripture from Matthew.

This instruction doesn't end here. There is another sentence that is often forgotten when being used out of context to denounce anyone from all judging.

"You hypocrite, first take the log out of your own eye, and then you will see clearly to take the speck out of your brother's eye" (Mt. 7:5, ESV).

Did you see that? Did you know that Jesus told us to get ourselves straightened out and stop committing the same sin we want to condemn another for so we can see clearly to help our brother remove that sin he has? This is us dealing with our own conviction of wrong, getting it right, and then showing a brother his own sin. Christ didn't say "Get the log out of your own eye and then let God convict your brother later as he is on his own path with the Lord."

This is a mandate to righteousness and judgment for the sake of two coming clean before the Lord. It isn't forbidding judgment. When we look at the message, Jesus is actually telling us to judge. There is a link between the fact that we are sinners, but it isn't that we aren't supposed to "judge" others in sin because we are sinners too or that everyone is in a different place and should be left in their sin waiting on God's perfectly timed conviction—you might just be the vessel for the conviction—and since our God has called us to righteous lives, Paul rebukes and exhorts strongly, and we are to mimic Christ, and even Paul, as he mimics Christ, we can know…

We are supposed to stop sinning first. We are not to be hypocritical and call our brothers and sisters out on sin that we are also committing because we can't see distinctly enough to help him or her. After we stop sinning though, we are supposed to judge our brother and help him get that speck out of his own eye. We are supposed to share our conviction.

Another facet from this section of Scripture is the concept that one who has already overcome the sin can be a huge encouragement in helping someone else come out of the same thing. They know how it felt, the challenges involved in quitting, or any other detail, and they know a way to successfully stop. The sin has to be stopped first, however. Setting up a support meeting for a bunch of alcoholics or addicts would be a complete failure if no one had yet come clean. They could console each other on how hard it is to quit while they look at someone they think drinks more and justify their drinking because "at least I'm not as bad as…" Sitting with people who won't stop their sin gives an illusion that it's okay to continue because everyone else is.

My last husband went to breakfast with a church elder for "counsel" on his porn addiction and left with a pat on the back like he'd just joined "the club." He told me, "If Dan is looking at porn and he's a church elder, then it's all right for me too." The same elder arranged for the church to hire him for a renovation project. It was all in the name of giving him opportunity to support his own family, but when they showed up to see how the progress was going and found his work truck outside but him nowhere to be found, nothing was said to him or asked of his whereabouts, and his hookups from the church parking lot were suddenly approved of in his mind. In fact, the only sort of restriction applied to my former husband was that he not go to the elder's home and be alone with his wife there. Everyone was buddies. Everything was good, except that it wasn't because it only made my and our children's suffering greater.

When we care about living righteously and being sanctified, we shouldn't really mind being called out or helped by another for helping us. The woman I knew from church who was on her second affair, my ex-husband, and those who do not want to be judged do not want to live righteously. Christianity shouldn't be based on the desires of the apostate.

We can't honestly conclude that it's okay to keep sinning but others cannot. Imagine an alcoholic telling another he has to stop drinking or a gossip telling another friend that she shouldn't talk about others. The Scriptures warn us not to find ourselves in this position.

"Therefore you have no excuse, O man, every one of you who judges. For in passing judgment on another you condemn yourself, because you, the judge, practice the very same things. We know that the judgment of God rightly falls on those who practice such things. Do you suppose, O man—you who judge those who practice such things and yet do them yourself—that you will escape the judgment of God?" (Rom. 2:1–3, ESV)

Paul reiterated the same concept Christ did with the parable of the speck and the log. We cannot be the pot calling the kettle black. We can't call a brother or sister out on a sin we are also committing too. But this does not mean we are to not judge anything. The problem in today's Christian culture is that we are so wrapped up in the idea that we're all so burdened with our flesh that we can't stop sinning ourselves. We've already excused the next person because we don't want to stop our own sins and tell them such.

It's ironic in ways that many refuse to live righteously and judge fellow believers in their sin but are eager to start debates and fights over varying church traditions, doctrines, or practices. It's as though Christianity is turned upside down. That which is right is wrong and that which is wrong is right in modern Christian culture. The judging that God does not want of us is within the parameters of how many churches function today and yet the same churches deny the biblical form of judgment and condemn others for doing that. There is anger and strife with a heavy dose of disunity within the body. It isn't that the members don't want to hurt feelings with a loving exhortation or there would be the same care and effort not to do so within the semantics of church life. Instead, there are fights and feuds over what color carpet the church should have or which foods should be served at the Vacation Bible School. There are believers who want to condemn others for the education they choose for their kids, whether they are allowed to watch Disney movies etc. There is discord and a readiness to jump on someone for not choosing the "right Christian looking things."

"As for the one who is weak in faith, welcome him, but not to quarrel over opinions. One person believes he may eat anything, while the weak person eats only vegetables. Let not the one who eats despise the one who abstains, and let not the one who abstains pass judgment on the one who eats, for God has welcomed him. Who are you to pass judgment on the servant of another? It is before his own master that he stands or falls. And he will be upheld, for the Lord is able to make him stand. One person esteems one day as better than another, while another esteems all days alike. Each one should be fully convinced in his own mind. The one who observes the day, observes it in honor of the Lord. The one who eats, eats in honor of the Lord, since he gives thanks to God, while the one who abstains, abstains in honor of the Lord and gives thanks to God. For none of us lives to himself, and none of us dies to himself. For if we live, we live to the Lord, and if we die, we die to the Lord. So then, whether we live or whether we die, we are the Lord's. For to this end Christ died and lived again, that he might be Lord both of the dead and of the living. Why do you pass judgment on your brother? Or you, why do you despise your brother? For we will all stand before the judgment seat of God; for it is written, 'As I live, says the Lord, every knee shall bow to me, and every tongue shall confess to God.' So then each of us will give an account of himself to God. Therefore let us not pass judgment on one another any longer, but rather decide never to put a stumbling block or hindrance in the way of a brother" (Rom. 14:1–13, ESV).

Notice the little quirks, beliefs, and customs some believers have are not to be quarreling points. When we are making choices to honor the Lord, it isn't any other believer's job to align us to their own beliefs. We can't take the verses that we've already looked at about judging and use it as a license to bash our brothers and sisters in Christ for having different religious traditions, practices, etc. One man may believe the diet of Daniel is what he and his family should eat. Another might believe God wants all kids to be homeschooled. One believer may believe the true Sabbath is Saturday and keep that day holy. We need to consider our motives if we are more concerned with others agreeing with us or putting down those who do not.

We can also look at the following passage to see that while sin is sin and God decided the code for all to follow, just as we've seen in previous scriptures, we are not called to be the condemning judge.

"But Jesus went to the Mount of Olives. Early in the morning he came again to the temple. All the people came to him, and he sat down and taught them. The scribes and the Pharisees brought a woman who had been caught in adultery, and placing her in the midst they said to him, 'Teacher, this woman has been caught in the act of adultery. Now in the Law, Moses commanded us to stone such women. So what do you say?' This they said to test him, that they might have some charge to bring against him. Jesus bent down and wrote with his finger on the ground. And as they continued to ask him, he stood up and said to them, 'Let him who is without sin among you be the first to throw a stone at her.' And once more he bent down and wrote on the ground. But when they heard it, they went away one by one, beginning with the older ones, and Jesus was left alone with the woman standing before him. Jesus stood up and said to her, 'Woman, where are they? Has no one condemned you?' (Jn. 8:1–10, ESV).

Notice the people wanted to condemn this woman. They wanted to cast the punishment on her for being caught in sin. This is the sort of "judgment," condemnation that we are not authorized for. Condemnation is different from exhortation and rebuke for the sake of bringing a brother back to righteous living.

"But exhort one another every day as long as it is called 'today' that none of you may be hardened by the deceitfulness of sin" (Heb. 3:16, ESV).

Exhort means (transitive verb) "to give warnings or advice, make urgent appeals" (https://www.merriam-webster.com/dictionary/exhort).

"Let the word of Christ dwell in you richly, teaching and admonishing one another in all wisdom, singing psalms and hymns and spiritual songs, with thankfulness in your hearts to God" (Col. 3:16, ESV).

Admonish means (transitive verb) to express warning or disapproval to especially in a gentle, earnest, or solicitous (concerned) manner" (https://www.merriam-webster.com/dictionary/admonish).

Again, once we see the sin, we are called to exhort our brother or sister (lovingly) for it. Whether it's our sin or our sibling's sin, we have been told to call it out (first in ourselves) so we are not hypocritical then in others so that we all can move in this process of sanctification to live more righteously. The purpose is to bring another back to right standing, not to win a battle, prove someone wrong, punish, or belittle a person to make us feel superior. That would be heinous of a "believer" to do, and God knows the motives of the heart. "Above all, keep loving one another earnestly, since love covers a multitude of sins" (1 Pet. 4:8, ESV).

"Do not speak evil against one another, brothers. The one who speaks against a brother or judges his brother, speaks evil against the law and judges the law. But if you judge the law, you are not a doer of the law but a judge. There is only one lawgiver and judge, he who is able to save and to destroy. But who are you to judge your neighbor?" (Jas. 4:11–12, ESV).

James (the brother of Jesus) is exhorting these "believers" to not speak evil of other brothers in Christ. Contrasting this to the verses about church discipline: "If your brother sins against you, go and tell him his fault, between you and him alone. If he listens to you, you have gained your brother. But if he does not listen, take one or two others along with you, that every charge may be established by the evidence of two or three witnesses. If he refuses to listen to them, tell it to the church. And if he refuses to listen even to the church, let him be to you as a Gentile and a tax collector. Truly, I say to you, whatever you bind on earth shall be bound in heaven, and whatever you loose on earth shall be loosed in heaven. Again I say to you, if two of you agree on earth about anything they ask, it will be done for them by my Father in heaven. For where two or three are gathered in my name, there am I among them" (Mt. 18:15–20, ESV).

Notice the mandate. We are to address the Christians sinning against us alone. There is no prior discussion with anyone else. Then if he doesn't listen, two or three others are to go as witnesses. It says if that doesn't work, then the one sinned against is to go to the church and the instruction is to treat the fellow brother as a tax collector. I've never seen church discipline in action in any of the churches I've attended. It's a practice largely avoided in our society of "don't offend anyone," but if we were doing this, there would be immediate consequences (authored by God himself) to hopefully restore a person back to the faith. Mind you, this is also a sin against another person…

When we pair this scripture with the one we were looking at in James, we can see that we aren't supposed to go around talking about other people's sins against us; we are supposed to address it with them personally. A few chapters prior to the one we're looking at in James, we read about being doers of the word and not hears.

When we're listening to others tell of another person's sin, we are being "hearers." Jesus gave us the requirements in Matthew for what is expected of us concerning sin. Paul also included various instructions as we've seen so far in this chapter. We also know that God hates gossips…and to be fit before our king that we are to "Let no corrupting talk come out of your mouths, but only such as is good for building up, as fits the occasion, that it may give grace to those who hear" (Eph. 4:29, ESV).

We also know that "Sin is not ended by multiplying words, but the prudent hold their tongues" (Prov. 10:19, NIV).

Therefore, we can see that there is no good coming from talking about another person's sin unless we are "doers" and actually following the Word of God and addressing the sin of a brother in a scriptural manner. Finally, we know that we are not the condemner but are merely brothers in Christ and should always have a heart for peaceful and gentle reconciliation to our Father by the one who is sinning against him. This is a seriously huge difference between judging in a slandering and gossiping sort of way than in the manner of helping a brother realize his blunder, sin, transgression, or iniquity so that he can be restored to right standing with God.

That woman I told you about earlier, the one who is pregnant from her second known affair, while she attends church, where she is being "loved on" for the sake of "loving her back to Christ," others tell their friends and families about her in the name of "pray for her." It's gossip by another name and just as wrong as it is that no one rebukes her for her sin.

We have to realize though that when we fail to "judge" ourselves or others and be exhorted or to exhort as necessary, we fail to walk in righteousness and are in danger of becoming hardened by deceitfulness of sin or even in danger of sickness and death.

"That is why many of you are weak and ill, and some have died. But if we judged ourselves truly, we would not be judged. But when we are judged by the Lord, we are disciplined so that we may not be condemned along with the world" (1 Cor. 13:30–32, ESV).

When we look the other way and refuse to help our brothers and sisters (or ourselves) to name the sin and repent from it, we let ourselves become desensitized to it. What was once known to be a grievous sin of yesteryears becomes tolerated and acceptable. What is tolerated and accepted becomes commonplace by even more.

Judge, lest ye be judged! Judge yourselves and your fellow believers now…lest you be judged by God.

The Bible commands us to judge—biblical context mandates godly and righteous judgment—with the exemption of condemnation. Love yourself and your neighbors so much that their eternal lives matter more than following after a contrived interpretation taken out of context that leads to darkness. Love our brothers and sisters in Christ with such earnest that we can tell them of their offense in such a way that we don't instead encourage them to continue in their sin but to be restored to righteousness. We do no good to them or ourselves if we fear to "judge" and tell them of their wrong as our silence or approval becomes their own validation to continue in denial that they aren't even wrong.

Chapter 11

There Is a Way

There is a way that seems right to a man, but its end is the way to death.
—Proverbs 14:12, ESV

For my whole life, I've heard people talk about a void within each person. It's a void, they say, that only God can fill. It's also a void that I've watched people scramble to fill with all sorts of things, like drugs, alcohol, homosexuality, and even relationships. I've even seen people fill the void with "God."

If God is the missing piece in the void, isn't that the right answer then? Sometimes it is. Other times it isn't. Let me explain.

We've heard of, or maybe been guilty of, running through the motions of Christianity and our religion. We can understand that happening. Everyone has highs and lows within their walk with the Lord, and sometimes, when we're not careful, that low is where we get stuck for a while. No one from the outside knows we're stale and just doing what we've done all along because we know how to do it. We know what "religion" looks like.

The problem is that there are some who never even realize they are missing the power of the gospel. Typically, these are the people who have been raised in church and or Christian families. Filling the void with a God but not the one true God could look like "real" faith. A person can say all the right things about his conversion experience or service in the ministries; he can be a deacon or a Sunday school teacher. She/he might lead a small group or any other facet of the known church today but be intellectually spiritual instead of full of the Holy Spirit and walking with God. If they're filling their life with religion and the things that look godly and going through the motions without the power of God driving God's "good works," they will become tired from all the religiousness! They will be exhausted from running on the proverbial hamster wheel doing religious works but accomplishing nothing and will be looking for someone to tickle their ears to tell them they don't have to. There will be a bait and switch-equating religion and religious deeds with those scriptures call "good works."

False preachers will fill their messages with passages about not being under Jewish law any longer and being under grace instead; therefore, they say, "Believers need to stop striving to do good works," as if good works equate to Jewish law. They preach to the weary souls who are not truly tired from good works but religious nonsense that is not the Jewish law either. It's a trickery of words from the deceiver to elude believers and lead them to believe their true gospel is grace. They prey on the tired who are already deluded by religiosity and relieve them through a false gospel that tells them they're tired from good deeds—and good deeds are law-based or a works-based religion they say. They call this the "true gospel" or the "gospel plus nothing," "grace." They convince many that to follow Christ is to do nothing but rest, with the overt implication that it is necessary to neglect biblical "good works" (which is the law of Christ, according to 1 Corinthians 9:21 and Galatians 6:2) in order to accept Christ's grace.

What these people need is the truth. They need the Holy Spirit and accuracy of Scriptures, not excuses to live by a grace that doesn't include the law of Christ. They need to know they're tired because they're being religious and filling their void with religious deeds that are not the same as "good works" described in our Scriptures. And they need to know that our Savior gave us the strength to do all things through him. If we're weary and tired, it's not God we need to redefine, it's our own faith. It's a warning to check our motives and our relationship with him.

"As for other matters, brothers and sisters, we instructed you how to live in order to please God, as in fact you are living. Now we ask you and urge you in the Lord Jesus to do this more and more. For you know what instructions we gave you by the authority of the Lord Jesus. It is God's will that you should be sanctified: that you should avoid sexual immorality; that each of you should learn to control your own body in a way that is holy and honorable, not in passionate lust like the pagans, who do not know God; and that in this matter no one should wrong or take advantage of a brother or sister. The Lord will punish all those who commit such sins, as we told you and warned you before. For God did not call us to be impure, but to live a holy life. Therefore, anyone who rejects this instruction does not reject a human being but God, the very God who gives you his Holy Spirit" (1 Thess. 4:1–8, NIV).

Christians have been instructed by the authority of the Lord Jesus how to live in order to please God. Verse 8 tells us precisely that anyone who rejects this instruction does not reject a human being but God, the very God who gives you his Holy Spirit! 1 Thessalonians 5:22, KJV, says, "Abstain from all appearance of evil."

"Not everyone who says to Me, 'Lord, Lord,' will enter the kingdom of heaven, but only he who does the will of My Father in heaven. Many will say to Me on that day, 'Lord, Lord, did we not prophesy in Your name, and in Your name drive out demons and perform many miracles?' Then I will tell them plainly, 'I never knew you; depart from Me, you workers of lawlessness!'" (Mt. 7:21–23).

There will be people who believe they've lived Christian lives for God and be turned away on the day of judgment. This single verse should have each of us checking ourselves and our lives. Notice again that these people were church people doing very churchy things. They prophesied, drove out demons, performed miracles... These are even more churchy than I see in mainstream Christendom today. I cannot recall a single instance in which I've seen demons been driven out and would get strange looks from fellow parishioners if I should mention the word "demon" even, so these are very churchy people who made it before the Son of God and thought they were going to spend eternity with him, but they are *not*.

Jesus Christ spent his time on Earth showing us and telling us how to live for him. He made it no secret. He gave us the Holy Spirit to make it possible to live for him as the Father desires. We really have no excuses…except that some would rather learn their theology from man and not open up to the Word of God and see for themselves what is written and how it clearly tells us to live our lives. Others use a few verses to quench their own desires, either by looking for the promises and ignoring their requirements or by taking pieces of scriptures out of context and fitting it to their own predetermined meanings.

Still others read the Bible as words on a page so they feel as though they are spiritual, all the while devoid of understanding and applying it. "But people who aren't spiritual can't receive these truths from God's Spirit. It all sounds foolish to them and they can't understand it, for only those who are spiritual can understand what the Spirit means" (1 Cor. 2:14, NLT).

A true seeking believer may not fully understand everything in the Bible, but a genuine pursuer of the Lord will read to understand and pray for wisdom to know what is meant by God. They might read searching for verses that link or topics that keep coming up, or they may read to find an answer to a controversial topic. I have been listing words and concepts on the top of the inside cover and color-coordinating tabs and highlights to gather every verse I can find about the topics I'm currently looking for. Currently, I have red tabs for the word *dunamis,* yellow for *grace,* orange for *faith,* green for *sabbath,* and so forth. Every time I find a verse with mention of these topics and others, I highlight it in the color I've assigned it and put a tab (sticky paper) in the same color on the side of my Bible so I can easily open to each verse per topic/color. Other times, I use the internet to do searches for verses about certain topics, such as the Sabbath. I wanted to know everything I could know about it so I could draw a conclusion about what God wants us to do on Sabbath and many other topics, and getting lists of verses is the fastest way to put them all together in one place to study them. Not everyone will read their Bibles or do searches in these manners, but they will read to understand. They will read looking to know more about the One True God and what they can do to love him. They will find conflict in what they are reading and what they hear in some of the current Christian pop songs, devotionals, Sunday School lessons, and sermons; and they will dig deeper, pray for illumination, and be convicted. Those who are spiritual can understand what the Spirit means and will look to understand more and more with a thirst that can't be quenched.

I know some prayer warriors, godly worshippers, and Spirit-filled believers, and I know others who talk about praying all the time, lift their hands while they sing songs along with the local Christian radio station or at church, and those who prophecy or speak in tongues regularly. There is a difference though with those who have filled the void with God versus filling the hole with a god. There are some going through the Christian motions they've learned from their families, church experiences, or friends, "thus nullifying the word of God by the tradition that has been handed down. And they do so in many such matters" (Mk. 7:13).

I saw a devotional page posted online to be encouragement for others. It read much like a horoscope telling readers to keep going on their journey; it's chosen by God. It's written as though God is speaking in the first person and telling readers that their path is going to be hard, that he won't give what is desired and expects the views to be dull, but Sundays will be highs as they sing and worship in church, and as long as they take one step in front of the other, they will have glittering wonders around the corner. It ended with a sentence that confirmed the dull paths are indeed what God wants for us with a gift of a high at church.

What a farce! There is nothing scripturally accurate about that but is a daily devotional that we've been conditioned to read instead of the Word and walk away, believing our lives are supposed to be mediocre and our joy is only derived from an emotional experience we could also feel at a rock concert or any other musical event. This is propagating false Christianity and luring believers to think getting a tingly feeling while singing a song is the epitome of walking with God. They are conned into believing that it's the evidence of being "touched by God" or feeling him during their worship, and they go out of the building living their ungodly, self-centered lives in the name of being under grace with proof of their salvation from a rush and having some "feelies" at church that past Sunday or at a religious event.

We know that this isn't truth from the one true God as he's looking for obedience with hearts after him. "Therefore, if anyone cleanses himself from what is dishonorable, he will be a vessel for honorable use, set apart as holy, useful to the master of the house, ready for every good work" (2 Tim. 2:21, ESV). He wants his people set apart and consecrated. He wants us to be holy.

"A new commandment I give you: Love one another. As I have loved you, so you also must love one another. By this everyone will know that you are My disciples, if you love one another" (Jn. 13:34–35, BSB).

Just as we know from 1 Corinthians 13:1–7, BSB it says, "If I speak in the tongues of men and of angels, but have not love, I am only a ringing gong or a clanging cymbal. If I have the gift of prophecy and can fathom all mysteries and all knowledge, and if I have absolute faith so as to move mountains, but have not love, I am nothing. If I give all I possess to the poor and exult in the surrender of my body, but have not love, I gain nothing. Love is patient, love is kind. It does not envy, it does not boast, it is not proud. It is not rude, it is not self-seeking, it is not easily angered, it keeps no account of wrongs. Love takes no pleasure in evil but rejoices in the truth. It bears all things, believes all things, hopes all things, endures all things."

Likewise in John 4:7–21 (ESV), we see the commission for us as believers is to love. "Beloved, let us love one another, for love is from God, and whoever loves has been born of God and knows God. Anyone who does not love does not know God, because God is love. In this the love of God was made manifest among us, that God sent his only Son into the world, so that we might live through him. In this is love, not that we have loved God but that he loved us and sent his Son to be the propitiation for our sins. Beloved, if God so loved us, we also ought to love one another. No one has ever seen God; if we love one another, God abides in us and his love is perfected in us. By this we know that we abide in him and he in us, because he has given us of his Spirit. And we have seen and testify that the Father has sent his Son to be the Savior of the world. Whoever confesses that Jesus is the Son of God, God abides in him, and he in God. So we have come to know and to believe the love that God has for us. God is love, and whoever abides in love abides in God, and God abides in him. By this is love perfected with us, so that we may have confidence for the day of judgment, because at he is so also are we in this world. There is no fear in love, but perfect love casts out fear. For fear has to do with punishment, and whoever fears has not been perfected in love. We love because he first loved us. If anyone says, 'I love God,' and hates his brother, he is a liar; for he who does not love his brother whom he has seen cannot love God whom he has not seen. And this commandment we have from him: whoever loves God must also love his brother."

As the risk of sounding repetitive, we must look at love again because of how important it is for our eternal security. God has given us a litmus test to determine the legitimacy of our salvation. While we know the only way to love God is to follow his commandments, and righteous living is imperative, it's completely interlinked with loving one another. We literally must be full of love to be a child of God. We must love him, and we must love our brothers, sisters, and everyone else. The fruit of this love is sweet and savory to the nostrils of our God Most High. "Live a life filled with love, following the example of Christ. He loved us and offered himself as a sacrifice for us, a pleasing aroma to God" (Eph. 5:2, NLT).

"But thanks be to God, who in Christ always leads us in triumphal procession, and through us spreads the fragrance of the knowledge of him everywhere" (2 Cor. 2:14, ESV).

By brethren, let's check our fruit together. Let us be sure that we offer a sweet aroma to our Father in heaven. Be leery not to fill the void in our lives with a form of God that is not right. Let our zeal for following after righteousness be matched with a zeal for love of others. Let us not "forsake our first love" (Rev. 2:4–5) by living religious lives with little or no righteousness, chock-full of "ministry" and "church" work but have true love for God first, producing in us a sweet, loving spirit that wants to give, help, and share the gospel.

When the Son of Man comes in His glory, and all the angels with Him, He will sit on His glorious throne. All the nations will be gathered before Him, and He will separate the people one from another, as a shepherd separates the sheep from the goats. He will place the sheep on His right and the goats on His left. Then the King will say to those on His right, 'Come, you who are blessed by My Father, inherit the kingdom prepared for you from the foundation of the world. For I was hungry and you gave Me something to eat, I was thirsty and you gave Me something to drink, I was a stranger and you took Me in, I was naked and you clothed Me, I was sick and you looked after Me. I was in prison and you visited Me.' Then the righteous will answer Him, 'Lord, when did we see You hungry and feed You or thirsty and give You something to drink? When did we see You a stranger and take You in or naked and clothe You? When did we see You sick or in prison and visit You?' And the King will reply, 'Truly I tell you, whatever you did for one of the least of these brothers of mine, you did for Me.'

Then He will say to those on His left, 'Depart from Me, you who are cursed, into the eternal fire prepared for the devil and his angels. For I was hungry and you gave me nothing to eat, I was thirsty and you gave Me nothing to drink, I was a stranger and you did not take Me in, I was naked and you did not clothe Me, I was sick and in prison and you did not visit Me.' And they too will reply, 'Lord, when did we see You hungry or thirsty or a stranger or naked or sick or in prison, and did not minister to You?' Then the King will answer, 'Truly I tell you, whatever you did not do for one of the least of these, you did not do for Me.' And they will go away into eternal punishment but the righteous into eternal life." (Mt. 25:31–46, BSB)

Be sheep! Do not be hearers of the gospel message, going out without the Spirit, trying to force it on others or looking down your noses at them. Guard your soul with love. Do not dutifully attend church, drop a donation in the church box, or even toss a few dollars out the window at a homeless beggar while singing a Christian song loudly to get some "feelies" and assume that you're following after God because of these things. Seek after God with your whole heart, mind, and soul to find his answers.

Pray for passionate love for others that consumes like a blazing fire. Speak to God with words that are full of meaning and not empty, like what you've heard others say. Be careful not to imitate what you see other believers do to fulfill your own Christianity. Be careful not to read the words of Scripture to accomplish a goal that isn't about seeking the glory of the Lord.

There is a scripture in Isaiah 55:11–13 that is often quoted in saying that "God's word does not come back void." This scripture specifically says, "So shall my word be that goes out from my mouth, it shall not return to me empty, but it shall accomplish that which I purpose and shall succeed in the thing for which I sent it." It is a powerful scripture that reminds us that the word of God is true! His promises will be upheld as he assures them.

I warn you though, reading our Bible is not enough. Memorizing scriptures does not make us godly. It is wonderful to be able to call upon a scripture for living well and encouraging other believers, but remember Satan knows scriptures and quotes them too. If Satan can memorize scripture and offer it to others, so can a person trying to fill a void with a form of godliness that does not require the repentance, death to self, or sanctification.

"If You are the Son of God," he said, "throw Yourself down. For it is written: 'He will command His angels concerning You, and they will lift You up in their hands, so that You will not strike Your foot against a stone'" (Mt. 4:6, BSB).

This verse is a direct quote from Satan, tempting Christ by using Psalm 91:11–12. "For the word of God is living and active, sharper than any two-edged sword, piercing to the division of soul and of spirit, of joints and of marrow, and discerning the thoughts and intentions of the heart" (Heb. 4:12, ESV). But if even Satan can quote it, beware that you are using scriptures to come to know God better, build your relationship with him, build others up, and "live in peace with one another. And we urge you, brothers, to admonish the unruly, encourage the fainthearted, help the weak, and be patient with everyone. Make sure that no one repays evil for evil. Always pursue what is good for one another and for all people. Rejoice at all times. Pray without ceasing. Give thanks in every circumstance, for this is God's will for you in Christ Jesus" (1 Thess. 5:13–16, BSB) and "Seek the Lord while he may be found; call upon him while he is near; let the wicked forsake his way, and the unrighteous man his thoughts; let him return to the Lord, that he may have compassion on him, and to our God, for he will abundantly pardon" (Isa. 55:6–7, ESV).

"All Scripture is breathed out by God and profitable for teaching, for reproof, for correction, and for training in righteousness" (2 Tim. 3:16, ESV) and ought to be used as such.

Remember that the fear of the Lord is to know him. "And unto man he said, 'Behold, the fear of the Lord, that is wisdom; and to depart from evil is understanding'" (Job 28:28, KJB).

It is a life-and-death matter at hand. Be sure to fill the void within your soul with the very Spirit of the living God. Examine your hearts and pray for God to give you a heart after him and not just after the things that look like him. Fervently pray for love of God and others as he wants us to love him and them and study your Bible, applying it to yourself, your life, and your relationship with the Lord.

Jesus Christ warned believers in the book of Mark: "What comes out of a man, that is what defiles him. For from within the hearts of men come evil thoughts, sexual immorality, theft, murder, adultery, greed, wickedness, deceit, debauchery, envy, slander, arrogance, and foolishness. All these evils come from within, and these are what defile a man" (Mk. 7:20–23, BSB).

Our Savior groups greed, envy, arrogance, and foolishness within a list of sins we would think are more heinous, like sexual immorality, theft, murder, adultery, wickedness, etc.

As we go through our Christian lives jealous of others for having things we want that they have, we commit a sin that Christ calls evil. "Do not covet from thy neighbor" is the tenth commandment we seem to forget about as we see others with something we immediately want to have too. It's the twenty-first century, and arrogance runs rampant. It is the epitome of pride. Be careful not to be puffed up with arrogance, needing others to see you as superior as you look down your nose on them. Even foolishness is listed within this grouping as a sin of defilement.

In the second letter to the Corinthians, Paul wrote to them with exhortation, *"For I am afraid that when I come, I may not find you as I want you to be, and you may not find me as you want me to be. I fear that there may be discord, jealousy, fits of rage, selfish ambition, slander, gossip, arrogance and disorder" (2 Cor. 12:20, NIV).*

Often, we see Paul distraught over the Corinthians and their state of salvation. The New Testament books as well as the old are full of warnings to clean up our lives. We want to believe these verses are talking about everyone else but us. Don't fall into the trap that blinds you of the log in your own eye. Tread carefully and examine your heart as you begin to pay attention to the words you speak. Watch that you are not a gossip, slanderer, or deceitful to gain more favor, sympathy, or possessions. Do not deceive your own selves with a form of godliness that could never fill the void God put there to fill with himself.

When we lean too heavily on the carnal man, we fall into theses sins ourselves. Some want to turn salvation into a package that includes endless grace. They want to argue and debate with others to prove themselves right and others wrong. It's the void that's still there; desperately, they try to fill it by harshly judging others and attacking them. Within their own hearts, they think if they can make someone else out to be worse than them, they will be superior and somehow godlier. There is no more Christ in a person trying to make another feel like a loser for not knowing about the truth of salvation than for the person who has not yet believed.

Check yourselves. Examine your motives. Great debaucheries have been committed in the name of the Lord. Peoples have been slaughtered, lands taken over, and hearts turned cold because of the arrogance of many conducting their own form of godliness but "in his name."

"But understand this, that in the last days there will come times of difficulty. For people will be lovers of self, lovers of money, proud, arrogant, abusive, disobedient to their parents, ungrateful, unholy, heartless, unappeasable, slanderous, without self-control, brutal, not loving good, treacherous, reckless, swollen with conceit, lovers of pleasure rather than lovers of God, having the appearance of godliness, but denying its power. Avoid such people" (2 Tim. 3:1–5, ESV).

This scripture is not talking about the inmates on death row. These sins are not those that could be prosecuted in a court of our laws. To our Father in heaven though, being a lover of self or of money, being proud and arrogant with such conceit to disobey parents, being ungrateful, unholy, heartless, lacking empathy and sympathy for others, lovers of pleasure, unappeasable (the exact culture of Americans today) has us on spiritual death row.

What is imperative for us all to realize is that God is not talking about the world in this passage. When he had Paul pen this second letter to Timothy, it was for the believers. It is a warning of the end times and the need for endurance. It was a cautioning to us that we avoid such people. We can't even be around them much less be like them. My brothers and sisters, take heed. Examine your hearts, actions, motives, and what you believe salvation is. Be sure that it matches up with our Father's plans because he is the author of the universe and the one who makes all the rules. We will not be able to swindle our ways into his heart when all is said and done. We will not be able to argue with him that we did good things. He is going to know where our hearts are whether right or for self. This is life and death. Fill the void with the one true God. Remember that while we are offered grace, it is not a license to continue sinning. It is not an acclaim for our humanness. *Grace is a gift from our Father to forgive us of our sins and a powerful tool of God*, "training us to renounce impiety and worldly passions, and in the present age to live lives that are self-controlled, upright, and godly while we wait for the blessed hope and the manifestation of the glory of our great God and Savior, Jesus Christ" (Titus 2:11–13 NRSV).

"Let us draw near with a sincere heart in full assurance of faith, having our hearts sprinkled to cleanse us from a guilty conscience and our bodies washed with pure water. Let us hold resolutely to the hope we profess, for He who promised is faithful. And let us consider how to spur one another on to love and good deeds. Let us not neglect meeting together, as some have made a habit, but let us encourage one another, and all the more as you see the Day approaching. If we deliberately go on sinning after we have received the knowledge of the truth, no further sacrifice for sins remains, but only a fearful expectation of judgment and of raging fire that will consume all adversaries" (Heb. 10:22–27, BSB).

"For if, after they have escaped the defilements of the world through the knowledge of our Lord and Savior Jesus Christ, they are again entangled in them and overcome, the last state has become worse for them than the first. For it would have been better for them never to have known the way of righteousness than after knowing it to turn back from the holy commandment delivered to them. What the true proverb says has happened to them: 'The dog returns to its own vomit, and the sow, after washing herself, returns to wallow in the mire'" (2 Pet. 2:20–22, ESV).

"So do not throw away your confidence. It holds a great reward. You need to persevere so that after you have done the will of God, you will receive what he has promised. 'For in just a little while, he who is coming will come and will not delay. But my righteous one will live by faith, and if he shrinks back, I will take no pleasure in him.' But we are not of those who shrink back and are destroyed but of those who have faith and preserve their souls" (Heb. 10:35–39, ESV).

"May the Lord direct your hearts into the love of God and into the steadfastness of Christ" (2 Thess. 3:5, ESV).

My family is in a new home. We live on top of a mountain ridge. The land is rocky and slopes one way or another. It's a wonderful place to live, except when you need a flat surface. Like now, we need a flat surface. We wanted to put up one of those cheap steel-frame pools for us to swim in. We went about it just as we've seen other successful pool builders do. We bought dirt. Not just dirt but sandy loam. It was going to be a great foundation for our pool. Well, since there are so many rocks on the land, we decided rather than to dig into the land to level it, we'd stack this loam. We went to work shoveling it and working it flat, making it thicker on one side than the other so we could level the land. I built up a stone-retaining wall of sorts (see those rocks were coming in handy after all). The next day, we started to fill it. I went around and put footings under each leg of the pool. We eyeballed it and thought it looked level and great.

Looks can be deceiving though. We used the same materials others use to put pools up, and it looked level and perfectly even until you got up close and saw how shallow it was going to be from the crookedness. The foundation wasn't built right. We didn't measure with a level. We eyeballed it. Our retaining wall was inferior while it looked good. We winged it and hoped for the best. We made it look like it was supposed to look, but we never made sure we had accurate footings in the correct spot. As I sit here now, I'm letting water out of the pool so I can lift the low side up with blocks and dig out from under the high side to make it more level.

We can make our Christianity look just right. We can wing it and do the things we see others doing, hide behind a mantra that we are covered by grace, carnal, and God knows it but loves us anyway, and we can even lead church, Sunday school classes, or Bible studies and still just be winging it with crooked lives. There is a purpose that so many pages of our sacred Bibles are filled with cautions, warnings, and instructions for us to live by. There's a reason the Lord spoke of "the way" as narrow. It is.

"For the gate is narrow and the way is hard that leads to life, and those who find it are few" (Mt. 7:14, ESV).

If for no other reason than to know we are pleasing God and giving him due glory, can we not live our lives with virtuous righteousness? Can we not find pleasure in knowing that we can please our Father by tapping into the power of his forgiveness and changed lives thereafter?

"Because you have kept the word of My perseverance, I also will keep you from the hour of testing, that hour which is about to come upon the whole world, to test those who dwell on the earth" (Rev. 3:10, NASB).

Our purpose on Earth, as the creation of our omnipotent God is to bring him glory. Let us, therefore, focus our lives on bringing this magnificence to our supreme Father.

"Then Jesus told His disciples, 'If anyone wants to come after Me, he must deny himself and take up his cross and follow Me. For whoever wants to save his life will lose it, but whoever loses his life for My sake will find it. What will it profit a man if he gains the whole world, yet forfeits his soul? Or what can a man give in exchange for his soul? For the Son of Man will come in His Father's glory with His angels, and then He will repay each one according to what he has done" (Mt. 16:24–27, ESV).

If we're going to live your life for God, then live it by his will, not in a way that just looks or sounds right. We must do according to his instructions as he's commanded and given us the ability to do through the saving blood of our Savior. Love because his Spirit dwells in us and loving others is not burdensome because of his power within us.

> What do I gain if, humanly speaking, I fought with beasts at Ephesus? If the dead are not raised, "Let us eat and drink, for tomorrow we die." Do not be deceived: "Bad company ruins good morals." Wake up from your drunken stupor, as is right, and do not go on sinning. For some have no knowledge of God. I say this to your shame. (1 Cor. 15:32–34, ESV)

> Make me to know your ways, O Lord; teach me your paths. Lead me in your truth and teach me, for you are the God of my salvation; for you I wait all the day long. (Ps. 25:4–5, ESV)

Chapter 12

Purpose

> *What does the worker gain from his toil? I have seen the burden that God has laid upon the sons of men to occupy them. He has made everything beautiful in its time. He has also set eternity in the hearts of men, yet they cannot fathom the work that God has done from beginning to end.*
> —Ecclesiastes 3:9–11, BSB

As our Savior walked this Earth over two thousand years ago, he spoke often of a new heaven and Earth. We have eternal lives that go on beyond this world. "But do not forget this one thing, dear friends: With the Lord a day is like a thousand years, and a thousand years are like a day" (2 Pet. 3:8, NIV).

Our lives are short. "For you are a mist that appears for a little time and then vanishes" (Jas. 4:14. ESV). We're here for but a moment in comparison to eternity as it's, well, eternal. While I contest that salvation is strictly about getting your "get out of hell" card, we really need to consider eternity and the details our Lord has left for us to know so that we can be prepared.

There seem to be a multitude of ideas about when Christ will return. The most popular one in today's time is that there will be a pre-tribulation rapture of all the saints. When I look for sermons on the topic of end times or of the antichrist, I find mostly preachers exclaiming that believers do not need to worry about such matters because the Lord will return and take his bride before any of it happens. That would be fantastic if that is the case. As we proceed with caution, let us remember, "No one knows about that day or hour, not even the angels in heaven, nor the Son, but only the Father" (Mt. 24:36 and Mk. 13:32).

Since we *cannot* know the day or time, we are not going to even try to figure that out. We do, however, need to know enough details to be prepared and ready for it. If we assume that we are not going to be here for any of the details, but do not confirm in our own Scriptures that this is true, we might not be ready for his return and find ourselves just as the five virgins.

"At that time the kingdom of heaven will be like ten virgins who took their lamps and went out to meet the bridegroom. Five of them were foolish, and five were wise. The foolish ones took their lamps but did not take along any extra oil. But the wise ones took oil in flasks along with their lamps. When the bridegroom was delayed, they all became drowsy and fell asleep. At midnight the cry rang out: 'Here is the bridegroom! Come out to meet him!' Then all the virgins woke up and trimmed their lamps. The foolish ones said to the wise, 'Give us some of your oil; our lamps are going out.' 'No,' said the wise ones, 'or there may not be enough for both us and you. Instead, go to those who sell oil and buy some for yourselves.' But while they were on their way to buy it, the bridegroom arrived. Those who were ready went in with him to the wedding banquet, and the door was shut. Later the other virgins arrived and said, 'Lord, lord, open the door for us!' But he replied, 'Truly I tell you, I do not know you.' Therefore keep watch, because you do not know the day or the hour" (Mt. 25:1–13, BSB).

This passage was a parable given by Jesus himself but not elaborated on like many of his others were. There is no explanation that we can look at a few verses later, but it's something to ponder and consider carefully. To begin, we are frequently called the bride of Christ as he is the bridegroom. This section of Scripture stirs an urging from deeper than within me to be sure that I have enough oil for my lamp. Without an explanation from Christ himself, we are left to figure out what this means. There are many theories from various theologians. Without arguing or debating any of their points though, I can be assured of two things from this parable. First, we are told to watch for his return. The instruction to watch for his return is repeated throughout the Scriptures and must hold some merit. This nullifies the current voices that tell us to not worry about any of the end time details. Those who claim that since "we can't know the hour or day and will be raptured first anyway" are not taking into account that our Savior warned us to be sure we were on the lookout. His parables give us direction for active participation in being sure we are anticipating his return.

Second, we are told to be ready. The fact that there are five (or half) of the virgins unprepared and turned away by Christ himself makes me think of the passage we looked at earlier, Matthew 7:23. There will be many who are living church-like lives and still be turned away. This is a huge wake-up call to the sleepy believers who err on the side of grace and deny the power of our redeeming Almighty Savior. "Behold, I am coming like a thief. Blessed is the one who remains awake and clothed, so that he will not go naked and let his shame be exposed" (Rev. 16:15, BSB).

We obviously need to know more about the last days so we know what to watch for and what to prepare for. The book of Daniel includes specific details we need to look at first before even going into the infamous book of Revelation.

"At that time Michael, the great prince who stands watch over your people, will rise up. There will be a time of distress, the likes of which will not have occurred from the beginning of nations until that time. But at that time your people—everyone whose name is found written in the book—will be delivered. And many who sleep in the dust of the earth will awake, some to everlasting life, but others to shame and everlasting contempt. Then the wise will shine like the brightness of the heavens, and those who lead many to righteousness will shine like the stars forever and ever. But you, Daniel, shut up these words and seal the book until the time of the end. Many will roam to and fro, and knowledge will increase" (Dan. 12:1–4, BSB).

Daniel had an encounter with Michael the archangel from on high. He recounts details given about distressful times to come, worse than have ever been seen before, and tells us that simultaneously, or at the same time, those whose names are written in the Lamb's Book of Life will be delivered. Daniel was commanded to shut up these words and seal the book until the time of the end.

A few verses later, we see that Daniel responds and says, "I heard, but I did not understand. So I asked, 'My lord, what will be the outcome of these things?' 'Go on your way, Daniel,' he replied, 'for the words are closed up and sealed until the time of the end. Many will be purified, made spotless, and refined, but the wicked will continue to act wickedly. None of the wicked will understand, but the wise will understand'" (Dan. 12:8–10, BSB).

Once again, the archangel tells Daniel to close up the words and seal them until the time of the end. We are given a comparison of the saved and the nonbelievers. In addition to this, we are told that while the wicked will continue to act wickedly and not understand, the wise will understand. The following verses give a huge clue and an important key phrase.

"And from the time the daily sacrifice is abolished and the abomination of desolation set up, there will be 1,290 days. Blessed is he who waits and reaches the end of the 1,335 days. But as for you, go on your way until the end. You will rest, and will arise to your inheritance at the end of the days" (Dan. 12:11–13, BSB).

We see in these verses that there are 1,290 days between the daily sacrifice being abolished and the abomination of desolation being set up. The following verse adds forty-five days and says those who wait and reach the end are blessed. The closing verses are to Daniel, telling him that he will be "asleep" by then and will "rest" and arise to his inheritance at the end of the days. The book of Thessalonians mirrors this information.

"By the word of the Lord, we declare to you that we who are alive and remain until the coming of the Lord will by no means precede those who have fallen asleep. For the Lord Himself will descend from heaven with a loud command, with the voice of an archangel, and with the trumpet of God, and the dead in Christ will be the first to rise. After that, we who are alive and remain will be caught up together with them in the clouds to meet the Lord in the air. And so we will always be with the Lord. Therefore encourage one another with these words" (1 Thess. 4:15–18, BSB).

It seems clear and accurate to say that those in Christ who have died before his second coming will be the first to be raised in the rapture. Those who are still alive will go with our Savior next. "Then there will be two men in the field; one will be taken and one will be left" (Mt. 24:40, NASB). "I tell you, on that night there will be two in one bed; one will be taken and the other will be left" (Lk. 17:34, BSB).

Clearly, there will be a rapture of the saints. Those who have lived and died before he comes will be taken up first, and then those who are still living on the earth at the time of the rapture will go to be with the Lord in the air. I fear, however, that if we conclude that this is all we need to know, "We've been saved, we went to church, Jesus will come take me before tribulation, and I will be all set," that we will not be prepared as we've been warned.

As I bring these next several passages to light, please pray for discernment. Read them with me and pray that God the Father will open our eyes to see what he is telling us through his Son and other writers of the Holy Scriptures.

There was a key phrase in Daniel 12. It was "abomination of desolation." It's written of at least seven other times in Scriptures. In the books of Matthew, Mark, and Luke, Jesus references the abomination of desolation as a sign of end times to occur before his second coming and the rapture of the church. Because of this, it's important to look at these verses to see if we can figure out what this might be so that we can be ready. Let us look at the first three books of the New Testament to get a better idea of the abomination of desolation.

"So when you see the abomination of desolation standing where it should not be (let the reader understand), then let those who are in Judea flee to the mountains" (Mk. 13:4, BSB).

"So when you see standing in the holy place "the abomination of desolation," described by the prophet Daniel (let the reader understand)" (Mt. 24:15, BSB).

We're going to have to look at the other verses about the abomination of desolation in the book of Daniel to best understand what is meant by this. Before we do that, let us look at the book of Luke for the parallel scripture: "But when you see Jerusalem surrounded by armies, you will know that her desolation is near" (Lk. 21:20, BSB).

Here we have a hint that the abomination of desolation will have something to do with armies surrounding Jerusalem. Daniel 11:25–27 also describes the desolation revolving around Jerusalem as it foretells of the rebuilding as well as "the troops of the prince who is to come" destroying the city, the sanctuary, and that then, the antichrist will make a strong covenant with many for one week.

It's interesting to realize that Jerusalem did not exist anymore until May 14, 1948, when Israel became a nation again. This prophecy could not have come to pass literally without the rebirth of this nation. It is also for this reason that many believe the end is eminent. Matthew 24:34, ESV comes after Christ tells his disciples of the signs of the end times. He says, "Truly, I say to you, this generation will not pass away until all these things take place." If the rebirth of Israel is the beginning of the signs to take place, they reason, then we are seventy-four years later and must be close to the end "for this generation not to pass away until all these things take place."

Because our Lord referenced the Prophet Daniel in his mentioning of the abomination of desolation, it is necessary to go back and look into Daniel.

"At the appointed time he will invade the South again, but this time will not be like the first. Ships of Kittim will come against him, and he will lose heart. Then he will turn back and rage against the holy covenant and do damage. So he will return and show favor to those who forsake the holy covenant. His forces will rise up and desecrate the temple fortress. They will abolish the daily sacrifice and set up the abomination of desolation. With flattery he will corrupt those who violate the covenant, but the people who know their God will firmly resist him. Those with insight will instruct many, though for a time they will fall by sword or flame, or be captured or plundered. Now when they fall, they will be granted a little help, but many will join them insincerely. Some of the wise will fall, so that they may be refined, purified, and made spotless until the time of the end, for it will still come at the appointed time" (Dan. 11:29–35, BSB).

This portion of Scripture gives more insight. We can see that there will be an invasion from the south again. There will be rage against the holy covenant and damage done. The enemy will show favor to those who forsake God and be able to rise up to desecrate the temple fortress. There is no temple of God literally standing in Jerusalem right now. It was destroyed twice, but this prophecy foretells that there will be a daily sacrifice that is abolished and the abomination of desolation set up. We know that the span between these two events is 1,290 days and that after the abomination of desolation, there will be forty-five more days in which the enemy will flatter the lost and convince them to violate the covenant of God. Those who stay true to God and resist the enemy will be killed by sword, flame, and captured or robbed. This forewarning includes the fact that some will join the enemy insincerely and be made spotless until the time of the end. It isn't a whole lot of information to go on that we be diligent in watchful, but we can glean enough from this to know that this event will most definitely happen in Jerusalem in the literal temple of God.

The Gospel of Luke goes on after mentioning the abomination of desolation to say the following: "Then let those who are in Judea flee to the mountains, let those in the city get out, and let those in the country stay out of the city. For these are the days of vengeance, to fulfill all that is written. How miserable those days will be for pregnant and nursing mothers! For there will be great distress upon the land and wrath against this people. They will fall by the edge of the sword and be led captive into all the nations. And Jerusalem will be trodden down by the Gentiles, until the times of the Gentiles are fulfilled. There will be signs in the sun and moon and stars, and on the earth dismay among the nations, bewildered by the roaring of the sea and the surging of the waves. Men will faint from fear and anxiety over what is coming upon the earth, for the powers of the heavens will be shaken. At that time, they will see the Son of Man coming in a cloud with power and great glory. When these things begin to happen, stand up and lift up your heads, because your redemption is drawing near" (Lk. 21:21–28, BSB).

This passage describes a miserable time. "These are the days of vengeance," "There will be a great distress upon the land" just as Daniel spoke of. There are more details listed of this devastating time, but notice here that there will be signs in the sun, moon, and stars…and later it is exclaimed that we will see the Son of Man coming in the cloud with power and great glory. These miserable times are to come before the church is raptured and Christ returns.

We see this same fact here: "Immediately after the tribulation of those days: 'The sun will be darkened, and the moon will not give its light; the stars will fall from the sky, and the powers of the heavens will be shaken. At that time the sign of the Son of Man will appear in heaven, and all the tribes of the earth will mourn. They will see the Son of Man coming on the clouds of heaven, with power and great glory. And He will send out His angels with a loud trumpet call, and they will gather His elect from the four winds, from one end of the heavens to the other" (Mt. 24:29–31, BSB).

This is recorded in Matthew. Jesus told us that "immediately after the tribulation of those days, the likes of which will not have occurred from the beginning of nations until that time" (Dan. 12:1) the sun will be darkened, the moon will give no light, and the stars will fall from the sky, and then at that time, the sign of the Son of Man will appear in heaven…*and they will gather his elect.* The rapture and the second coming are after the worst tribulation the world has ever seen.

Christ comes after there is the greatest tribulation this earth has ever seen. Luke specifies that "on the earth dismay among the nations, bewildered by the roaring of the sea and the surging of the waves. Men will faint from fear and anxiety over what is coming upon the earth for the powers of the heavens will be shaken."

Christ warns us in Luke 21:10–19: "Nation will rise against nation, and kingdom against kingdom. There will be great earthquakes, famines, and pestilences in various places, along with fearful sights and great signs from heaven. But before all this, they will seize you and persecute you. On account of My name they will deliver you to the synagogues and prisons, and they will bring you before kings and governors. This will be your opportunity to serve as witnesses. So make up your mind not to worry beforehand how to defend yourselves. For I will give you speech and wisdom that none of your adversaries will be able to resist or contradict. You will be betrayed even by parents and brothers and relatives and friends, and some of you will be put to death. And you will be hated by everyone because of My name. Yet not even a hair of your head will perish. By your patient endurance, you will gain your souls."

These are the reasons our Lord has warned us and given us instruction to watch and be ready. There will be earthquakes, famine, pestilence, and persecution of the saints, and he tells us to make up our minds now, not to worry about how to defend ourselves. He is going to give us his power! "You know of Jesus of Nazareth, how God anointed Him with the Holy Spirit and with power, and how He went about doing good and healing all who were oppressed by the devil, for God was with Him" (Acts 10:38, BSB).

We've been looking at scriptures providing insight in how the Lord gave the Holy Spirit to us to live like Christ. There are many verses throughout the texts that describe the Holy Spirit as an anointing on Christ and believers as well. It is because of these verses that many believe there is a direct correlation in symbolism to oil and the Holy Spirit. As we look at the Lord's words about being set in our minds not to worry about how to defend ourselves and that he will give us speech and wisdom, I am reminded of other verses we've looked at regarding the Holy Spirit and how he gives us the sounds and utterances in prayer when we do not know what to pray (Rom. 8:26) "for the Holy Spirit will teach you in that very hour what you ought to say" (Lk. 12:12, NASB).

Immediately, I wonder if the five virgins who were without enough oil to burn their lamps were without the Holy Spirit for before our bridegroom comes to take us away, he's warned us that we will be persecuted but given "speech and wisdom that none of your adversaries will be able to resist or contradict." We will not be able to do this without the power of the Holy Spirit.

Up to this point, I've felt God giving me an urgency to speak out on behalf of the power of him in us through the Holy Spirit given to us upon the ascension of Christ to the right hand of the father (Acts 2). As we look at the end of times and the attention given to our need in preparedness, it shouldn't come as a surprise that we still need to remember the Holy Spirit is the one who gives us the power of God to do that which we couldn't on our own. "And do not grieve the Holy Spirit of God in whom you were sealed for the day of redemption" (Eph. 4:30).

The day of redemption is referring to the end of the times. "But when these things begin to take place, straighten up and lift up your heads because your redemption is drawing near" (Lk. 21:28, NASB). As we hypothesize that the five virgins who did not bring enough oil for their lamps to burn could be connected to a lack of the Holy Spirit of God, it puts another verse in my mind that we've used before as we discussed just how indispensable the presence of the Holy Spirit is within our Christian lives. Paul warns, "In the last days, terrible times will come. For men will be lovers of themselves, lovers of money, boastful, arrogant, abusive, disobedient to their parents, ungrateful, unholy, unloving, unforgiving, slanderous, without self-control, brutal, without love of good, traitorous, reckless, conceited, lovers of pleasure rather than lovers of God, having a form of godliness but denying its power…" (2 Tim. 3:1–5, ESV).

"'In the last time there will be mockers, following after their own ungodly lusts.' These are the ones who cause divisions, worldly-minded, devoid of the Spirit" (Jude 1:18–19, BSB).

Be mindful not to be religious without the power of God by listening to the popular Christian verses that paint a false picture of God and the life he wants for his children, "seeking" only through short daily devotionals and other ear-tickling messages that make you feel "good" but leave you devoid of the one true God. Pray that God will give you wisdom, knowledge, and understanding. Pray that He will fill you with His Holy Spirit daily so that your lamps will have enough oil until he comes to take his bride. Humble yourselves before God, die to yourselves and your flesh, and ask for his Spirit to fill you.

> For the time will come when men will not tolerate sound doctrine, but with itching ears they will gather around themselves teachers to suit

their own desires. So they will turn their ears away from the truth and turn aside to myths. But you, be sober in all things, endure hardship, do the work of an evangelist, fulfill your ministry. For I am already being poured out like a drink offering, and the time of my departure is at hand. I have fought the good fight, I have finished the race, I have kept the faith. From now on there is laid up for me the crown of righteousness, which the Lord, the righteous Judge, will award to me on that day—and not only to me, but to all who crave His appearing. (2 Tim. 4:3–8, BSB)

Chapter 13

The Segue

> *This gospel of the kingdom shall be preached in the whole world as a testimony to all the nations, and then the end will come.*
> —Matthew 24:14, NASB

Our God has given us specific signs to watch for to know that the end is near. As we look throughout history, we can find that even the earliest of Christians were expecting his return in their lifetimes. Essentially, we can't know for certain when Christ is coming or if it's going to be in our own generation, but that doesn't mean we should not be prepared and watching. The parable of the virgins should give us the reminder we need to be vigilant. As we look at what's going on in the world around us and see how sins of our times have openly multiplied, we can compare it to the days of Noah.

Genesis chapter 6 gives an account for what Noah's times were like. "The lord saw that the wickedness of man was great in the earth and that every intention of the thoughts of his heart was only evil continually" (Gen. 6:5, ESV). "Now the earth was corrupt in God's sight, and the earth was filled with violence. And God saw the earth, and behold, it was corrupt, for all flesh had corrupted their way on the earth" (Gen. 6:11–12, ESV).

"For the coming of the Son of Man will be just like the days of Noah" (Mt. 24:37, NASB). "Just as it was in the days of Noah, so will it be in the days of the Son of Man. They were eating and drinking and marrying and being given in marriage, until the day when Noah entered the ark, and the flood came and destroyed them all" (Lk. 17:26–27, ESV).

We are living in evil times. The evil we see in our world has prevailed historically. There have been eras of great apostasy. Holodomor, the Holocaust, China's Great Leap Forward, and so many other travesties dot our timelines of the past. We have certainly experienced times like Noah's with horrific tragedies that have left millions suffering, starving, killed, and even eaten by their own parents. While we know that the end will be like the days of Noah and our current international policies could easily be compared to those times described in Genesis chapter 6, we cannot go solely by these heinous atrocities. We do have other signs to look for while I believe living as God has commanded will prepare us for these times; remember Jesus Christ told us to watch and be prepared, so again, it's worth it to look at the signs.

"In the last days, God says, I will pour out My Spirit on all people. Your sons and daughters will prophesy, your young men will see visions, your old men will dream dreams. Even on My menservants and maidservants I will pour out My Spirit in those days, and they will prophesy" (Acts 2:17–18, BSB).

Here we have "the last days" specified once again. We can easily look at this section of scripture as an isolated verse and say that the Spirit of the living God will be poured out in the last days. There is an explanation that there will be prophecies, visions, and dreams… what we need to look at though, is the verse preceding this and know that Peter is quoting the Prophet Joel and clarifying that the Holy Spirit has come and is from that moment until the end going to be poured out. "For we know in part and we prophesy in part, but when the perfect comes, the partial passes away" (1 Cor. 13:9–10, BSB). So while this is a sign of the end, it is also not particularly telling of how close we are to the end.

There are other signs given by Christ our Lord in Matthew 24, "All these are the beginning of birth pains. Then they will deliver you over to be persecuted and killed, and you will be hated by all nations because of My name. At that time, many will fall away and will betray and hate one another, and many false prophets will arise and mislead many… For false Christs and false prophets will appear and perform great signs and wonders that would deceive even the elect, if that were possible. See, I have told you in advance" (Mt. 24:8–11, 24–25, BSB).

The phrase "if that were possible" caught my attention.

After pairing Matthew 24:24 with 1 Timothy 4:1, it says, "Now the Spirit expressly says that in later times some will depart from the faith by devoting themselves to deceitful spirits and teachings of demons." The phrase that stuck out in Matthew is even more intriguing. "If it were possible" implies that the elect cannot fall away because it is not possible.

Paul, however, did not include that in his warning of the same thing. We can simply agree that Paul meant that but didn't say it because he assumed we already knew it and go on or we can begin digging to find out what "if it were possible" means. I went to the lexicon to discover what Greek word was interpreted to "possible" in our English Bibles. The Greek word is "*dunation*," the origin is "*dunamis.*" It's a rather common word used throughout the New Testament 199 times and means "strong, mighty, powerful" (Mt. 24:24 lexicon: "For false Christs and false prophets will arise and will show great signs and wonders, so as to mislead, if possible, even the elect. biblehub.com). Biblestudytools.com gives a more thorough definition as "inherent power, power residing in a thing by virtue of its nature, or which a person or thing exerts and puts forth, power for performing miracles, moral power and excellence of soul" (Bible Study Tools, "*dunamis*," biblestudytools.com).

Using some of the 199 verses *dunamis* is found in our scriptures will help us define the word meaning and understand if it actually means "Christians cannot possibly fall away (in the end of times)."

"No one who is born of God practices sin because his seed abides *in him, and he cannot* sin because he is born of God" (1 Jn. 3:9, NASB). "In him, and he cannot" is the interpretation of the very same Greek word *dunamis* and means the same here: "to be able, to have power" (1 Jn. 3:9 lexicon: "No one who is born of God practices sin, because His seed abides in him; and he cannot sin, because he is born of God. biblehub.com). It's a verb, an action from God, given to the believer.

Our Father in heaven gives us inherent power to perform the miracle of moral power and excellence of soul. Either we're living with that power and we won't fall away, or we are holding onto our fleshly lives crying that "God knows we're human and didn't really mean we are supposed to actually do anything within our faith." We can claim that it's not possible for the false prophets to deceive us if we are walking in this *dunamis* and we abide in him, without sin, or we can get real and realize we *need* this *dunamis* from our loving Abba Father and get right with him to be able to not be deceived.

Dunamis is a supernatural power and ability. In these scriptures that we've looked at, this *dunamis* is from God. In the end though, Satan will give the antichrist his own supernatural power, or *dunamis*. This power is so strong the antichrist will be able to heal himself of a mortal wound and preform miraculous signs and wonders. Certainly, if Satan can give that amount of power, then the *dunamis* from our Father is even greater.

We talked about this concept within the first several chapters of this book as we searched for truth. In the third chapter, we focused on the book of Romans and what righteousness was. In Romans 8, Paul made a case for power given to us through the Holy Spirit of God. We looked at verses 1–15 previously to get a better idea of how to live as Christians and be distinguished between the fleshly and sinful man versus the godly man made new through the power of our Father through salvation. In verse seven, we can see the word *dunamis* used again and get a better idea of what Jesus meant in Matthew 24:24.

"For the mind set on the flesh is death, but the mind set on the Spirit is life and peace, because the mind set on the flesh is hostile toward God; for it does not subject itself to the law of God, for it is not even able *to do so*, and those who are in the flesh cannot please God" (Rom. 8:6–8, NASB). According to the lexicon, this passage means that a fleshly man is unable to subject himself to God's law (Romans 8:7 lexicon: "because the mind set on the flesh is hostile toward God; for it does not subject itself to the law of God, for it is not even able to do so." biblehub.com).

There is a crystal clear explanation of how *dunamis* is the supernatural power bestowed to believers and is the *only power* humanity has *to be able to* be saved and follow God, and it is when we look at these verses in Matthew: "When the disciples heard this, they were greatly astonished and asked, 'Who then can be saved?' Jesus looked at them and said, 'With man this is *impossible*, but with God all things are *possible*'" (Mt. 19:25–26, BSB; emphasis added). *Impossible* is derived from "*adunaton*", meaning *without* power (a derivation of "*dunamis*"). The last word of the verse, "possible," is derived from "*dunata*" (also a derivation of "*dunamis*"). Christ is explaining to his disciples and us that believers have the divine power to be saved and the ability to please God through *dunamis*. Without this power, we run the risk of possibly being lead astray by false christs and false prophets.

The flesh does not have the divine power, the *dunamis*, to follow after God on its own. Our God is almighty and gives us the ability to do his will through his *dunamis*. We have supernatural power to live without sin and even perform the miracles as Christ told us in John 14:12 ESV: "Truly, truly, I say to you, whoever believes in me will also do the works that I do; and greater works than these will he do, because I am going to the Father."

Jesus told us in Matthew 24:25 (NASB), "Behold, I have told you in advance that the end times are going to be perilous."

"But understand this, that in the last days there will come times of difficulty. For people will be lovers of self, lovers of money, proud, arrogant, abusive, disobedient to their parents, ungrateful, unholy, heartless, unappeasable, slanderous, without self-control, brutal, not loving good, treacherous, reckless, swollen with conceit, lovers of pleasure rather than lovers of God, having the appearance of godliness, but denying its power. Avoid such people. For among them are those who creep into households and capture weak women, burdened with sins and led astray by various passions, always learning and never able to arrive at a knowledge of the truth" (2 Tim. 3:1–7, ESV).

As we look at this scripture warning us about the last days, it's important to note that the word *dunamis* comes up again. "Always learning and never *dunamis* to arrive at a knowledge of truth" (verse 7). Do not be the person always learning about God, having an appearance of godliness but denying it's power, the *dunamis*, or you will be one who falls away just as foretold by Jesus, his apostles, and his prophets. "For false christs and false prophets will arise and will provide great signs and wonders so as to mislead, if possible, even the elect" (Mt. 24:24, BSB). We need to be careful that we are not "believers" with the description of those described in 2 Timothy 3:1–7 because these people do not have the *dunamis* Christ spoke of in Matthew 24:24 when he warns us that many will be misled. This is why Paul said the same thing, and we do not see an "if it were possible" clause. The accurate translation seems to be lost by using the word "possible," and we need to be sure to look at the other scriptures warning of the same falling away that will happen as well as looking at the valid definition of *dunamis* to see that we can have the God-given and divine power to endure as long as we are not "believers" with an appearance of godliness that denies that power (*dunamis*).

A sign of the times will be that there are false prophets and those with a form of religion and godliness that is not of the one true God. As we study these end times and look for the signs, it's most important that we are right with the Lord not having given our lives to him as younger selves but living with fleshly motivations "covered by a grace" that will not sustain anyone but instead live lives full of *dunamis*. It is the only way to be prepared and to have the *dunamena* to resist the evil ones.

"Examine yourselves to see whether you are in the faith; test yourselves. Can't you see for yourselves that Jesus Christ is in you—unless you actually fail the test? And I hope you will realize that we have not failed the test" (2 Cor. 13:5–6, BSB).

Imagine walking into a telephone booth a plain man and popping out as Superman. We have this gift from God. As we navigate through life, come up against someone poised to argue or something frustrating happens pop into your prayer closet, even if you stay put and simply pray silently in your mind and ask your Father in heaven for his power. He already promised he'd give it to us. *"Lord, this is hard. I don't know how to respond, I feel angry, etc. Fill me with your dunamis to do what is right, holy, and would be honorable to you."*

The book of Revelation gives us insight into the way God looks at his church found to have *dunamis*. "And to the angel of the church in Philadelphia write… 'I know your deeds. Behold, I have put before you an open door which no one can shut, because you have a little power, and have followed My word, and have not denied My name… Because you have kept My word of perseverance, I also will keep you from the hour of the testing, that *hour* which is about to come upon the whole world, to test those who live on the earth. I am coming quickly; hold firmly to what you have, so that no one will take your crown. The one who overcomes, I will make him a pillar in the temple of My God, and he will not go out from it anymore; and I will write on him the name of My God, and the name of the city of My God, the new Jerusalem, which comes down out of heaven from My God, and My new name. The one who has an ear, let him hear what the Spirit says to the churches'" (Rev. 3:7–13, NASB).

Verse 8 includes the word *dunamin*. He says, "You have a little *dunamin* and have followed my word and have not denied my name." Verses 11–13 speaks to a church that has a little of God's power and tells them he is coming quickly. "Hold firmly to what you have so that no one will take your crown." In the verses prior to this, in the letter to Sardis, there is a warning that sounds much like this, "So remember what you have received and heard; and keep *it*, and repent. Then if you are not alert, I will come like a thief, and you will not know at what hour I will come to you. But you have a few people in Sardis who have not soiled their garments; and they will walk with Me in white, for they are worthy. The one who overcomes will be clothed the same way, in white garments; and I will not erase his name from the book of life, and I will confess his name before My Father and before His angels" (Rev. 3:3–5, NASB).

We have an active role in our Christianity. Even with a little *dunamis*, we have enough power to endure, but we are called to receive this power through the Holy Spirit and then to overcome so that God will not erase our name from the Book of Life.

I fear we've been taught with such strong veracity that we are locked in, saved because we professed belief, and are unable to lose our salvation that any one of us could be like those in the churches who are not enduring or those described in the third chapter of 2 Timothy. It's so important to read the word of God for ourselves and to check ourselves, our fruit, and be willing to be exhorted. Whether we can lose our salvation or never had it in the first place isn't going to matter. There will be people who thought they were converted believers standing before Jesus and naming great feats they accomplished "in his name," and our Savior will turn them away and tell them to depart from Him, he never knew them (Mt. 7:23). It really doesn't matter if they lost their salvation or never had it; what's important is that we take this into account as we address our own salvation and work it out with fear and trembling (Phil. 2:12).

There are many believers preparing for hard times. They are "preppers" and working with the tenacity of an ant to prepare for bad times to come. There is so much effort going into the preservation of physical lives, even by believers, that I fear the efforts are being wasted and only serving as a pseudo preparation. God requires that we walk with him, unsoiled, and in search of fulfilling his will. "The road to hell is paved with good intentions."

No matter what we do in the name of Christ, if it is not in accordance to the Word and in obedience to his commandments through the power of the Holy Spirit of God, (this *dunamis*) we run the risk of not being the fulfillment of Revelation 3:5 and being the ones whose names are erased as we get turned away. Being saved is simple "if you confess with your mouth that Jesus is Lord and believe in your heart that God raised him from the dead, you will be saved" (Rom. 10:9, ESV). It's that "believe in you heart" part that creates an unquenchable desire to love God that we must be sure it's there for our lives to be saved. This is the part of us that is full of the Holy Spirit, seeking God, living righteously with love for our neighbors, as he called us to. And the part that was missing in the believers standing before the Lord in Matthew 7:22–23 when our Savior tells them to "depart from me, I never knew you."

I've searched YouTube for sermons on the end times, looking for what is taught by preachers of our time. There are scores of sermons based on the concept of who the "false teachers" are. Some name names, but mostly, they are warning us of the "prosperity gospel" and the "name it and claim it" preachers we can find on television or in the odd church scattered across America. What if these are not all that is meant when our Word tells us that we are to beware of false prophets and false teachers. What if it's them *and* those who preach such a watered-down version of the gospel that "the power" is denied? What if the false prophets include teachers who tell us that we are "too human" to go and sin no more and that grace covers all, praising God for the "grace" to keep sinning, yet still be saved?

As we actively prepare ourselves for the day of our Lord, whether it be before we die or afterward, the urgency to get right with God is the same. We must love God with our whole hearts, minds, and souls, love our neighbors as ourselves, help the afflicted, and live righteously with the power of the Holy Spirit and *dunamis* to keep us from stumbling. While we have an advocate if we sin, we need to focus our lives around living for Christ and not hanging our salvation on a grace that knows we're still human and, therefore, unable to stop living in sin. We need to live our lives believing God is stronger than the world and "You, little children, are from God and have overcome them, because greater is He who is in you than he who is in the world" (1 Jn. 4:4, BSB).

Much like Luke tells us, "People were eating and drinking, marrying and being given in marriage, up to the day" (Lk. 17:27, BSB). Peter warns us also that "Most importantly, you must understand that in the last days scoffers will come, scoffing and following their own evil desires. 'Where is the promise of His coming?' they will ask. 'Ever since our fathers fell asleep, everything continues as it has from the beginning of creation'" (2 Pet. 3:4, BSB).

We must be ready. We must realize that we will be able to see the signs of the end, but scoffers will try to sway us and mock the very idea of an end being near as they continue in their own merrymaking and the world seems to go on. As ridiculers follow their own evil desires, we must be careful not to let that which is common skew our own faith.

Peter warns us also that "Most importantly, you must understand that in the last days scoffers will come, scoffing and following their own evil desires"(2 Pet. 3:3, BSB). How is a scoffer following his own evil desires any different than the supposed believers "covered by a grace" that deems them unable to live righteously and after God but to continue on in their own evil desires? Didn't Timothy warn us about not being lovers of pleasure in 2 Timothy 3:4?

As far back as I can remember, I've loved to read mysteries. I wanted to figure out what was going to happen before it happened and keep reading to see if I had gotten it right. Now, I can get the same thrill from an "escape room." My husband and I took two of our older kids to one right after Christmas. We were locked into a room with clues everywhere that had to be pieced together to figure out the next clue. We couldn't get out until we figured out where the key was and how to get it out. We looked under tables, behind furniture, in clocks, and every obvious place. We looked under rugs and pressed against the wall to find secret openings that might hold other clues. We found pieces of clues that went to other clues and could only figure out the meaning once we put them together. In the end, we figured out just enough to get out. We actually hadn't solved each riddle but managed to escape.

The end times is just like that. We don't have to have the entire thing figured out to endure to the end. There is so much information throughout the Holy Scriptures that we can put together to extrapolate truth for the end times as well as righteous Christian living. Looking for symbolism is like finding the clues to a puzzle and trying to solve a riddle. Until the end is here, we can't know this for sure, but it would be exciting to find that this is a clue given by the Father in our own preparation for this day and that he's given us an ear to…hear what the Spirit says (Mt. 11:15, Rev. 3:13, Rev. 2:29, Mk. 4:9, Rev. 3:6, Rev. 2:17, Rev. 2:11, Rev. 2:7, Rev. 3:22, Mk. 4:23, Mt. 13:9).

I think I may have found some clues. "Beloved, do not let this one thing escape your notice: With the Lord a day is like a thousand years, and a thousand years are like a day. The Lord is not slow in keeping His promise as some understand slowness, but is patient with you, not wanting anyone to perish but everyone to come to repentance" (2 Pet. 3:8–9, BSB).

As our Savior walked this earth over two thousand years ago, he spoke often of a new heaven and Earth and that "Alas for the day! For the day of the LORD is near, and as destruction from the Almighty it comes" (Joel 1:15, ESV).

If a day is as a thousand years, then in the year 2022, we are in the wee hours of the third day now… Wouldn't it be uncanny of God to bring Christ back on the "third day"? We can look at signs, make educated guesses; "however, no one knows the day or hour when these things will happen, not even the angels in heaven or the Son himself. Only the Father knows" (Mt. 24:36, NLT). Actually, even if he comes back on the "third day," there are still 988 years left in the "third-day concept." We still don't know the hour of the day, just that it is coming…

"But the Day of the Lord will come like a thief…" (2 Pet. 3:11, BSB).

It's a good thing to think about these hints and consider possibilities of when and what some of these details could actually end up being; after all, Christ told us to be prepared and to watch for his return, but the main point we need to be focusing on is our lives in Christ.

"Since everything will be destroyed in this way, what kind of people ought you to be? You ought to conduct yourselves in holiness and godliness as you anticipate and hasten the coming of the day of God, when the heavens will be destroyed by fire and the elements will melt in the heat. But in keeping with God's promise, we are looking forward to a new heaven and a new earth, where righteousness dwells. Therefore, beloved, as you anticipate these things, make every effort to be found at peace—spotless and blameless in His sight" (2 Pet. 3:11–14, BSB).

"Therefore, beloved, since you already know these things, be on your guard so that you will not be carried away by the error of the lawless and fall from your secure standing. But grow in the grace and knowledge of our Lord and Savior Jesus Christ. To Him be the glory both now and to the day of eternity. Amen" (2 Pet. 3:17–18, BSB).

Beloved, although I made every effort to write to you about the salvation we share, I felt it necessary to write and urge you to contend earnestly for the faith entrusted once for all to the saints. For certain men have crept in among you unnoticed—ungodly ones who were designated long ago for condemnation. They turn the grace of our God into a license for immorality, and they deny our only Master and Lord, Jesus Christ. Although you are fully aware of this, I want to remind you that after Jesus had delivered His people out of the land of Egypt, He destroyed those who did not believe. And the angels who did not stay within their own domain but abandoned their proper dwelling—these He has kept in eternal chains under darkness, bound for judgment on that great day. In like manner, Sodom and Gomorrah and the cities around them, who indulged in sexual immorality and pursued strange flesh, are on display as an example of those who sustain the punishment of eternal fire. Yet in the same way, these dreamers defile their bodies, reject authority, and slander glorious beings. But even the archangel Michael, when he disputed with the devil over the body of Moses, did not presume to bring a slanderous charge against him but said, "The Lord rebuke you!" These men, however, slander what they do not understand, and like irrational animals, they will be destroyed by the things they do instinctively. Woe to them!

They have traveled the path of Cain; they have rushed headlong into the error of Balaam; they have perished in Korah's rebellion. These men are hidden reefs in your love feasts, shamelessly feasting with you but shepherding only themselves. They are clouds without water, carried along by the wind; fruitless trees in autumn, twice dead after being uprooted. They are wild waves of the sea, foaming up their own shame; wandering stars, for whom blackest darkness has been reserved forever. Enoch, the seventh from Adam, also prophesied about them: "Behold, the Lord is coming with myriads of His holy ones to execute judgment on everyone, and to convict all the ungodly of every ungodly act of wickedness and every harsh word spoken against Him by ungodly sinners.'

These men are discontented grumblers, following after their own lusts; their mouths spew arrogance; they flatter others for their own advantage. But you, beloved, remember what was foretold by the apostles of our Lord Jesus Christ when they said to you, "In the last times there will be scoffers who will follow after their own ungodly desires." These are the ones who cause divisions, who are worldly and devoid of the Spirit. But you, beloved, by building yourselves up in your most holy faith and praying in the Holy Spirit, keep yourselves in the love of God as you await the mercy of our Lord Jesus Christ to bring you eternal life. And indeed, have mercy on those who doubt: save others by snatching them from the fire; and to still others show mercy tempered with fear, hating even the clothing stained by the flesh.Now to Him who is able to keep you from stumbling and to present you unblemished in His glorious presence, with great joy—to the only God our Savior be glory, majesty, demons, and authority through Jesus Christ our Lord before all time, and now, and for all eternity. Amen. (Jude 1:3–24, BSB)

Chapter 14

Black and Red Is Black and White

Peter included other signs of the end of times to watch for in the book of Acts. "I will show wonders in the heavens above and signs on the earth below, blood and fire and billows of smoke. The sun will be turned to darkness and the moon to blood before the coming of the great and glorious day of the Lord. And everyone who calls on the name of the Lord will be saved" (Acts 2:19–21, NIV).

Likewise, Joel, Christ, Isaiah, Ezekiel, and Amos tell us the same thing.

"Before them the earth quakes, the heavens tremble, the sun and the moon grow dark and the stars lose their brightness" (Joel 2:10, BSB).

"The sun shall be turned to darkness, and the moon to blood, before the great and awesome day of the LORD comes" (Joel 2:31, ESV).

"The sun and moon grow dark and the stars lose their brightness" (Joel 3:15, NASB).

"Immediately after the tribulation of those days the sun will be darkened, and the moon will not give its light, and the stars will fall from heaven, and the powers of the heavens will be shaken" (Mt. 24:29, ESV).

"But in those days, after that tribulation, the sun will be darkened and the moon will not give its light" (Mk. 13:24, NASB).

"There will be signs in sun and moon and stars, and on the earth dismay among nations, in perplexity at the roaring of the sea and the waves" (Lk. 21:25, BSB).

"For the stars of heaven and their constellations will not flash forth their light; The sun will be dark when it rises and the moon will not shed its light" (Isa. 13:10, NASB).

"'It will come about in that day,' declares the Lord God, 'That I will make the sun go down at noon and make the earth dark in broad daylight'" (Am. 8:9, NASB).

"And when I extinguish you, I will cover the heavens and darken their stars; I will cover the sun with a cloud, and the moon will not give its light" (Ezek. 32:7, NASB).

Just as we look at biblical history to find clues, we can know that when Jesus was hung on the cross and breathed his last breath, the sun turned dark then too. "It was now about the sixth hour, and darkness came over all the land until the ninth hour. The sun was darkened, and the veil of the temple was torn down the middle. Then Jesus called out in a loud voice, 'Father, into Your hands I commit My Spirit.' And when He had said this, He breathed His last" (Lk. 23:44–46, BSB). "From the sixth hour until the ninth hour darkness came over all the land. At the ninth hour, Jesus cried out in a loud voice, '*Eloi, Eloi, lema sabachthani?*' which means, 'My God, My God, why have You forsaken Me?'" (Mk. 15:33 and Mt. 27:45, BSB).

It isn't a coincidence that God will use the darkened sun to announce the arrival of his Son. "When the centurion and those with him who were guarding Jesus saw the great earthquake and all that had happened, they were terrified and said, 'Truly this was the Son of God'" (Mt. 27:54, BSB).

The signs surrounding the second coming of Christ will herald the validity of our Savior's return. These signs are given many times as a caution to us. You see, Christ warns us that many will come in the end, claiming to be the Son of God. "At that time, if anyone says to you, 'Look, here is the Christ!' or 'There He is!' do not believe it. For false christs and false prophets will appear and perform great signs and wonders that would deceive even the elect, if that were possible" (Mt. 24:23–24, BSB).

By knowing that the sun will turn dark, the moon will turn red, etc. before the rapture and Christ's second coming, we can be sure when the Son of God returns and not be deceived by any other performing miracles, signs, and wonders. This is essential to know as we get closer to the end. If we don't know that there will be a great earthquake, the mountains and islands will be removed, the sun will turn black, the moon will turn red, and the stars will fall from the sky, we could be swayed into believing a false Christ is the one true Messiah. It would be a terrible mistake that could cause one to spend an eternity in hell instead of heaven with our Savior and our God.

There is one other place that we can see the reference to the sun turning black and the moon turning red prior to the second coming of the Lord. It is a sign that the Apostle John gives us in Revelation.

"And when I saw the Lamb open the sixth seal, there was a great earthquake, and the sun became black like sackcloth of goat hair, and the whole moon turned blood red" (Rev. 6:12, BSB).

This is reference to the sixth seal though. There are five more ahead of this one and other signs to look for before the sun turns dark and the moon turns red and even another seal after this one. Remember this detail as we get to the scriptures describing the opening of the seals.

"Now concerning the coming of our Lord Jesus Christ and our being gathered together to Him, we ask you, brothers, not to be easily disconcerted or alarmed by any spirit or message or letter seeming to be from us, alleging that the Day of the Lord has already come. Let no one deceive you in any way, for it will not come until the rebellion occurs and the man of lawlessness—the son of destruction—is revealed. He will oppose and exalt himself above every so-called god or object of worship. So he will seat himself in the temple of God, proclaiming himself to be God" (2 Thess. 2:1–4, BSB).

Even in biblical times, new believers were confused and misled to believe Christ had already returned. Paul is being specific with details leading up to the second coming to make a point to the Thessalonians that there are signs to watch for, and these had not yet happened. They have still not happened. So Christ cannot come in the clouds at any moment as many errantly say at present time. The antichrist has not been revealed or the abomination of desolation, which will be his seating himself in the temple of God, proclaiming himself to be God.

Previously, when we looked at the abomination of desolation mentioned by Christ in Matthew 24:15, we saw his reference to Daniel, the prophet, and learned from Daniel 12:11–13 that there are 1,290 days between the daily sacrifice being abolished and the abomination of desolation being set up. The following verse added forty-five days and says those who wait and reach the end are blessed.

"Then I was given a measuring rod like a staff, and I was told, 'Rise and measure the temple of God and the altar and those who worship there, but do not measure the court outside the temple; leave that out, for it is given over to the nations, and they will trample the holy city for forty-two months. And I will grant authority to my two witnesses, and they will prophesy for 1,260 days, clothed in sackcloth'" (Rev. 11:1, ESV).

This verse corresponds with the one we have already looked at in Daniel: "…and the troops of the [antichrist] shall come destroy the city and the sanctuary. Its end shall come with a flood, and to the end there shall be war" (Dan. 9:26 NRSV).

There are thirty days here that are unaccounted for, but this section of the book of Revelation sheds light on what might be happening during the majority of the 1,290 days between the daily sacrifice being abolished and the abomination being set up.

Remember though that the temple of God is still not built as of today (February 2022). It has previously been destroyed (twice). Daniel 11:25 is telling us that the rebuilding is to come during tribulate times. "Know therefore and understand that from the going forth of the command to restore and build Jerusalem until Messiah the Prince, there shall be seven weeks and sixty-two weeks; The street shall be built again, and the wall even in troublesome times."

Predominantly, I want to be prepared for the Lord. I want to be aware of the things that have been spelled out for us in the Scriptures, but I can't help but try to put the clues together and wait to see what actually happens.

The closing verse of this section in Daniel (12:13) is to Daniel, telling him that he will be "asleep" by then and will "rest" and arise to his inheritance at the end of the days. The book of 1 Thessalonians 4:15–18 mirrored this information in explanation of the dead in Christ rising first to meet him in the clouds before those who remain alive on the last day. You see, Christ (Mt. 24:15, Mk. 13:4, and Lk. 21:20) and Paul were making it clear that this abomination of desolation would occur before the rapture of the church and the second coming of Christ.

Paul clarified that the man of lawlessness, also known as the antichrist, will be at the seat of the abomination of desolation. Both his revelation and his taking his seat as a god in the Temple Mount must occur before our Lord returns and the elect are gathered. It is clearly written in black and white. "But in those days, after that tribulation: 'The sun will be darkened, and the moon will not give its light; the stars will fall from the sky, and the powers of the heavens will be shaken.' At that time they will see the Son of Man coming in the clouds with great power and glory. And He will send out the angels to gather His elect from the four winds, from the ends of the earth to the ends of heaven" (Mark 13:24–27, BSB).

Believers are going to have to know about the antichrist. Those of us who are alive at the end of times will have to endure the hardships of his reign before the rapture takes us up into the clouds.

To know more about the antichrist, we must open our Bibles. Daniel chapters 2 and 7, Isaiah 10:5, and Micah 5:5 refer to the Antichrist's origin. There is a contrast in beliefs. Some say the Antichrist will be from Rome. Fewer know of the verses that speak of the Antichrist as an Assyrian. I think both will be true. I would not be surprised if the reigning Antichrist will have roots in both the Roman Empire and the Assyrian Empire, neither of which have the same ancient borders. Many modern countries were one part of the Roman Empire, but not any longer: Britain (excluding Scotland), Italy, France, Portugal, Spain, Greece, Turkey, Germany, Switzerland, Egypt, Levant, Crimea, and the northern coast of Africa. The former

Assyrian Empire was comprised of modern-day Iraq, Syria, Turkey, Iran, Saudi Arabia, and Lebanon. In Revelation 13, we find a description that is hard to understand. While I will not begin to unearth all the possibilities that this symbolism might represent, there are facts embedded within the text. There are truths we can take away from this passage.

"And I saw a beast rising out of the sea, with ten horns and seven heads, with ten diadems on its horns and blasphemous names on its heads. And the beast that I saw was like a leopard; its feet were like a bear's, and its mouth was like a lion's mouth. And to it the dragon gave his power and his throne and great authority. One of its heads seemed to have a mortal wound, but its mortal wound was healed, and the whole earth marveled as they followed the beast. And they worshiped the dragon, for he had given his authority to the beast, and they worshiped the beast, saying, 'Who is like the beast, and who can fight against it?' And the beast was given a mouth uttering haughty and blasphemous words, and it was allowed to exercise authority for forty-two months. It opened its mouth to utter blasphemies against God, blaspheming his name and his dwelling, that is, those who dwell in heaven. Also it was allowed to make war on the saints and to conquer them. And authority was given it over every tribe and people and language and nation, and all who dwell on earth will worship it, everyone whose name has not been written before the foundation of the world in the book of life of the Lamb who was slain. If anyone has an ear, let him hear" (Rev. 13:1–9, ESV). Let's remember that Revelation 11:1 tells us that during this time, the nations trample over the court of the temple, and the two witnesses are prophesying for 1,260 days in sackcloth.

"The beast that you saw—it was, and now is no more, but is about to come up out of the Abyss and go to its destruction. And those who dwell on the earth whose names were not written in the Book of Life from the foundation of the world will marvel when they see the beast that was, and is not, and yet will be. This calls for a mind with wisdom. The seven heads are seven mountains on which the woman sits. There are also seven kings. Five have fallen, one is, and the other has not yet come; but when he does come, he must remain for only a little while. The beast that was, and now is not, is an eighth king, who belongs to the other seven and is going into destruction. The ten horns you saw are ten kings who have not yet received a kingdom, but will receive one hour of authority as kings, along with the beast. These kings have one purpose: to yield their power and authority to the beast" (Rev. 17:8–13, BSB).

"And the woman you saw is the great city that rules over the kings of the earth" (Rev. 17:18, BSB).

The dragon is Satan. "And the great dragon was thrown down, that ancient serpent, who is called the devil and Satan, the deceiver of the whole world—he was thrown down to the earth, and his angels were thrown down with him" (Rev. 12:9, ESV).

Satan gives the beast (also known as the antichrist or man of lawlessness) his power (his *dunation*). There is a mortal wound on the head of this antichrist that has healed and caused the whole earth to marvel and follow him. The dragon and the beast will be worshipped, and a chant will fill the air from their followers "Who is like the beast and who can fight against it?"

Notice that the beast will be allowed to exercise authority for forty-two months. This is the equivalence of 1,260 days. It's so important to keep in mind that the antichrist is being worshipped. He has set himself up as a false god, bestowing signs, wonders, and miracles that fool mankind, even the "elect" if they are without *dunation*. He is being worshipped, not feared, for three and a half years.

"Then he shall confirm a covenant with many for one week; But in the middle of the week He shall bring an end to sacrifice and offering. And on the wing of abominations shall be one who makes desolate, even until the consummation, which is determined, is poured out on the desolate" (Dan. 9:27, NKJV).

In this passage we see that the antichrist will confirm a covenant with many for one week. This could be a peace covenant created to end a war waging between all the nations (recorded in Matthew 24 and Mark 13 as signs of the end), and the way he wins over the world's heart to be trusted, praised, and worshipped. He shall bring an end to sacrifice and offerings. It is so uncanny how similar this prophecy is to the ones we have already read about in both Daniel and Revelation. Many look at this "one week" as seven years (not days) and halfway through is three and half years (not days), which would be forty-two months, or 1,260 days. If we bring in Revelation 11 and the scripture about the two witnesses, we can surmise that this is likely happening simultaneously.

"And when they (the two witnesses) have finished their testimony the beast that rises from the bottomless pit will make war on them and conquer them and kill them, and their dead bodies will lie in the street of the great city that symbolically is called Sodom and Egypt, where their Lord was crucified. For three and a half days some from the peoples and tribes and languages and nations will gaze at their dead bodies and refuse to let them be placed in a tomb, and those who dwell on the earth will rejoice over them and make merry and exchange presents, because these two prophets had been a torment to those who dwell on the earth" (Rev. 11:7–10, ESV).

The antichrist will kill the two witnesses. The world will be so strongly against anything of God that this will mark a celebration, and the people will party! According to the prophesies of Daniel and referenced by Christ, the Lord has not returned or raptured his bride yet. Those 1,260 days plus thirty and another forty-five are the days the saints are to endure and wait on the Lord. They will be perilous times. We will be persecuted as believers. "Then they will deliver you to tribulation, and will kill you, and you will be hated by all nations because of My name" (Mt. 24:9, BLB).

Remember also that we've been warned that Christians will be under heavy persecution. We are going to be the enemy during the time when the rest of the world is safely guarded by this peace covenant. It will be a heavy temptation to join the ranks of the unbelievers to spare our own lives. The Holy Scriptures have given us these warnings so that we will be prepared, have oil in our lamps, and be there when our Bridegroom comes in the clouds to gather us to the wedding table.

"I have told you these things so that you will not fall away. They will put you out of the synagogues. In fact, a time is coming when anyone who kills you will think he is offering a service to God. They will do these things because they have not known the Father or Me.

But I have told you these things so that when their hour comes, you will remember that I told you about them" (Jn. 16:1–4, BSB).

"And the king shall do as he wills. He shall exalt himself and magnify himself above every god, and shall speak astonishing things against the God of gods. He shall prosper till the indignation is accomplished; for what is decreed shall be done. He shall pay no attention to the gods of his fathers, or to the one beloved by women. He shall not pay attention to any other god, for he shall magnify himself above all. He shall honor the god of fortresses instead of these. A god whom his fathers did not know he shall honor with gold and silver, with precious stones and costly gifts. He shall deal with the strongest fortresses with the help of a foreign god. Those who acknowledge him he shall load with honor. He shall make them rulers over many and shall divide the land for a price" (Dan. 11:36–39, ESV).

The antichrist will be so convincing that he is above the true Messiah that he will convince so many to kill and persecute the believers as an act of service to God/him. There is going to be a way for everyone to know who is a believer in Christ Jesus and who is not. As the antichrist reigns during these three and a half years, forty-two months, or 1,260 days with *dunation* from Satan, the dragon, he will be performing signs and wonders that trick people into thinking he is their Savior. Remember there will be wars and rumors of wars. Nations will rise against nations… The antichrist will rise up during times of a great war. The "mortal wound" he recovers from could come from this warring time possibly.

Look at this passage in Daniel again: "At the time of the end, the king of the south shall attack him, but the king of the north shall rush upon him like a whirlwind, with chariots and horsemen, and with many ships. And he shall come into countries and shall overflow and pass through. He shall come into the glorious land. And tens of thousands shall fall, but these shall be delivered out of his hand: Edom and Moab and the main part of the Ammonites. He shall stretch out his hand against the countries, and the land of Egypt shall not escape. He shall become ruler of the treasures of gold and of silver, and all the precious things of Egypt, and the Libyans and the Cushites shall follow in his train. But news from the east and the north shall alarm him, and he shall go out with great fury to destroy and devote many to destruction. And he shall pitch his palatial tents between the sea and the glorious holy mountain" (Dan. 11:40–45, ESV).

He will come with help (Rev. 17:13) and other leaders who will direct their nations to worship the beast. He will bring such peace and healing to the world that has been decimated by war, and many will be easily tricked into believing he is a deity. There are no verses that deliberately state this is the time the temple is rebuilt, but notice the antichrist (referred to as a king in Daniel) pitches his palatial tents between the sea and the glorious holy mountain. We can't also forget that Christ warned us to watch for Jerusalem being surrounded by armies so that we will know that her desolation is near (Lk. 21:20).

I want to be one with an ear, who is wise, but I also want to be prepared. If we listen to modern Christendom tell us that we will all be raptured before any of this happens and, therefore, we don't need to know any of the details, we are not going to be equipped and risk the consequences of such.

The worshippers of the antichrist and anyone else who is not prepared with the knowledge of end times, given through scriptures, will be offered a mark. "And he causes all, the small and the great, and the rich and the poor, and the freemen and the slaves, to be given a mark on their right hand or on their forehead, and he provides that no one will be able to buy or to sell, except the one who has the mark, either the name of the beast or the number of his name" (Rev. 13:16–17, BLB).

True believers will need God's power ever so greatly during these times. The *dunamis* of God will be the only thing to keep believers enduring during this persecution. Remember the world is going to be looking at Christians like they are the adversary. They will be thought to be evil for not following after the beast who has tricked them into thinking he is the great "I Am" and Savior of the world. After all, he will have survived a mortal wound and caused world peace that we hear politicians only talk about and wish they could credit to themselves. The world is going to think we're enemies of God and we're going to suffer as we try to survive without this mark.

When I was a child, I wondered what this mark could be. I imagined an identifying tattoo or the proverbial barcode, but as I grew older and watched technology advance, computers become commonplace, then credit cards and pets being chipped, it became clear that this mark is going to be something that seems commonplace and makes life more convenient to most. Without the mark, anyone who survives the brutality given out to Christians will be hard-pressed to survive in a world that we can't buy food in any longer. "This calls for wisdom. Let the person who has insight calculate the number of the beast, for it is the number of a man. That number is 666" (Rev. 13:18, NIV).

This mark is going to be universal, and most have heard will be identified as the number 666. "In the Greek language, certain letters were given numerical value, so the actual Greek is *chi, xi, stigma*. It literally means 600, 60, and 6" (Kelley, Jack. "Was 666 Translated Incorrectly?" Grace thru faith). The verse in Revelation 13:18 leads me to believe that 666 or the derivation is *not* going to be obvious, but I do believe that the mark itself is going to be clearly "the mark of the beast" to all those who are consecrated to God, love him, seek him, and have lived their lives with *dunamis* so that they did not stumble but lived for God with their whole hearts, souls, and minds. Let no one deceive you. These are the things our Father in heaven has shown us so that we will be prepared to endure up to the second coming of our Lord and Savior; endure and run the good race that we might hear "well done, my good and faithful servant" (Mt. 25:23).

Those taking the mark are not without eternal punishment: "And a third angel followed them, calling out in a loud voice, 'If anyone worships the beast and its image, and receives its mark on his forehead or on his hand, he too will drink the wine of God's anger, poured undiluted into the cup of His wrath. And he will be tormented in fire and sulfur in the presence of the holy angels and of the Lamb. And the smoke of their torment rises forever and ever. Day and night there is no rest for those who worship the beast and its image, or for anyone who receives the mark of its name.' Here is a call for the perseverance of the saints who keep the commandments of God and the faith of Jesus" (Rev. 14:9–12, BSB).

Believers who refuse the mark will receive the promise but not before they are persecuted by the evil people: "Indeed, all who desire to live a godly life in Christ Jesus will be persecuted, while evil people and impostors will go on from bad to worse, deceiving and being deceived. But as for you, continue in what you have learned and have firmly believed, knowing from whom you learned it and how from childhood you have been acquainted with the sacred writings, which are able to make you wise for salvation through faith in Christ Jesus" (2 Tim. 3:12–15, ESV).

If we are faithful, the Holy Spirit will keep us secure in Christ. "And do not grieve the Holy Spirit of God, in whom you were sealed for the day of redemption" (Eph. 4:30, NIV). "Therefore settle *it* in your hearts not to meditate beforehand on what you will answer; for I will give you a mouth and wisdom which all your adversaries will not be able to contradict or resist" (Lk. 21:14–15, NKJ).

Jesus told us clearly that those living at the end will *not* be raptured before the great tribulation, but his Spirit will be our strength and our protector. "Then He said to them, 'Nation will rise against nation, and kingdom against kingdom. And there will be great earthquakes in various places, and famines and pestilences; and there will be fearful sights and great signs from heaven. But before all these things, they will lay their hands on you and persecute *you*, delivering *you* up to the synagogues and prisons. You will be brought before kings and rulers for My name's sake. But it will turn out for you as an occasion for testimony. Therefore settle *it* in your hearts not to meditate beforehand on what you will answer; for I will give you a mouth and wisdom which all your adversaries will not be able to contradict or resist. You will be betrayed even by parents and brothers, relatives and friends; and they will put *some* of you to death. And you will be hated by all for My name's sake. But not a hair of your head shall be lost. By your patience possess your souls" (Lk. 21:10–19, NKJ).

> He who dwells in the shelter of the Most High will abide in the shadow of the Almighty. I will say to the Lord, "My refuge and my fortress, my God, in whom I trust." For he will deliver you

from the snare of the fowler and from the deadly pestilence. He will cover you with his pinions, and under his wings you will find refuge; his faithfulness is a shield and buckler. You will not fear the terror of the night, nor the arrow that flies by day, nor the pestilence that stalks in darkness, nor the destruction that wastes at noonday. A thousand may fall at your side, ten thousand at your right hand, but it will not come near you. You will only look with your eyes and see the recompense of the wicked. Because you have made the Lord your dwelling place—the Most High, who is my refuge. No evil shall be allowed to befall you, no plague come near your tent. For he will command his angels concerning you to guard you in all your ways. On their hands they will bear you up, lest you strike your foot against a stone. You will tread on the lion and the adder; the young lion and the serpent you will trample underfoot. "Because he holds fast to me in love, I will deliver him; I will protect him, because he knows my name. When he calls to me, I will answer him; I will be with him in trouble; I will rescue him and honor him. With long life I will satisfy him and show him my salvation." (Ps. 91, ESV)

Chapter 15

Calling All Saints!

> *Blessed is the one who reads aloud the words of this prophecy, and blessed are those who hear and obey what is written in it, because the time is near.*
> —Revelation 1:3, BSB

The book of Revelation begins with warnings to the seven churches. We've looked at three of these churches as we've gone through this book so far and gotten incredibly valuable information from them. The Church of Laodicea is an example to us and cautions us not to be lukewarm. The Church of Philadelphia has a little *dunamis* and is saved. The Church of Sardis reminds us to keep our faith in God and our garments spotless before him to be saved as well. There are four other churches we have not looked at yet but give us great warnings as well.

> To the angel of the church in Ephesus write: 'The words of him who holds the seven stars in his right hand, who walks among the seven golden lampstands. "'I know your works, your toil and your patient endurance, and how you cannot bear with those who are evil, but have tested those who call themselves apostles and are not, and found them to be false. I know you are

> enduring patiently and bearing up for my name's sake, and you have not grown weary. But I have this against you, that you have abandoned the love you had at first. Remember therefore from where you have fallen; repent, and do the works you did at first. If not, I will come to you and remove your lampstand from its place, unless you repent. Yet this you have: you hate the works of the Nicolaitans, which I also hate. He who has an ear, let him hear what the Spirit says to the churches. To the one who conquers I will grant to eat of the tree of life, which is in the paradise of God.' (Rev. 2:1–7, ESV)

Be the believer who has an ear and conquer through this life with the power of the Holy Spirit and with the love of God that "bears all things, believes all things, hopes all things, endures all things" (1 Cor. 13:7, ESV).

> And to the angel of the church in Smyrna write: 'The words of the first and the last, who died and came to life. "'I know your tribulation and your poverty (but you are rich) and the slander of those who say that they are Jews and are not, but are a synagogue of Satan. Do not fear what you are about to suffer. Behold, the devil is about to throw some of you into prison, that you may be tested, and for ten days you will have tribulation. Be faithful unto death, and I will give you the crown of life. He who has an ear, let him hear what the Spirit says to the churches. The one who conquers will not be hurt by the second death.' (Rev. 2:9–11, ESV)

This church is known for its tribulation and poverty but note that it is rich. Because you say "I am rich, and have become wealthy, and have need of nothing, and you do not know that you are wretched and miserable and poor and blind and naked" (Rev. 3:17, ESV). The Lord is speaking of the heart of those of the Church of Smyrna. He sees they are truly poverty-stricken in their faith and spirit. God is foretelling that he will allow them to suffer at the hands of Satan as a test. He tells them to be faithful unto death so that they can conquer and endure in their belief to avoid the wrath of judgment upon the second death.

> And to the angel of the church in Pergamum write: 'The words of him who has the sharp two-edged sword. "I know where you dwell, where Satan's throne is. Yet you hold fast my name, and you did not deny my faith even in the days of Antipas my faithful witness, who was killed among you, where Satan dwells. But I have a few things against you: you have some there who hold the teaching of Balaam, who taught Balak to put a stumbling block before the sons of Israel, so that they might eat food sacrificed to idols and practice sexual immorality. So also you have some who hold the teaching of the Nicolaitans. Therefore repent. If not, I will come to you soon and war against them with the sword of my mouth. He who has an ear, let him hear what the Spirit says to the churches. To the one who conquers I will give some of the hidden manna, and I will give him a white stone, with a new name written on the stone that no one knows except the one who receives it." (Rev. 2:13–17, ESV)

The warning to this church is for their allowance of certain sins to prevail and religions that are not of God included into their practices. The Lord tells them to repent from holding to teachings of false religions and sexual immorality, or he himself will war against them. Contrast this to our average American churches today and consider how sexual immorality is at best ignored, if not celebrated. We have scores of traditions embedded within our church culture that were first pagan and "Christianized" to be practiced by churchgoers. To those who have an ear to hear, feel the conviction of the Holy Spirit, and repent.

> And to the angel of the church in Thyatira write: 'The words of the Son of God, who has eyes like a flame of fire, and whose feet are like burnished bronze. "'I know your works, your love and faith and service and patient endurance, and that your latter works exceed the first. But I have this against you, that you tolerate that woman Jezebel, who calls herself a prophetess and is teaching and seducing my servants to practice sexual immorality and to eat food sacrificed to idols. I gave her time to repent, but she refuses to repent of her sexual immorality. Behold, I will throw her onto a sickbed, and those who commit adultery with her I will throw into great tribulation, unless they repent of her works, and I will strike her children dead. And all the churches will know that I am he who searches mind and heart, and I will give to each of you according to your works. But to the rest of you in Thyatira, who do not hold this teaching, who have not learned what some call the deep things of Satan, to you I say, I do not lay on you any other burden. Only hold fast what you have until I come. The one who conquers and who keeps my works until the end, to him I will give authority over the nations, and he will rule them with a rod of iron, as when earthen pots are broken in pieces, even as I myself have received authority from my Father. And I will give him the morning star. He who has an ear, let him hear what the Spirit says to the churches.' (Rev. 2:18–29, ESV)

This is another church with sexual immorality among them. They are tolerating a spirit of Jezebel. We are living in a time where Christians are called haters if they do not tolerate all walks of life (and of the spirits). We must look at this twofold. First, we know sexual immorality runs rampant within our "body of believers." I know firsthand that little is done even when they know of "indiscretions." If fact, we are watching many "great" preachers fall from their thrones with sexual scandals coming out regularly. It isn't just that our Christianity turns a blind eye to the "believers" committing such sins, but the leaders themselves who are being caught have significantly increased lately. The other part of this is about Jezebel and the testing of the "saints" to see who will commit adultery with her. In 1 Kings, we learn that Jezebel killed the prophets of her time. "And when Jezebel cut off the prophets of the Lord, Obadiah took a hundred prophets and hid them by fifties in a cave and fed them with bread and water" (1 Kings 18:4, ESV).

Jezebel was an instigator of evil. "There was none who sold himself to do what was evil in the sight of the Lord like Ahab, whom Jezebel his wife incited" (1 Kings 21:25, ESV).

Frequently, the spirit of Jezebel is associated with narcissism when looked at in a spiritual basis. She cut off prophets and incited evil in her own husband, and this church is tolerating her.

One of the points that stands out to me is that she killed the prophets. The prophets are the messengers of truth and warnings. This Church of Thyatira has allowed truth and God's convicting spirit to be cut off. It is a church led into evil by their own toleration and swayed away from that which is right into tolerating narcissism, evil, sexual immorality, and adultery. She cuts off the truth from the church.

God has given us ample time, warnings, and instruction to be right with him before the end times begin. If we will heed his Word and live for him with the power he puts inside of us upon conversion and through daily prayer, with a determination to live righteously in love, we will conquer and prevail until the end when the Lord comes back in the clouds. We know the signs of the end times.

We are called to endure to the end with righteous lives filled with wholehearted love (*agapēn*), "goodwill" (1 Cor. 13:1 lexicon: "If I speak with the tongues of men and of angels, but do not have love, I have become a noisy gong or a clanging cymbal." biblehub.com), toward others and God. We have been given a Bible full of passages and scriptures that will clearly tell us that we can have *dunamis* from our Father and must lean on his power to overcome the fleshly, sinful nature of the nonbelieving man. We are children of God, not left helpless when we know to seek him, be filled with his Holy Spirit, and to be truly repentant of our sinfulness.

God has set up the rules, the requirements, and the actions; he's looking for his followers to fulfill with pure motives. He's told us that our old selves were crucified with his Son and that we are able to do all things through him who strengthens us. The Greek word for "him who strengthens us" is a derivation of *dunamis* again. The word *endunamounti* means to "empower"; the prefix "*en*" gives additional meaning to *dunamis*, in that God, Christ, the Holy Spirit of God, empowers us to do all things unto the will of God. It is the will of God that we live righteously, seeking after him; therefore, we have that power.

Are you right with God? Have you inspected your fruit and tested your faith as Paul instructed the believers of Corinth? Do you have the Holy Spirit and his gifts?

Paul prayed for the Ephesians "that the God of our Lord Jesus Christ, the Father of glory, may give to (them) a spirit of wisdom and of revelation in the knowledge of him" (Eph. 1:17, BSB).

Have you prayed for wisdom and revelation in the knowledge of him? Do you obey God to illustrate your love to him and to receive his Holy Spirit? (Acts 5:32)

"There are different gifts, but the same Spirit. There are different ministries, but the same Lord. There are different ways of working, but the same God works all things in all people. Now to each one the manifestation of the Spirit is given for the common good. To one there is given through the Spirit the message of *wisdom*, to another the message of *knowledge* by the same Spirit, to another *faith* by the same Spirit, to another gifts of *healing* by that one Spirit, to another the working of *miracles*, to another *prophecy*, to another *distinguishing between spirits*, to another *speaking in various tongues*, and to still another the *interpretation of tongues*. All these are the work of one and the same Spirit who apportions them to each one as he determines" (1 Cor. 12:4–11, BSB).

Has the Spirit been manifest in your life? Have you prayed for his gifts? Do you live with his fruit?

"But the fruit of the Spirit is love, joy, peace, patience, kindness, goodness, faithfulness, gentleness, and self-control. Against such things there is no law" (Gal. 5:22–23, BSB).

Has your flesh been crucified with Christ so that it is obvious you have the Spirit indwelling you? Or are your gut reactions and deeds described more in the flesh than the fruit?

"So I say, walk by the Spirit, and you will not gratify the desires of the flesh. For the flesh craves what is contrary to the Spirit and the Spirit what is contrary to the flesh. They are opposed to each other, so that you do not do what you want. But if you are led by the Spirit, you are not under the law. The acts of the flesh are obvious: sexual immorality, impurity, and debauchery, idolatry and sorcery, hatred, discord, jealousy, and rage; rivalries, divisions, factions, and envy; drunkenness, orgies, and the like. I warn you, as I did before, that those who practice such things will not inherit the kingdom of God. But the fruit of the Spirit is love, joy, peace, patience, kindness, goodness, faithfulness, gentleness, and self-control. Against such things there is no law. Those who belong to Christ Jesus have crucified the flesh with its passions and desires. Since we live by the Spirit, let us walk in step with the Spirit. Let us not become conceited, provoking and envying one another" (Gal. 5;16–26, BSB).

We are not slaves to our flesh. If you are still slave to it and find yourself struggling to fight it, you are not living with the power from God, *dunamis*, which is given freely to anyone who loves the Lord God, repents of their sins, and receives the Holy Spirit.

"But you will receive power when the Holy Spirit has come upon you, and you will be my witnesses in Jerusalem and in all Judea and Samaria, and to the end of the earth" (Acts 1:8, ESV).

The "power received" in this verse is the Greek word *dunamis*—receiving the Holy Spirit comes with a supernatural power that gives us the ability to do God's will—to manifest his Spirit's gifts and to live our lives with the fruit of the Spirit. We will be able to obey God and his commandments and easily love our neighbor. We will have love, joy, peace, patience, kindness, goodness, faithfulness, gentleness, and self-control. We will share the gospel through lives that are distinguished from that of unbelievers and have the words we need to speak from a Holy Spirit indwelling in us.

"You, however, have an anointing from the Holy One, and all of you know the truth. I have not written to you because you lack knowledge of the truth, but because you have it and because no lie comes from the truth… And as for you, the anointing you received from Him remains in you, and you do not need anyone to teach you. But just as His true and genuine anointing teaches you about all things, so remain in Him as you have been taught. And now, little children, remain in Christ, so that when He appears, we may be confident and unashamed before Him at His coming. If you know that He is righteous, you also know that everyone who practices righteousness has been born of Him" (1 Jn. 2:20–21, 27–29, BSB).

When we walk with the anointing of the Holy Spirit, his will is natural. He bestows a supernatural power within us that sets us apart. Many have repented once and been baptized but have not received this anointing because of a lack in faith in the one true God. They have given in to the notion that Christianity is about forgiveness from a merciful God who accepts us with grace that covers our practice of unrighteousness. Wake up! Repent of your sins. Come before the Lord with a grieving heart that knows he is a God of righteousness and of power who can forgive you of your ignorance and who wants to forgive you of this ignorance and the sinfulness that continued even in your born-again lives. Come before him and pray that he forgives you. Pray that he will give you wisdom, knowledge, discernment, and the anointing of the Holy Spirit. Pray for forgiveness that you've not lived with faith in his *dunamis* and have succumbed to a life of mediocrity lacking in the power of God.

God wants his children to be free in his power. He wants us to live under his grace. "Therefore, beloved, since you already know these things, be on your guard so that you will not be carried away by the error of the lawless and fall from your secure standing. But grow in the grace and knowledge of our Lord and Savior Jesus Christ. To Him be the glory both now and to the day of eternity. Amen" (2 Pet. 3:17–18, BSB).

"Grow in his grace." Pray for his knowledge. Ask the Father above for the power of the Holy Spirit in your life. Do not settle for a memory of a moment in time where you felt the inkling of his presence but failed to accept his *dunamis* and live righteously thereafter, through the power of the Holy Spirit in you, full of the fruit of the Spirit and with supernatural powers freely given to those who ask.

"Earnestly pursue love and eagerly desire spiritual gifts, especially the gift of prophecy. For he who speaks in a tongue does not speak to men, but to God. Indeed, no one understands him; he utters mysteries in the Spirit. But he who prophesies speaks to men for their edification, encouragement, and comfort. The one who speaks in a tongue edifies himself, but the one who prophesies edifies the church" (1 Cor. 14:1–4, BSB).

Pray for these gifts that you may be spiritually edified and that you may edify the church, the whole body of believers. "If any of you lacks wisdom, let him ask God, who gives generously to all without reproach, and it will be given him" (Jas. 1:5, ESV).

This world is not our home. "Therefore let us be grateful for receiving a kingdom that cannot be shaken, and thus let us offer to God acceptable worship, with reverence and awe" (Heb. 12:28, ESV).

Let us come before God with worship like he has described he wants. Let us not look for a fleeting high or for a moment we received chills to fulfill something in us but with reverence and awe that gives God glory. Let our faith in him not be a religious experience or our doctrine be based on what we hear others speak of. Let us not be hypocrites with our Bibles open or daily devotionals read and not live lives with *dunamis* from our Father in heaven. Let our worship not be empty or for a selfish and false security in nothing more than feelings and false doctrine. Let us pray to our heavenly Father to give us eyes that see and ears to listen to the words left behind by our Savior, the prophets, and apostles of God so that we can actively pursue God. Pray that you read the Holy Scriptures to seek after God and that you will desire wisdom and the ability to live after Christ's example. Keep praying for this daily so that you will endure.

Have you tried to pray and earnestly sought God in prayer for these things but felt nothing added unto you? Could there be iniquity in your life that blocks you from receiving what God has promised. Have you not judged yourself properly?

In the first letter Paul wrote to the Corinthians, Paul quoted Christ on the importance of communion. "For I received from the Lord what I also passed on to you: The Lord Jesus, on the night He was betrayed, took bread, and when He had given thanks, He broke it and said, 'This is My body, which is for you; do this in remembrance of Me.' In the same way, after supper He took the cup, saying, 'This cup is the new covenant in My blood; do this, as often as you drink it, in remembrance of Me.' For as often as you eat this bread and drink this cup, you proclaim the Lord's death until He comes" (1 Cor. 11:23–26, NIV).

Paul went on, however, to rebuke anyone for taking communion in a shameful way. The exhortation went so far as to explain that the improper handling of breaking bread together is the very reason many among them were sick, weak, or had died.

"Therefore, whoever eats the bread or drinks the cup of the Lord in an unworthy manner will be guilty of sinning against the body and blood of the Lord. Each one must examine himself before he eats of the bread and drinks of the cup. For anyone who eats and drinks without recognizing the body eats and drinks judgment on himself. That is why many among you are weak and sick, and a number of you have fallen asleep. Now if we judged ourselves properly, we would not come under judgment. But when we are judged by the Lord, we are being disciplined so that we will not be condemned with the world" (1 Cor. 11:27–32, BSB).

"We know that God does not listen to sinners, but if anyone is a worshiper of God and does his will, God listens to him" (Jn. 9:31, ESV).

If we're struggling to receive the Holy Spirit, see fruit in our lives, and claim any of the *dunamis* we're promised as believers, it is imperative to examine yourself deeply. Are you worshipping God and doing his will, or could you be going along with the "right Christian motions" with no true relationship? Have you repented within a one time "sinner's prayer" and held fast to a notion that God expects you to keep struggling in the flesh so that your repentance was not truly turning from your sin? Do you hold strong to your iniquity because you enjoy it too much?

"If I had cherished iniquity in my heart, the Lord would not have listened" (Ps. 66:18, ESV).

"The Lord is far from the wicked, but He hears the prayer of the righteous" (Prov. 15:29).

"He fulfills the desires of those who fear Him; He hears their cry and saves them" (Ps. 145:19, BSB).

It's time to be right with the Lord. Throw down the strongholds in your life! Commit to the Father and follow him in obedience.

God looks at sin very seriously! In Matthew, Christ tells the believers, "So if you are offering your gift at the altar and there remember that your brother has something against you, leave your gift there before the altar. First go and be reconciled to your brother; then come and offer your gift" (Mt. 5:23–24, BSB).

We can't expect to sit around in sin with such a callous view of Christianity that God doesn't care about it; he does! Implore the Lord to search your heart. Ask that he reveal wrong motives you have in your pursuit for your own life, liberty, and freedom. Beseech the Father to reveal sins in your life. Genuinely give yourself to God that he shows you all the iniquity you commit. This is not lip service or words from a song you sing to feel like you're getting closer to God; this is a real sincere appeal to the Creator of the universe that he shows you the transgression within your lives which keeps you from being heard him. Pray, too, that you get past the traditional Christian mantra and religion that has you believing everyone is in sin and it's all okay. Be real with God and legitimately look to him that he shows you arrogance, pride, laziness, foolishness, and anything else that might keep you from receiving the gifts of God and his Holy Spirit.

As crazy as it may sound, I had placed my former husband on an idol pedestal. It wasn't because I worshipped him in awe; no, it was because I feared him. His reactions were always so unpredictable that I stayed on my toes to keep him happy. I worked hard to do what he would like best and focused so much of my energy on "being a good wife" so that I could keep him from getting angry. His affection and attention were so limited that I found myself talking to him, telling him things, making jokes, anything to get a response from him. I was so eager to be loved by him and avoid his wrath that our lives revolved around him. I kept my behavior tempered. I remained copacetic. I looked for ways to make him happy.

I had made him an idol. This sin was one that became illuminated for me as I worked my way through scriptures before I was able to escape him. Perhaps, all those years of prayers and pleadings before God to help me out of that misery were hindered due to my own making an idol of him? We can make almost anything an idol really. Where is your focus? What do you spend your time doing? What or who are you worshipping instead of the Lord God Almighty?

The book of Revelation is the last book in the Bible. It is a last call to the children of God to heed his words, his cautions, his plea to repent from our sins. When we get to the end or die before coming to this saving knowledge, we will have no other time to get it right. This is a free gift for eternal life that we can only get through true repentance. It is a salvation described for the believers who endure to the end.

Chapter 16

Will You Worship the Dragon or Messiah?

The sixth chapter of Revelation begins the opening of the Seals. The Lamb who was slain is the only one found to be worthy of opening them. Artists, theologians, and the curious have looked at these seals and the horses and horsemen that come with them as the epitome of the end. The horses and their riders are painted and depict the rider of the first white horse as the Messiah. Let's look at the verses in context and compare to that which we already know.

"Then I watched as the Lamb opened one of the seven seals, and I heard one of the four living creatures say in a thunderous voice, 'Come!' So I looked and saw a white horse, and its rider held a bow. And he was given a crown, and he rode out to overcome and conquer" (Rev. 6:1–2, BSB).

With so many people praising God today and posting memes and sermons about God already overcoming and conquering Satan, it's easy to read these verses and see a savior come to overcome and conquer. This rider has a crown—like we'd expect the Prince of Peace, our Jesus Christ, the Messiah to wear—but he holds a bow. Never, in any other scripture recorded in description of our Lord, has he ever held a bow to conquer. In fact, I'm going to show you in Revelation chapter 19, thirteen chapters from this text, that there is another description of a white horse with Christ upon it. Notice the differences.

"Then I saw heaven standing open, and there before me was a white horse. And its rider is called Faithful and True. With righteousness He judges and wages war. He has eyes like blazing fire, and many royal crowns on His head. He has a name written on Him that only He Himself knows. He is dressed in a robe dipped in blood, and His name is The Word of God. The armies of heaven, dressed in fine linen, white and pure, follow Him on white horses. And from His mouth proceeds a sharp sword with which to strike down the nations, and He will rule them with an iron scepter. He treads the winepress of the fury of the wrath of God the Almighty. And He has a name written on His robe and on His thigh: *King of kings and lord of lords*" (Rev. 19:11–16).

> A white horse
> A bow
> Given a Crown
> Came to overcome and conquer. (Revelation 6:1–2)

> A white horse
> A sharp sword and iron scepter
> Many Royal Crowns on His Head
> Rider called Faithful and True
> With righteousness—judges and wages war
> Eyes like blazing fire
> A name written on Him that only He knows
> He is dressed in a robe dripping with blood
> His name is "The Word of God"
> The Armies of Heaven, dressed in white linen follow him on white horses.
> *King of kings and lord of lords* on his thigh and his robes. (Rev. 19:11-16)

The first white horse is a fraud; the rider is the antichrist, a mocker of our Savior, but one who will come and deceive many into believing he is the true Messiah. He is "the one that was, and is not, and yet will be" (Rev. 17:8), not "who was and is and is to come" (Rev. 1:4 and 8).

It is absolutely not possible for this first seal to be describing the Messiah because we know the details leading up to Christ's true return. The antichrist comes before the Lord returns, and he is the one who overcomes and conquers as we've seen through many scriptures God has given us. It's important to realize that this is the antichrist, or we could fall victim to the ways of this false teacher and lawless one. It is exactly how Satan wants it. The more he can fool and get to take the mark of this beast, the more he takes with him into the lake of fire. "And the beast was seized, and with him the false prophet who performed the signs in his presence by which he deceived those who had received the mark of the beast and those who worshipped his image. These two were thrown alive into the lake of fire which burns with brimstone" (Rev. 19:20, NASB).

"Also (the beast) was allowed to make war on the saints and to conquer them. And authority was given it over every tribe and people and language and nation" (Rev. 13:7, ESV).

Notice that the beast "conquers" the saints. As we made our way to this information, we looked at the sixth seal and saw that the sun turned black and the moon turned red after the fifth seal was opened. Since Christ and so many of the apostles and prophets have all told us that Christ does not come to rapture his church or return for his second coming until after these celestial signs happen, we know that it is impossible for this first horse to be the Son of God. Satan is crafty. Don't let him deceive you or lead you astray. "Now the serpent was more crafty than any beast of the field which the Lord God had made" (Gen. 3:1). "But I am afraid that, as the serpent deceived Eve by his craftiness, your minds will be led astray from the simplicity and purity of devotion to Christ" (2 Cor. 11:3, NASB). "Satan himself masquerades as an angel of light" (2 Cor. 11:14, BSB).

The antichrist is going to be revealed before Christ returns, but he is going to masquerade as the Son of God, and anyone who is not careful to know the Word will be led astray from the simplicity and purity of devotion to Christ. The prophet Isaiah writes of the antichrists reign and records the multitudes who go to worship him erroneously, believing him that he is lord. We know part of his abomination of desolation is going to be that he seats himself on the throne of God and elevates himself above God. It should be no surprise that many will fall for his schemes.

The Prophet Isaiah recorded what he saw "concerning Judah and Jerusalem. It shall come to pass in the latter days that the mountain of the house of the Lord shall be established as the highest of the mountains, and shall be lifted up above the hills; and all the nations shall flow to it, and many peoples shall come, and say: 'Come, let us go up to the mountain of the Lord, to the house of the God of Jacob, that he may teach us his ways and that we may walk in his paths.' For out of Zion shall go forth the law, and the word of the Lord from Jerusalem. He shall judge between the nations, and shall decide disputes for many peoples; and they shall beat their swords into plowshares, and their spears into pruning hooks; nation shall not lift up sword against nation, neither shall they learn war anymore. O house of Jacob, come, let us walk in the light of the Lord" (Isa. 2:1–5 and Mic. 4:1–3).

The New Living Translation mistakenly labels this text as "The Lords Future Reign"; it is obviously a mistake as we look ahead in this very chapter to discover hysteria, confusion, and an appeal from God that they walk in the light of the Lord. "O house of Jacob, come, let us walk in the light of the LORD" (Isa. 2:5, ESV). It is an appeal to come out of the darkness that would deceive the world into believing the antichrist is the Lord himself as described in the first four verses of Isaiah 2. Looking even further into this book, we see, "For the Lord of hosts has a day against all that is proud and lofty, against all that is lifted up—and it shall be brought low…against all the lofty mountains and against all the uplifted hills" (Isaiah 2:12 and 14 BSB). These verses contrast the false lord described previously in this chapter, who established the mountain of the house of the lord as the highest of mountains and lifted above the hills (Isaiah 2:2). Just ten verses later, we can see that the Antichrist and all those who went up to him, revering him as the Lord, will be taken down by the one true Lord and Messiah.

The quick switch to judgment, in the following verses, of the deceived who are not walking with the Lord is the giveaway that this is not of the Lord's future reign at all but the corruption of the world, believing that the antichrist is a god to worship.

"For you have rejected your people, the house of Jacob, because they are full of things from the east and of fortune-tellers like the Philistines, and they strike hands with the children of foreigners. Their land is filled with silver and gold, and there is no end to their treasures; their land is filled with horses, and there is no end to their chariots. Their land is filled with idols; they bow down to the work of their hands, to what their own fingers have made. So man is humbled, and each one is brought low—do not forgive them! Enter into the rock and hide in the dust from before the terror of the Lord, and from the splendor of his majesty. The haughty looks of man shall be brought low, and the lofty pride of men shall be humbled, and the Lord alone will be exalted in that day" (Isa. 2:6–11, ESV).

Look at how the house of Jacob is judged for having things from the east and of fortune-tellers like the Philistines. They are chastised for making deals with children of foreigners. Their land is full of treasures and wealth and idols. We cannot have read about the "Lord's future reign and his worship" and their judgment for idol worship at the same time. We know the Lord does not tolerate idol worship and certainly isn't going to be reigning on Earth and allowing it.

Look closely again at this passage in Isaiah: "Come, let us go up to the mountain of the Lord, to the house of the God of Jacob, that he may teach us his ways and that we may walk in his paths." "For out of Zion shall go forth the law, and the word of the Lord from Jerusalem. He shall judge between the nations, and shall decide disputes for many peoples; and they shall beat their swords into plowshares, and their spears into pruning hooks; nation shall not lift up sword against nation, neither shall they learn war anymore" (Isa. 2:3–4).

The antichrist swoons the nations to become defenseless.

When our Lord returns (Rev. 19:11, 15, BSB), he wages war righteously "And from His mouth proceeds a sharp sword with which to strike down the nations, and He will rule them with an iron scepter. He treads the winepress of the fury of the wrath of God the Almighty."

"'In that day,' declares the Lord, 'I will remove your horses from among you and wreck your chariots. I will remove the cities of your land and tear down all your strongholds. I will cut the sorceries from your hand, and you will have no fortune-tellers. I will also cut off the carved images and sacred pillars from among you, so that you will no longer bow down to the work of your own hands. I will root out the Asherah poles from your midst and demolish your cities. I will take vengeance in anger and wrath upon the nations that have not obeyed Me" (Mic. 5:10–15, BSB).

If Isaiah 2 and Micah 4:1–3 were about our Lord's second coming and him sitting on the throne, then these people would be coming to the mountain of the Lord to worship the Lord. They say they want to be taught the ways of this leader and that he settles disputes between nations and people. It is a description of peace in which the people are deceived into believing he is a god and comes with miraculously signs, creating peace in a world that has never seen happen in all world history. *He is the antichrist* as described in passages that we've already seen.

"So if they tell you, 'There He is in the wilderness,' do not go out; or, 'Here He is in the inner rooms,' do not believe it. For just as the lightning comes from the east and flashes as far as the west, so will be the coming of the Son of Man. Wherever there is a carcass, there the vultures will gather" (Mt. 24:26–28, BSB). I promise, this man on the mountaintop is the carcass as proven when the signs Christ has given us do not align. Remember, he gave those signs so we would not be confused or lured into believing a false Christ is he. This "lord" on the "mountain of the Lord to the house of God" is a direct correlation to the antichrist taking his seat in the Temple Mount and claiming deity.

Realize that this antichrist comes on a white horse to mimic Christ. Remember Christ warns us in Matthew and Mark, "Jesus answered, 'See to it that no one deceives you. For many will come in My name, claiming, "I am the Christ," and will deceive many. You will hear of wars and rumors of wars, but see to it that you are not alarmed. These things must happen, but the end is still to come. Nation will rise against nation, and kingdom against kingdom. There will be famines and earthquakes in various places. All these are the beginning of birth pains" (Mt. 24:4–8, BSB).

He will come to quell war on Earth at first. There will be three and a half years of "peace" from a false god. He settles disputes between nations and disarms them all or their weapons and armies. "They will beat their swords into plowshares and their spears into pruning hooks. Nation will no longer take up the sword against nation, nor train anymore for war" (Isa. 2:4, BSB).

"And the king shall do as he wills. He shall exalt himself and magnify himself above every god, and shall speak astonishing things against the God of gods. He shall prosper till the indignation is accomplished; for what is decreed shall be done. He shall pay no attention to the gods of his fathers, or to the one beloved by women. He shall not pay attention to any other god for he shall magnify himself above all. He shall honor the god of fortresses instead of these. A god whom his fathers did not know he shall honor with gold and silver, with precious stones and costly gifts. He shall deal with the strongest fortresses with the help of a foreign god. Those who acknowledge him he shall load with honor. He shall make them rulers over many and shall divide the land for a price" (Dan. 11:36–39, ESV).

"Then he shall confirm a covenant with many for one week, *but in the middle of the week he shall bring an end to sacrifice and offering*. And on the wing of abominations shall be one who makes desolate, even until the consummation, which is determined, is poured out on the desolate" (Dan. 9:27, BSB, emphasis added)

This scripture explains why the antichrist would have the nations destroy their own weapons and stop training their armies for war (as foretold in Isaiah 2:4). He has the nations tricked into believing he is the Messiah, above God even. They trust the covenant and believe that there is permanent world peace, falling right into the trap of Satan baited with the beast (the antichrist, the lawless one, the man of sin), they will allow him to set the world up for failure and destruction. God has allowed this and foretold the details leading up to the Second Coming of Christ and the rapture of his saints.

Chapter 17

Still Going…

Now that we've gone through all these scriptures to establish the fact that the first seal is in fact the coming of the antichrist, we've got to back up some (Rev. 6:1–2). The antichrist comes to overcome and conquer. The second seal comes close at the heels of this antichrist's arrival. "And when the Lamb opened the second seal, I heard the second living creature say, 'Come!' Then another horse went forth. It was bright red, and its rider was granted permission to take away peace from the earth and to make men slay one another. And he was given a great sword" (Rev. 6:3–4, BSB).

"And when the Lamb opened the third seal, I heard the third living creature say, 'Come!' Then I looked and saw a black horse, and its rider held in his hand a pair of scales. And I heard what sounded like a voice from among the four living creatures, saying, 'A quart of wheat for a denarius, and three quarts of barley for a denarius, and do not harm the oil and wine'" (Rev. 6:5–6, BSB).

This is an alarming prospect, considering it is only the first acts of violence within the great tribulation "suffering" which Daniel 12:1–2 and Matthew 24:21 both explain is worse than the world has ever seen *or* will ever see.

Our true Messiah has already warned us in the gospels when he told us that there would be famine. "There will be great earthquakes, and in various places famines and pestilences. And there will be terrors and great signs from heaven" (Lk. 21:11, ESV). This is what Christ referenced when he foretold of the signs to watch for signifying his near return.

"And when the Lamb opened the fourth seal, I heard the voice of the fourth living creature say, 'Come!' Then I looked and saw a pale green horse. Its rider's name was Death, and Hades followed close behind. And they were given authority over a fourth of the earth, to kill by sword, by famine, by plague, and by the beasts of the earth" (Rev. 6:7–8, ESV).

There are currently 7.9 billion people on earth right now (Worldometer. "World Population Clock: 7.9 Billion People, 2021, worldometers.info). One quarter of today's population would be about two billion people dying. It will be 1.8 billion more than we saw in the COVID-19 death numbers over the course of 2020 and 2021. This seal, therefore, cannot have been opened yet.

There will be no peace. Remember we've already looked at the fact that the antichrist is going to solve this war and bring world peace. The Prophet Daniel shed light on this war. I will not pretend to know who the king of the south is or who the king of the north will be, but here is the prophecy detailing this war: "At the time of the end, the king of the south shall attack him, but the king of the north shall rush upon him like a whirlwind, with chariots and horsemen, and with many ships. And he shall come into countries and shall overflow and pass through. He shall come into the glorious land. And tens of thousands shall fall, but these shall be delivered out of his hand: Edom and Moab and the main part of the Ammonites. He shall stretch out his hand against the countries, and the land of Egypt shall not escape. He shall become ruler of the treasures of gold and of silver, and all the precious things of Egypt, and the Libyans and the Cushites shall follow in his train. But news from the east and the north shall alarm him, and he shall go out with great fury to destroy and devote many to destruction. And he shall pitch his palatial tents between the sea and the glorious holy mountain" (Dan. 11:40–45, ESV).

Likely, the beast will receive his fatal wound on his head during this time while all eyes are on him, and it will miraculously heal.

"One of the heads of the beast appeared to be mortally wounded. But the mortal wound was healed, and the whole world marveled and followed the beast. They worshiped the dragon who had given authority to the beast, and they worshiped the beast, saying, 'Who is like the beast and who can wage war against it?'" (Rev. 13:3–4, BSB).

He'll perform signs and wonders from the *dunamis* of Satan, the dragon, and convince most people that he is the true lord. He's going to solve this world hunger, cure plagues, diseases, pestilences, and end wars that have come with the second, third, and fourth seals opening. He will sign a covenant that offers peace for seven days or possibly years, but remember he only commits to this treaty for three and a half days (or years). Do not worship the beast or be fooled into it as is written in Isaiah 2. "Then he shall confirm a covenant with many for one week; But in the middle of the week, He shall bring an end to sacrifice and offering. And on the wing of abominations shall be one who makes desolate, even until the consummation, which is determined, is poured out on the desolate" (Dan. 9:27, NKJV).

Recall, as the antichrist goes back on his peace treaty, that he has already created a world where weapons and skills of war have been voluntarily removed. "…and they shall beat their swords into plowshares, and their spears into pruning hooks; nation shall not lift up sword against nation, neither shall they learn war anymore" (Isa. 2:4).

The people will be defenseless once he breaks the peace covenant. They will suffer at the hands of this enemy because they trusted him and did not know the Father or his Word, so they were not prepared, couldn't identify this fraud is not their savior, and could not endure.

"For you yourselves know full well that the day of the Lord will come just like a thief in the night. While they are saying, 'Peace and safety!' then destruction will come upon them suddenly like labor pains upon a woman with child, and they will not escape. But you, brethren, are not in darkness, that the day would overtake you like a thief; for you are all sons of light and sons of day. We are not of night nor of darkness, so then let us not sleep as others do, but let us be alert and sober" (1 Thess. 5:2–6, NASB).

This "peace and safety!" mentioned in the previous verse could likely be what we know as have the week mentioned in Daniel's prophecy and described in Isaiah 2. The saints are not going to know "this (false) peace" unless they receive the mark of the beast and fail to endure for Christ, which would make them false believers or apostate (fallen away). As for the nonbelievers, they will be deluded into following after the beast. We know from Revelation 17:12–13 that the beast is going to have helpers in leaders of other nations. Likely these leaders will be persuading or even forcing citizens to receive the mark and follow the beast: "The ten horns you saw are ten kings who have not yet received a kingdom but will receive one hour of authority as kings, along with the beast. These kings have one purpose, to yield their power and authority to the beast."

"The beast was given a mouth to speak arrogant and blasphemous words, and authority to act for 42 months. And the beast opened its mouth to speak blasphemies against God and to slander his name and his tabernacle—those who dwell in heaven. *Then the beast was permitted to wage war against the saints and to conquer them*, and it was given authority over every tribe and people and tongue and nation. And all who dwell on the earth will worship the beast— all whose names have not been written from the foundation of the world in the Book of Life belonging to the Lamb who was slain" (Rev. 13:5–8, BSB, emphasis added).

Likewise, we can read about the same prophecy given to Daniel and explained in chapter 7. "This is what he said: 'The fourth beast is a fourth kingdom that will appear on the earth, different from all the other kingdoms, and it will devour the whole earth, trample it down, and crush it. And the ten horns are ten kings who will rise from this kingdom. After them another king, different from the earlier ones, will rise and subdue three kings. He will speak out against the Most High *and oppress the saints of the Most High*, intending to change the appointed times and laws; and the saints will be given into his hand for a time, and times, and half a time" (Dan. 7:23–25, BSB, emphasis added).

I am not sure what a time and times and a half a time equals, but I would be willing to bet it's forty-two months. "The Hebrew word *for 'time' is 'mô'êd,' which also can mean 'a year.'" ("Here's Why the Tribulation of the End Times is 7 Years." prophecyproof.org). Revelation 17 explains some of the symbolism. Once the wars have ended and peace ensues for the earth, the antichrist will be given power to "act for 42 months" (Rev. 13:5).*

Notice plainly within both texts that the saints, or believers, are absolutely present during the reign of the antichrist. We will see that as the trumpets are sounded and plagues poured out, *no one* repents. Therefore, these saints cannot be postrapture converts; furthermore, we have not come to any scripture describing Christ in the sky or angels gathering the saints for rapture as recorded in Matthew 24 etc. It's important for us to find that moment of rapture when the saints are called out of the world and not simply assume that we are taken out before any of the tribulation occurs because of the prevailing doctrine that has no scriptural backing.

The church has simply not been raptured yet; there has been no red moon, black sun, or falling stars yet. We can be assured that the living saints will live through these times and many will be martyred for their faith. "If anyone is to be taken captive, to captivity he goes; if anyone is to be slain with the sword, with the sword must he be slain. Here is a call for the endurance and faith of the saints" (Rev. 13:10, ESV).

"You will be betrayed even by parents and brothers and relatives and friends, and some of you will be put to death. And you will be hated by everyone because of My name" (Lk. 21:16–17, BSB).

These warnings are given to the saints, or believers, so that anyone living during this time will be prepared.

"Let no one deceive you in any way. For that day will not come, unless the rebellion comes first, and the man of lawlessness is revealed, the son of destruction, who opposes and exalts himself against every so-called god or object of worship, so that he takes his seat in the temple of God, proclaiming himself to be God" (2 Thess. 2:3–4).

The Lord does not return for his bride until after the antichrist comes is known and sits himself on the throne of God as a false god. When the fifth seal is opened, notice there are still no raptured saints, only those who have been martyred or slain for the world of God and testimony of our Savior, Christ Jesus.

"And when the Lamb opened the fifth seal, I saw under the altar the souls of those who had been slain for the word of God and for the testimony they had upheld. And they cried out in a loud voice, 'How long, O Lord, holy and true, until You avenge our blood and judge those who dwell upon the earth?' Then each of them was given a white robe and told to rest a little while longer, until the full number of their fellow servants, their brothers, were killed, just as they had been killed" (Rev. 6:9–11, ESV).

Remember we will be persecuted as believers during this great tribulation. These people described here could be us. As for those who live through to the end of times, we are going to be killed for our faith in Christ.

These are only the first five seals. We have already looked at the sixth seal when we saw how many times our Father told us that one of the signs *before* our Christ returns is a red moon and a black sun. Here is the scripture with the description of the sixth seal again.

"And when I saw the Lamb open the sixth seal, there was a *great earthquake*, and the *sun became black* like sackcloth of goat hair, and the whole *moon turned blood red*, and the stars of the sky fell to the earth like unripe figs dropping from a tree shaken by a great wind. *The sky receded like a scroll* being rolled up, and *every mountain and island was moved from its place*. Then the kings of the earth, the nobles, the commanders, the rich, the mighty, and every slave and freeman hid in the caves and among the rocks of the mountains. And they said to the mountains and the rocks, 'Fall on us and hide us from the face of the One seated on the throne and from the wrath of the Lamb.' For the great day of Their wrath has come, and who is able to withstand it?" (Rev. 6:12–17, ESV).

Our Savior has still not come as this sixth seal is opened. Notice the sun is black, the moon is red, there will be great earthquakes, and the great day of the wrath has now come, but we do not read yet of the rapture. Essentially, we have to get to this seal before we can legitimately look to the sky for his return in the clouds, but the

Bible does not yet tell of God's calling the people up from the earth or Christ coming in the clouds. We have to keep reading to find this.

This is where we start to see overlapping, not repetition mind you, but overlapping of the end times details. We will use these clues to put together a rough outline and truths that we must know in order to be prepared for the end. Included in the appendix.

Let us look again at Isaiah 2:10 (NLT), "Crawl into caves in the rocks. Hide in the dust from the terror of the Lord and the glory of his majesty."

Isaiah 2:19–22 (BSB) also parallels these scripture, "And people shall enter the caves of the rocks and the holes of the ground, from before the terror of the Lord, and from the splendor of his majesty, when he rises to terrify the earth. In that day mankind will cast away their idols of silver and their idols of gold, which they made for themselves to worship, to the moles and to the bats, to enter the caverns of the rocks and the clefts of the cliffs, from before the terror of the Lord, and from the splendor of his majesty, when he rises to terrify the earth. Stop regarding man in whose nostrils is breath, for of what account is he?"

Finally, we see this same foretelling in Luke 23:28–30 (BSB), "Daughters of Jerusalem, do not weep for Me, but weep for yourselves and for your children. Look, the days are coming when people will say, 'Blessed are the barren women, the wombs that never bore, and breasts that never nursed!' At that time 'they will say to the mountains, "Fall on us!" and to the hills, "Cover us!"'"

Notice that this is the same time period spoken of by Isaiah in chapter 2 as we uncovered the truth about who was sitting in the Holy Mountain of God. This parallel is proof through Scripture that the antichrist has set himself up to be thought of as a god who can settle all the disputes of the nations etc., and at the time of the opening of the sixth seal, we see nonbelievers trying to hide (and die) from the wrath of God.

We have seen six seals open and destruction fall on Earth. We already know that Christ told us he would not take his bride until after the moon turns red and the sun turns black: "Immediately after the tribulation of those days: 'The sun will be darkened, and the moon will not give its light; the stars will fall from the sky, and the powers of the heavens will be shaken.' At that time the sign of the Son of Man will appear in heaven, and all the tribes of the earth will mourn. They will see the Son of Man coming on the clouds of heaven, with power and great glory. And He will send out His angels with a loud trumpet call, and they will gather His elect from the four winds, from one end of the heavens to the other" (Mt. 24:29–31, ESV).

I expected to see a verse or two that says "It is done" and "Come out of her, my people," something that would indicate that the Lord had come in the clouds and the rapture of his bride had come. I kept reading and reading, anticipating something that would tell of this great event that would save us from the rest of what was to come.

As I failed to find evidence of a rapture to take the saints away before any further turmoil, distress, and suffering, I remembered something important: both our Lord (in Matthew 24:21) and the Prophet Daniel (in Daniel 12:1–2) specified that the tribulation will be the greatest suffering the world has ever seen and will ever see, and immediately after the tribulation, the details of seal six will take place. The Son of Man will come on the clouds. But if you've ever read ahead in the book of Revelation, you know that the seven trumpet blasts and the seven bowls or plagues usher in a far worse tribulation than the six seals do so far. If Christ returns before these fourteen blasts and bowls, then they can't be worse because the Savior comes after the worst the world has ever seen and will ever see.

As I dug deeper, the descriptions of seals six and seven, trumpet seven, and bowl seven also began to overlap and together fulfill the prophecy of the prophets, gospels, and epistles describing the end times leading up to the rapture of the church and the return of Christ.

The word *wrath* in Revelation 6:17 (used after the sun turns black and the moon turns red, etc.) comes from the Greek word *orgēs*. In 1 Thessalonians 1:10 and 5:9, as well as Romans 5:9 (BSB), we see the same word, *wrath*: "Therefore, since we have now been justified by his blood, much more shall we be saved by him from the wrath of God." This word also comes from the Greek word *orgēs*. God is not a liar, and his word will not contradict itself. So since we were promised to be saved from the wrath but do not see the visual coming of the Lord and rapture described in Revelation 1:7 (ESV), "Behold, he is coming with the clouds, and every eye will see him, even those who pierced him, and all tribes of the earth will wail on account of him..." but we know that after the sixth seal is opened "the great day of their wrath has come, who is able to survive it?" we have to be spared from the wrath. Furthermore, the wrath spoken of in Revelation 15:1, NRSV comes from the Greek word *thumos* (seen as the derivative *thumou* many times in scriptures. "Then I saw another portent in heaven, great and amazing: seven angels with seven plagues [or bowls in other translations] which are the last, for with them the wrath of God is ended." We see that the bowls are not actually part of the "orgēs"—wrath we are promised to be spared from.

This is another clue to me that there is an overlapping of these three different types of events describing the same thing. One theory I have is that the seven seals close one document. The entire document cannot be opened until all the seals are opened; therefore, the description of the tribulation described in the seals are not the happenings of the tribulation right then but the official "ribbon-cutting ceremony," if you will, of the end. The opening of the seals of this document could be ushering in the end-time tribulations as well and beginning the birth pains described by Christ. "For many will come in My name, claiming, 'I am the Christ,' and will deceive many. You will hear of wars and rumors of wars, but see to it that you are not alarmed. These things must happen, but the end is still to come. Nation will rise against nation, and kingdom against kingdom. There will be famines and earthquakes in various places. All these are the beginnings of birth pains" (Matt. 24:5–8, BSB).

Picture a scroll sealed with seven wax seals. The document itself gives a description of what is to come, as well as the exact birth pains described by Christ himself needed to happen prior to the beginning of the tribulation. Once the scroll is fully opened, the birth pains will end, and delivery of the end times will begin. This explanation helps me understand how the first three seals describe that which were previously described as the birth pains, as well as how it is that the sixth and seventh seals both hold the details that are described in trumpet 7 and bowl 7 (which we will see later). If the seals usher in the tribulation and the trumpets and bowls overlap in some way or are descriptions of the same things from different angles and points of view, it would make sense that each of the final seals, trumpets, and bowls could all describe the same last event prior to "the wrath," rapture, return of Christ, and marriage supper of the lamb. This would explain why we do not see any saints being raptured after the description of the sun turning black and the moon turning red, etc.

Chapter 18

It Is Done!

We haven't looked at the seventh seal yet, so before I get ahead of myself, let's see what that is about. "When the Lamb opened the seventh seal, there was silence in heaven for about half an hour. And I saw the seven angels who stand before God, and they were given seven trumpets..." (Rev. 8:1–2).

This seal opens the trumpets. Paul told us we will be raptured "at the last trumpet." Considering my theory that the seals open a document that usher in the tribulation and is not the tribulation itself, it would make sense that the trumpets are released upon the last seal's opening.

"Listen, I tell you a mystery: We will not all sleep, but we will all be changed in an instant, in the twinkling of an eye, *at the last trumpet. For the trumpet will sound, the dead will be raised imperishable, and we will be changed*" (1 Cor. 15:51–52, BSB, emphasis added).

Christ also told us in Matthew 24:30–31, BSB "At that time the sign of the Son of Man will appear in heaven, and all the tribes of the earth will mourn. They will see the Son of Man coming on the clouds of heaven, with power and great glory. And He will send out His angels with a loud trumpet call, and they will gather His elect from the four winds, from one end of the heavens to the other."

As we pulled scriptures together to build the picture of the last days, please remember Jesus Christ told us to watch for him *and* to be prepared. "But see to it that you are not alarmed. These things must happen, but the end is still to come" (Mt. 24:6, BSB).

The details of these seals are described in the remaining parts of Revelation. There are so many mysteries and riddles. There is a back and forth within the chapters of Revelation and a need to pair scriptures with scriptures from throughout the Holy Book to figure out what is being told. We read about the seals in the sixth and seventh chapters of Revelation, including the antichrist's coming, but the details of the beast aren't found until later in the twelfth and thirteenth chapters of Revelation. There is a woman who has "clothed in the sun, with the moon under her feet and a crown of twelve stars on her head. She was pregnant and crying out in the pain and agony of giving birth" (Rev. 12:1, BSB). It coincidentally speaks of sun, moon, stars, and labor pains in this section just as Christ referenced in Matthew 24 and Mark 13. Is this woman figurative or literal?

"After this I saw four angels standing at the four corners of the earth, holding back its four winds so that no wind would blow on land or sea or on any tree. And I saw another angel ascending from the east, with the seal of the living God. And he called out in a loud voice to the four angels who had been given power to harm the land and the sea: 'Do not harm the land or sea or trees until we have sealed the foreheads of the servants of our God'" (Rev. 7:1–3, BSB, emphasis added).

In Matthew 24:29, these same angels will gather the elect from the four winds when Christ returns and the church ascends to heaven. If the angels are here at the first trumpet holding back the winds. These angels are still in place at the sounding of the first trumpet, so the saints can't have been raptured yet.

There is an interlude between the revelation of the sixth seal and the seventh seal being opened. Typically, we want to read chronologically into these verses and chapters. I look forward to one day knowing exactly how this all unfolds, but for now, I'm trying to piece it together logically with scripture interpreting scripture and holding to the inerrancy of Christ's prophesies, and chronological or sequential happenings do not seem to be that. The following section of scripture lies between the sixth and seventh seals. We find that the saints who have endured and lived through tribulation thus far will receive their own mark. They will be sealed on the foreheads as servants of our God. This is a direct contrast to the mark of the beast all the nonbelievers will have taken.

> And I heard the number of those who were sealed, 144,000 from all the tribes of Israel: From the tribe of Judah 12,000 were sealed, from the tribe of Reuben 12,000, from the tribe of Gad 12,000, from the tribe of Asher 12,000, from the tribe of Naphtali 12,000, from the tribe of Manasseh 12,000, from the tribe of Simeon 12,000, from the tribe of Levi 12,000, from the tribe of Issachar 12,000, from the tribe of Zebulun 12,000, from the tribe of Joseph 12,000, and from the tribe of Benjamin 12,000. After this I looked and saw a multitude too large to count, from every nation and tribe and people and tongue, standing before the throne and before the Lamb. They were wearing white robes and holding palm branches in their hands. And they cried out in a loud voice: "Salvation to our God, who sits on the throne, and to the Lamb!" And all the angels stood around the throne and around the elders and the four living creatures. And they fell facedown before the throne and worshiped God, saying, "Amen! Blessing and glory and wisdom and thanks and honor and power and strength be to our God forever and ever! Amen."
>
> Then one of the elders addressed me: "These in white robes," he asked, "who are they, and where have they come from?" "Sir," I answered, "you know." So he replied, "These are the ones who have come out of the great tribulation; they have washed their robes and made them white in the blood of the Lamb. For this reason, they

> are before the throne of God and serve Him day and night in His temple; and the One seated on the throne will spread His tabernacle over them. Never again will they hunger, and never will they thirst; nor will the sun beat down upon them, nor any scorching heat.' For the Lamb in the center of the throne will be their shepherd. 'He will lead them to springs of living water,' and 'God will wipe away every tear from their eyes.' (Rev. 7:4–17, BSB)

The 144,000 and the multitude described in chapter 7 are the saints who were sealed. We read that they will hunger, thirst, cry, and scorch no more. John was told that the ones who were sealed are those who have come out of the great tribulation, but I don't believe this indicates that they are raptured and in heaven between these two seals. We will look at evidence to support this.

It's important to consider that given the sounding of the fifth trumpet (Rev. 9:4) recorded much later than the seals are recorded, the locusts that come from the pits of hell are forbade to damage the grass, trees, *or any of the people with the seal of God on their forehead*. This is in fulfillment of Christ's prophecy. "Yet not even a hair of your head will perish. By your patient endurance you will gain your souls" (Lk. 21:18–19, BSB). Look at Revelation 7:1–3 again as John wrote that the angels are not to harm the land or sea until the servants of God are sealed on their forehead. This way, when the locusts come from the pits of hell and are forbidden to damage the people with the seal of God on their foreheads, they will know who the sealed are, and this is the sounding of the fifth trumpet in which we are well into the tribulation—we as in the wicked who have taken the mark of the beast and the saints who have not.

Those marked with the seal of God must still be present on Earth, not raptured, and that interlude describing the saints *being sealed* probably happens at that point, but the explanation to John that he shares with us (Rev. 7:9–17) is still future tense up to this point and not to be confused with being a "mid-tribulation rapture" since obviously, Christ told us himself that he would come after the tribulation.

Just before the trumpets are blown, "the smoke of the incense, with the prayers of the saints, went up before God out of the angel's hand" (Rev. 8:4, BSB).

Here we see again that the saints are still on Earth below God and praying to their Father in heaven a chapter later and after all seven seals were opened.

> And the seven angels with the seven trumpets prepared to sound them. Then the *first* angel sounded his trumpet, and hail and fire mixed with blood were hurled down upon the earth. A third of the earth was burned up, along with a third of the trees and all the green grass. Then the *second* angel sounded his trumpet, and something like a great mountain burning with fire was thrown into the sea. A third of the sea turned to blood, a third of the living creatures in the sea died, and a third of the ships were destroyed. Then the *third* angel sounded his trumpet, and a great star burning like a torch fell from heaven and landed on a third of the rivers and on the springs of water. The name of the star is Wormwood. A third of the waters turned bitter like wormwood oil, and many people died from the bitter waters. Then the *fourth* angel sounded his trumpet, and a third of the sun and moon and stars were struck. A third of the stars were darkened, a third of the day was without light, and a third of the night as well. And as I observed, I heard an eagle flying overhead, calling in a loud voice, "Woe! Woe! Woe to those who dwell on the earth, because of the trumpet blasts about to be sounded by the remaining three angels!"

Then the *fifth* angel sounded his trumpet, and I saw a star that had fallen from heaven to earth, and it was given the key to the pit of the Abyss. The star opened the pit of the Abyss, and smoke rose out of it like the smoke of a great furnace, and the sun and the air were darkened by the smoke from the pit. And out of the smoke, locusts descended on the earth, and they were given power like that of the scorpions of the earth. They were told not to harm the grass of the earth or any plant or tree, *but only those who did not have the seal of God on their foreheads*. The locusts were not given power to kill them, but only to torment them for five months, and their torment was like the stinging of a scorpion. In those days men will seek death and will not find it; they will long to die, but death will escape them (Rev. 8:6–13, 9:1–6, BSB).

"Then the *sixth* angel sounded his trumpet, and I heard a voice from the four horns of the golden altar before God saying to the sixth angel with the trumpet, "Release the four angels who are bound at the great River Euphrates." So the four angels who had been prepared for this hour and day and month and year were released to kill a third of mankind. And the number of mounted troops was two hundred million; I heard their number. Now the horses and riders in my vision looked like this: The riders had breastplates the colors of fire, sapphire, and sulfur. The heads of the horses were like the heads of lions, and out of their mouths proceeded fire, smoke, and sulfur. A third of mankind was killed by the three plagues of fire, smoke, and sulfur that proceeded from their mouths. For the power of the horses was in their mouths and in their tails; indeed, their tails were like snakes, having heads with which to inflict harm. Now the rest of mankind who were not killed by these plagues still did not repent of the works of their hands. They did not stop worshipping demons and idols of gold, silver, bronze, stone, and wood, which cannot see or hear or walk. *Furthermore, they did not repent of their murder, sorcery, sexual immorality, and theft.*" (Rev. 9:13–21, BSB)

Notice there will be no one repenting of their sins during these times. Since there are no more being added to the saints, those with the seal of God had to have already been converted prior to the tribulation and *still* present on Earth.

As previously noted, the details of the sixth and seventh seal coincide with the seventh trumpet and seventh bowl. There is an imbrication between the four that appear to be describing the same one event.

"Then the seventh angel sounded his trumpet, and loud voices called out in heaven: 'The kingdom of the world has become the kingdom of our Lord and of His Christ, and He will reign forever and ever.' And the twenty-four elders who sit on their thrones before God fell on their faces and worshipped God, saying: 'We give thanks to You, O Lord God Almighty, the One who is and who was, because You have taken Your great power and have begun to reign. The nations were enraged, and your wrath has come. The time has come to judge the dead and to reward your servants the prophets, as well as the saints and those who fear Your name, both small and great—and to destroy those who destroy the earth.' Then the temple of God in heaven was opened, and the ark of His covenant appeared in His temple. And there were flashes of lightning, and rumblings, and peals of thunder, and an earthquake, and a great hailstorm" (Rev. 11:15–19, BSB).

Let's compare these events within the sixth and seventh seal, the seventh trumpet and the seventh bowl: each describes a great earthquake happening. Likewise, the sky opening like a scroll is recorded in the sixth seal and the seventh trumpet. There are peels of thunder, rumbling, and flashing lights in the seventh seal, trumpet, and bowl (as we will see later when we look at the bowls poured out).

The time of judgment coincides with the last trumpet being blown. "Listen, I tell you a mystery: We will not all sleep, but we will all be changed—in an instant, in the twinkling of an eye, at the last trumpet. For the trumpet will sound, the dead will be raised imperishable, and we will be changed" (1 Cor. 15:51–52, BSB).

But still, we see no rapture. As I studied through the seals, trumpets, and bowls, and saw the interconnected details that could only be describing the same one event. This supports my theory that the opening of the seals, bowls, and trumpets must overlap as they open but are recorded separately. Remember that Christ tells us that there will be a great tribulation that is worse than what the world has ever seen before and shall ever see again (Matt. 24:21) *and* that he will come for his bride *after* the tribulation (Matt. 24:29). As we read the details of the seals and then the trumpets, we can see the suffering and devastation to the world will get worse (if it is *not* simultaneously occurring). Therefore, it's impossible to say that the tribulation of the world has ended before the trumpets and bowls transpire while they describe suffering, devastation, and tribulation far greater than that which we read of in the seals.

There is another problem with the idea of a rapture at seal 6 with trumpets and bowls to follow afterward as the "believers" are to be spared the wrath of the scorpion-like creatures released at trumpet 5. And we already noted that the scriptures spell out that no one repents and turns to God during these times—so they can't be post-rapture Christians as some theorize. There will not be any. Additionally, we would also have to conclude that the sky would open like a scroll during the opening of the sixth seal, close up, and then open again at the seventh trumpet. We'd also have to believe that the mountains and islands would disappear at seal 6 then come back so they can disappear again at bowl 7. These and other repetitive details are likely the overlapping descriptions of the same events happening once. The revelation of the seals, trumpets, and bowls should likely not be read as chronological details. This is not to say that each of the seven (all, twenty-one) are opened at the same time but overlap in some way (see the chart in the appendix).

At some point within the midst of the apocalyptic events, the abomination of desolation will be set up. Forty-two months will go by as these seals and plagues are unveiled. The abomination of desolation will take place and still forty-five more days will play out before the final end, the rapture, and the coming of our Lord as the King of kings.

Revelation chapters 12 and 13 specifically reference the beast and the war waged on the saints: "And the dragon was enraged at the woman, and went to make war with the rest of her children, who keep the commandments of God and hold to the testimony of Jesus" (Rev. 12:17, BSB).

"*Then the beast was permitted to wage war against the saints and to conquer them*, and it was given authority over every tribe and people and tongue and nation. And all who dwell on the earth will worship the beast—all whose names have not been written from the foundation of the world in the Book of Life belonging to the Lamb who was slain… Here is a call for the perseverance and faith of the saints" (Rev. 13:7–10, BSB) so that they do not take the mark of the beast and will endure through the hardships that will come as they cannot buy or sell etc. without it.

John is specific in his writings. "Here is a call for the perseverance and faith of the saints." It's recorded in Revelation 14:12 as well as Revelation 13:10.

In these later chapters, the saints are absolutely present when the beasts are waging war and terror; there is no one repenting as noted during the trumpet blasts, and there has been nothing mentioned yet of the rapture of the church, which is clearly prophesied to happen with the return of Christ in the clouds.

The mark of the beast will be presented and forced on the earth along with the worship of the antichrist, the beasts, and the dragon, and we know from chapter 14 verse 9–11 (Revelation) that those who take the mark will not be spared God's wrath. "And a third angel followed them, calling out in a loud voice, 'If anyone worships the beast and its image, and receives its mark on his forehead or on his hand, he too will drink the wine of God's anger, poured undiluted into the cup of His wrath (thumou). And he will be tormented in fire and sulfur in the presence of the holy angels and of the Lamb. And the smoke of their torment rises forever and ever. Day and night there is no rest for those who worship the beast and its image, or for anyone who receives the mark of its name.'" Remember, this is a different type of wrath than the wrath describing the bowls (or plagues) in chapter 15, verse 1 of Revelation ("orgēs" vs "thumos"), so believers will not be receiving the "orgēs" wrath, save for those who worship the beast and its image and receive its mark on their forehead or their hand. But so far, without a visible non-secret rapture taking place, the saints are still present to live through the "thumos" wrath about to be unleashed with the pouring out of the bowls.

Be prepared brothers and sisters in Christ. There will be great tribulation like the earth has never seen, and we will either die before tribulation, be persecuted and killed during it, or endure to the end when that last trumpet sounds. God gave us these scriptures so that we will know what to expect. We are promised by Christ in Matthew 24:22 and Mark 13:23, "If those days had not been cut short, nobody would be saved. But for the sake of the elect, those days will be cut short." For this reason, I tend to believe the "week" or seven years will end up being cut short sometime after the three-and-a-half-year point (about forty-five days longer). "And from the time the daily sacrifice is abolished and the abomination of desolation set up, there will be 1,290 days. Blessed is he who waits and reaches the end of the 1,335 days" (Dan. 12:11–12 BSB). We see in these verses that there are 1,290 days between the daily sacrifice being abolished and the abomination of desolation being set up. The following verse adds 45 days and says those who wait and reach the end are blessed.

We will begin to look at the bowls being poured out and look for the same overlapping details as well as indications that the saints have still not been raptured, and no one is repenting.

> Then I saw another great and marvelous sign in heaven: seven angels with the seven final plagues,

with which the wrath of God is completed. And I saw something like a sea of glass mixed with fire, beside which stood those who had conquered the beast and its image and the number of its name. They were holding harps from God, and they sang the song of God's servant Moses and of the Lamb: "Great and wonderful are your works, O Lord God Almighty! Just and true are Your ways, O King of the nations! Who will not fear You, O Lord, and glorify Your name? For You alone are holy. All nations will come and worship before You for Your righteous acts have been revealed.' After this I looked, and the temple—the tabernacle of the Testimony—was opened in heaven. And out of the temple came the seven angels with the seven plagues, dressed in clean and bright linen and girded with golden sashes around their chests. Then one of the four living creatures gave the seven angels seven golden bowls full of the wrath (thumou) of God, who lives forever and ever. And the temple was filled with smoke from the glory of God and from his power; *and no one could enter the temple until the seven plagues of the seven angels were completed.* (Rev.15, BSB)

Looking through the end-times scriptures, we know how important it is to "endure" and to be prepared as believers of the Lord. Revelation chapter 16 describes the wrath (thumou) of six bowls.

> Then I heard a loud voice from the temple saying to the seven angels, "Go, pour out on the earth the seven bowls of God's wrath." So the *first* angel went and poured out his bowl on the earth, and loathsome, malignant sores broke out on those who had the mark of the beast and worshipped

its image. And the *second* angel poured out his bowl into the sea, and it turned to blood like that of the dead, and every living thing in the sea died. And the *third* angel poured out his bowl into the rivers and springs of water, and they turned to blood. And I heard the angel of the waters say: "Righteous are You, O Holy One, who is and was because You have brought these judgments. For they have spilled the blood of saints and prophets, and You have given them blood to drink as they deserve." And I heard the altar reply: "Yes, Lord God Almighty, true and just are Your judgments."

Then the *fourth* angel poured out his bowl on the sun, and it was given power to scorch the people with fire. And the people were scorched by intense heat, and they cursed the name of God who had authority over these plagues; yet they did not repent and give Him glory. And the *fifth* angel poured out his bowl on the throne of the beast, and its kingdom was plunged into darkness, and men began to gnaw their tongues in anguish and curse the God of heaven for their pains and sores; yet they did not repent of their deeds. And the *sixth* angel poured out his bowl on the great river Euphrates, and its water was dried up to prepare the way for the kings of the East. And I saw three unclean spirits that looked like frogs coming out of the mouths of the dragon, the beast, and the false prophet. These are demonic spirits that perform signs and go out to all the kings of the earth, to assemble them for battle on the great day of God the Almighty... And they assembled the kings in the place that in Hebrew is called Armageddon. (Rev. 16:1–14, 16, BSB, emphasis added)

After these bowls are poured out, Christ gives a warning in the fifteenth verse, "Behold, *I am coming like a thief.* Blessed is the one who remains awake and clothed, so that he will not go naked and let his shame be exposed" (Rev. 16:15, BSB, emphasis added).

This is very similar to that which we are warned of in 2 Peter 3:10, "But the Day of the Lord will come like a thief. The heavens will disappear with a roar, the elements will be destroyed by fire, and the earth and its works will be laid bare" (1 Thess. 5:2 and 4, and Rev. 3:3). This parallel is revealing. Paul, Peter, and Christ warned us that the Lord would come like a thief in the night. The verbiage is intentional. It's a clue for those who have an ear to hear (Mt. 11:15, 13:9, 13:43; Mk. 4:9, 4:23; Lk. 8:8, 14:35). Christ warned us four times in the New Testament that the rapture and his second coming would be like a thief in the night. Notice this reminder about Christ coming like a thief comes just before the last bowl is poured out. Pay attention also to the details given that overlap the sixth and seventh seal, the seventh trumpet, and the seventh bowl that we looked at earlier. Peter says the heavens will disappear with a roar, the elements will be destroyed by fire, and the earth will be laid bare, just like the descriptions given for what happens in the final seal, trumpet, and bowl. These details describing the coming of Christ match up and, unfortunately, do not describe a pretribulation rapture but the presence of the saints at the end of a tribulation that the world has never seen the likes of before.

Finally, we come to the seventh bowl. Notice the great hailstones, which is also an overlapping detail between the seventh trumpet (Rev. 11:19) and the sixth and seventh seals (Rev. 6:14 and 8:5). There are additional correlations between the second through sixth trumpets and bowls (see chart in the appendix). Finally, notice in the following passage, verse 18 will tell us that "there were flashes of lightning, and rumblings, and peals of thunder, and a great earthquake the likes of which had not occurred since men were upon the earth" (Rev. 16:18). Remember that Christ told us in Matthew 24:21 that the tribulation would be greater than what the world has ever seen and will ever see, and this earthquake described upon the opening of the seventh bowl literally says it's worse than what the world has ever seen since men were upon the earth. This is a huge detail to clue us in on the timing of the rapture and the second coming as well as the unfortunate fact that we will be raptured "after the great tribulation and suffering" (Matt. 24:29). It's important to note that we have still not found any scripture that indicates the end of the tribulation or the calling out of the bride from the world. Read the following scripture carefully.

"Then the seventh angel poured out his bowl into the air, and a loud voice came from the throne in the temple, saying, '*It is done!*' And there were flashes of lightning, and rumblings, and peals of thunder, and a great earthquake the likes of which had not occurred since men were upon the earth—so mighty was the great quake. The great city was split into three parts, and the cities of the nations collapsed. And God remembered Babylon the great and gave her the cup of the wine of the fury of His wrath (orgēs). Then every island fled, and no mountain could be found. And great hailstones weighing almost a hundred pounds each rained down on them from above. And men cursed God for the plague of hail, because it was so horrendous" (Rev. 16:18–20, BSB, emphasis added).

There it is. We've been looking for this! "It is done!" We had to get to the last bowl to see the Lord declare "the end."

"Then I heard another voice from heaven say: '*Come out of her, My people*, so that you will not share in her sins or contract any of her plagues'" (Rev. 18:4, BSB, emphasis added).

The rapture of the bride has finally come as foretold in Matthew 24:31, after the greatest tribulation the world has ever seen and could ever see again. The earth lies barren, destroyed by fire, earthquakes, and hail; the last trumpet blasts; we're reminded that the Lord will come like a thief in the night; the final bowl is poured out; a loud voice coming from the throne says, "It is done"; and then we literally read of our Father calling his bride out (the rapture). All of this will happen just like we were foretold in 2 Peter 3:10 and so many more passages in the Holy Scriptures. Then the Lord of lords and King of kings is seen in the clouds and descends as promised also in Matthew 24:31. All this, just before the cup of the wine of his fierce wrath (orgēs) is poured out on Babylon. Just as promised, believers were spared the wrath (orgēs).

"Then I saw heaven standing open, and there before me was a white horse. And its rider is called Faithful and True. With righteousness He judges and wages war. He has eyes like blazing fire, and many royal crowns on His head. He has a name written on Him that only He Himself knows. He is dressed in a robe dipped in blood, and His name is The Word of God. The armies of heaven, dressed in fine linen, white and pure, follow Him on white horses. And from His mouth proceeds a sharp sword with which to strike down the nations, and He will rule them with an iron scepter. He treads the winepress of the fury of the wrath of God the Almighty. And He has a name written on His robe and on His thigh: *King of kings and lord of lords*" (Rev. 19:11–16, BSB). Here is our great Savior coming on the clouds as promised!

We know we need only to cling to the Lord to be filled with his Holy Spirit and to continue on in the good works until it is finished.

"But watch yourselves, or your hearts will be weighed down by dissipation, drunkenness, and the worries of life—and that day will spring upon you suddenly like a snare. For it will come upon all who dwell on the face of all the earth. So keep watch at all times, and pray that you may have the strength to escape all that is about to happen and to stand before the Son of Man" (Lk. 21:34–36, BSB).

Notice our Savior warns us in Luke to keep watch and pray that we may have the strength to escape all that is about to happen. It is similar to the scripture in Revelation 3:10: "Because you have kept my word about patient endurance, I will keep you from the hour of trial that is coming on the whole world to try those who dwell on the earth." Look at how believers have been kept from not only "the wrath" but from "the hour" as promised by our Father.

"The hour" is a very important and key phrase here. Many look at this verse and believe that it means they will be raptured prior to the great tribulation. There are other verses that speak of this same "hour." In Matthew 25:13, Jesus tells his disciples to "watch therefore, for you know neither the day nor *the hour*." Luke 12:40, 46 tells us, "you too, be ready; for the Son of Man is coming at *an hour* that you do not expect…the master of that slave will come on a day when he does not expect him and at *an hour* he does not know and will cut him in pieces, and assign him a place with the unbelievers."

The hour is clearly speaking of the end of times, and Revelation 3:10 is definitely promising that the believer will be kept from "the hour of trial."

The important detail we need to understand is that "the hour" is not speaking of the actual tribulation that comes through the seals, the trumpets, and the bowls. Look at Revelation 14:7: "And he said with a loud voice, 'Fear God and give him glory, because *the hour* of his judgment has come, and worship him who made heaven and earth, the sea and the springs of water.'"

Look at the following verses: "Then a second angel followed, saying, 'Fallen, fallen is Babylon the great, who has made all the nations drink the wine of the passion of her immorality'" (Rev. 14:8–9, BSB).

Now, let us go right back to Revelation 18:5–24, the verse just after the Lord calls out his people. We see the utter destruction of Babylon. All those who were not taken upon the call of God to be raptured after it was done were left on the earth and are in shock, lament, terror, and torment. This is "the hour." Look at the italicized verses and how this fall of Babylon which does indeed occur after "It is done," the Bride is called out of the world, and our Savior comes on his white horse ready to wage war on his enemies. In the exact order prophesied, with no "secret," "pre-trib" rapture, or Christ coming partway to get us raptured and then going back up until this part of the end.

> "For her sins are piled up to heaven, and God has remembered her iniquities. Give back to her as she has done to others; pay her back double for what she has done; mix her a double portion in her own cup. As much as she has glorified herself and lived in luxury, give her the same measure of torment and grief. In her heart she says, 'I sit as queen; I am not a widow and will never see

grief.' Therefore her plagues will come in one day—death and grief and famine—and she will be consumed by fire for mighty is the Lord God who judges her." Then the kings of the earth who committed sexual immorality and lived in luxury with her will weep and wail at the sight of the smoke rising from the fire that consumes her. In fear of her torment, they will stand at a distance and cry out: "Woe, woe to the great city, the mighty city of Babylon! *For in a single hour, your judgment has come.*"

And the merchants of the earth will weep and mourn over her, because there is no one left to buy their cargo—cargo of gold, silver, precious stones, and pearls; of fine linen, purple, silk, and scarlet; of all kinds of citron wood and every article of ivory, precious wood, bronze, iron, and marble; of cinnamon, spice, incense, myrrh, and frankincense; of wine, olive oil, fine flour, and wheat; of cattle, sheep, horses, and chariots; of slaves and souls of men. And they will say, "The fruit of your soul's desire has departed from you; all your luxury and splendor have vanished, never to be seen again." The merchants who sold these things and grew their wealth from her will stand at a distance, in fear of her torment. They will weep and mourn, saying, "Woe, woe to the great city, clothed in fine linen and purple and scarlet, adorned with gold and precious stones and pearls! *For in a single hour such fabulous wealth has been destroyed!*"

Every shipmaster, passenger, and sailor, and all who make their living from the sea, will stand at a distance and cry out at the sight of the smoke rising from the fire that consumes her. "What city was ever like this great city?"

they will exclaim. Then they will throw dust on their heads as they weep and mourn and cry out: "Woe, woe to the great city, where all who had ships on the sea were enriched by her wealth! *For in a single hour she has been destroyed.*" Rejoice over her, O heaven, O saints and apostles and prophets, because God has pronounced for you His judgment against her. Then a mighty angel picked up a stone the size of a great millstone and cast it into the sea, saying: "With such violence the great city of Babylon will be cast down, never to be seen again. And the sound of harpists and musicians, of flute players and trumpeters will never ring out in you again. Nor will any craftsmen of any trade be found in you again, nor the sound of a millstone be heard in you again. The light of a lamp will never shine in you again, and the voices of a bride and bridegroom will never call out in you again. For your merchants were the great ones of the earth because all the nations were deceived by your sorcery." And there was found in her the blood of prophets and saints, and of all who had been slain on the earth. (Rev. 18:5–24, BSB)

Remember when we read in Matthew 24:37–38 that Jesus told us that "the last days will be like the days of Noah, people were eating, drinking, marrying and giving in marriage, up to the day Noah entered the ark…" We also see the same sentiments in 1 Thessalonians 5:3 (BSB): "While people are saying, 'peace and security,' destruction will come upon them suddenly, like labor pains on a pregnant woman, and they will not escape." I've heard it argued that the rapture of Christ's church has to take place before the tribulation (seals, trumpets, and bowls) are released because no one would be doing all these things described as in "the days of Noah" or calling life on earth as peaceful or secure once the tribulation had begun. We've read of the devastation the seals, trumpets, and bowls unleash and know it's going to be like something the earth has never endured before, and I too would imagine life *not* going on as usual. But look at what we just read in Revelation 18. The merchants of the earth will weep and mourn over the loss of their biggest consumer (Babylon). The shipmaster, passenger, and sailor will weep and mourn as they lose the wealth they were enriched with (by Babylon). Even in the midst of the tribulation, apparently life will go on. So Babylon gets destroyed in an hour of wrath. God will remember her iniquities and pay her back double. Look at the verses italicized and see "for a single hour your judgment has come; for in a single hour, such a fabulous wealth has been destroyed; for a single hour she has been destroyed."

This destruction comes as a judgment on all those who followed the beast and worshipped him and his image. These are the people who did not believe in Christ or repent of their sins. These are the ones spoken of who were *not* patiently enduring as spoken of by our Savior, John, and the other apostles in warning us. There is no evidence or scripture that says the church is raptured before any of this happens, and indeed, the Lord follows through on his promise given in Revelation 3:10 "to keep us from *the hour* of trial that is coming on the whole world." It isn't until Revelation 18:5, after all the seals, trumpets, and bowls have been opened, sounded, and poured out, that we finally see the children of God be called out—just before those who were not expecting Christ to return, who were joyfully making money and prospering in the great city—and who we've just read are judged. "…For in a single hour your judgment has come" (Rev. 18:10). This is *that* hour! This is that judgment we will be spared from as foretold by our Savior. Do not be deceived my fellow believers. We will have to have strength to endure and to escape this last judgment.

Look also at this warning in Mark 13:32–37, Matthew 24:36–51, and in Luke:

"Be dressed for service and keep your lamps burning. Then you will be like servants waiting for their master to return from the wedding banquet, so that when he comes and knocks, they can open the door for him at once. Blessed are those servants whom the master finds on watch when he returns. Truly I tell you, he will dress himself to serve and will have them recline at the table, and he himself will come and wait on them. Even if he comes in the second or third watch of the night and finds them alert, those servants will be blessed. But understand this: If the homeowner had known at what hour the thief was coming, he would not have let his house be broken into. You also must be ready, because the Son of Man will come at an hour you do not expect.

"'Lord,' said Peter, 'are You addressing this parable to us, or to everyone else as well?' And the Lord answered, 'Who then is the faithful and wise manager, whom the master puts in charge of his servants to give them their portion at the proper time? *Blessed is that servant whose master finds him doing so when he returns.* Truly I tell you, he will put him in charge of all his possessions. But suppose that servant says in his heart, "My master will be a long time in coming," and he begins to beat the menservants and maidservants, and to eat and drink and get drunk. The master of that servant will come on a day he does not expect and at an hour he does not anticipate. Then he will cut him to pieces and assign him a place with the unbelievers. That servant who knows his master's will but does not get ready or follow his instructions will be beaten with many blows. But the one who unknowingly does things worthy of punishment will be beaten with few blows. From everyone who has been given much, much will be required; and from him who has been entrusted with much, even more will be demanded'" (Lk. 12:35–48, BSB, emphasis added).

Look at this closely, in verses 45 and 46: "But suppose that servant says in his heart, 'My master will be a long time in coming,' and he begins to beat the menservants and maidservants, and to eat and drink and get drunk. The master of that servant will come on a day he does not expect and at an hour he does not anticipate. Then he will cut him to pieces and assign him a place with the unbelievers."

"Then he will cut him to pieces and assign him a place with the unbelievers…" These servants who were not ready to endure and who fell away from righteous living did not heed the call to patiently endure. They will be cast into the abyss with the antichrist, his image, and all the other unbelievers.

Saints must endure to the end!

Our Scriptures tell us that the marriage supper of the lamb comes after his children are called out and before our Lord and Savior heads out on his white horse to wage war on those who were left behind.

We've been warned but we've also been promised, "…But for the sake of the elect, those days will be cut short" (Mt. 24:22).

Christ told us in Luke 21:10–19, BSB "Nation will rise against nation, and kingdom against kingdom. There will be great earthquakes, famines, and pestilences in various places, along with fearful sights and great signs from heaven. But before all this, they will seize you and persecute you. On account of My Name they will deliver you to the synagogues and prisons, and they will bring you before kings and governors. *This will be your opportunity to serve as witnesses. So make up your mind not to worry beforehand how to defend yourselves. For I will give you speech and wisdom that none of your adversaries will be able to resist or contradict.* You will be betrayed even by parents and brothers and relatives and friends, and some of you will be put to death. And you will be hated by everyone because of My name. Yet not even a hair of your head will perish. By your patient endurance you will gain your souls."

We have watched all the warnings and prophesies unfold within the book of Revelation. Of course, this is not an exhaustive commentary on the entire book of Revelation or of end times, but we have looked at enough scriptures, pairing, paralleling, and allowing scripture to reveal scripture. The bottom line for the saints is to realize how important it is to endure, live by the spirit, and glorify Christ in our lives.

Chapter 19

Eternity

"And I heard a sound like the roar of a great multitude, like the rushing of many waters and like a mighty rumbling of thunder, crying out: 'Hallelujah! For the Lord our God the Almighty reigns. Let us rejoice and be glad and give Him the glory. For the marriage of the Lamb has come, and His bride has made herself ready. She was given clothing of fine linen, bright and pure.' For the fine linen she wears is the righteous acts of the saints. Then the angel told me to write, 'Blessed are those who are invited to the marriage supper of the Lamb.' And he said to me, 'These are the true words of God'" (Rev. 19:6–9, BSB).

The bride of Christ has made it to the wedding feast. All those who had the oil and Holy Spirit inside to endure to the end of their lives or of tribulation have made it to the table for the marriage supper of the Lamb. We've made it, but the beast, the dragon, and all the demons who followed after them will still need to be dealt with.

"Then I saw an angel coming down from heaven with the key to the Abyss, holding in his hand a great chain. He seized the dragon, that ancient serpent who is the devil and Satan, and bound him for a thousand years. And he threw him into the Abyss, shut it, and sealed it over him, so that he could not deceive the nations until the thousand years were complete. After that, he must be released for a brief period of time" (Rev. 20:3, BSB).

The great deceiver has been bound up and sealed into the abyss for one thousand years. Christ is about to reign on earth for what many call the millennial reign. "Then I saw the thrones, and those seated on them had been given authority to judge. And I saw the souls of those who had been beheaded for their testimony of Jesus and for the word of God, and those who had not worshiped the beast or its image, and had not received its mark on their foreheads or hands. And they came to life and reigned with Christ for a thousand years" (Rev. 20:4).

Christ already told us that the twelve disciples of Christ are those seated on the thrones and given authority to judge. "Jesus said to them, 'Truly, I say to you, in the new world, when the Son of Man will sit on his glorious throne, you who have followed me will also sit on twelve thrones, judging the twelve tribes of Israel'" (Mt. 19:28, ESV).

There is great reward for those who endure the hardships of tribulation and hold onto their faith. For one thousand years, Christ will reign with those who went through tribulation and did not receive the mark of the beast, didn't follow him, and those who were killed in the name of Christ.

"The rest of the dead did not come back to life until the thousand years were complete. This is the first resurrection. Blessed and holy are those who share in the first resurrection! The second death has no power over them, but they will be priests of God and of Christ, and will reign with Him for a thousand years" (Rev. 20:5–6, BSB).

Notice it says "the rest of the dead"—those who reign with Christ are the ones who were martyred, killed, or endured to the end of Tribulation—the only other believers not present would be those who died before the tribulation. Notice no mention of the pre-tribulation raptured saints who wouldn't have been "dead" because there are *none*, no such thing occurred. The true rapture and the second coming of Christ happened in Revelation chapter 16 and 18. There are only two sets of believers, those who made it through or died for their faith in Christ during the tribulation and those who were already dead and gone…"the rest of the dead."

In the last chapter, we looked at Revelation 18 and read of "the kings of the earth who committed sexual immorality and lived in luxury with her will weep and wail at the sight of the smoke rising from the fire that consumes her. In fear of her torment, they will stand at a distance and cry out." The merchants, shipmasters, passengers, and sailors "will stand [also] at a distance, in fear of her torment." This description gives us information often overlooked. At this point, the church has been raptured, Babylon has been destroyed, but the rest of the wicked will stand at a distance and mourn. We are not told of anything happening to them. This gives a more significant understanding to the context of Revelation 20:6: "But they will be priests of God and of Christ and will reign with Him for a thousand years." It seems plausible that those who were not saints of God who neither turned or repented continue to live outside of the new Jerusalem for the thousand-year reign. The very last chapter of Revelation says, "Blessed are those who wash their robes, so that they will have the right to the tree of life and may enter the city by the gates. Outside are the dogs and sorcerers and fornicators and murderers and idolaters, and everyone who loves and practices falsehood" (verses 14–15) This section is often lumped together into the description of the new heaven and earth; but there will be no dogs and sorcerers, fornicators, murderers, idolaters. And everyone who loves and practices falsehoods are to stay outside of the gate of the city. If this were the second heaven, these sinners would have already been thrown into the lake of fire, therefore, I'm pretty certain this is a description of the millennial reign, not the second heaven.

Between the blowing of the sixth and seventh trumpet, we read of these very same people: "The rest of humankind, who were not killed by these plagues, did not repent of the works of their hands or give up worshiping demons and idols of gold and silver and bronze and stone and wood, which cannot see or hear or walk. And they did not repent of their murders or their sorceries or their fornication or their thefts" (Rev. 9:20, NRSV).

We see that after the thousand years are complete, Satan is released and allowed to go out to deceive the nations but is cut off by our Lord and Savior and thrown into the lake of fire and then the judgment of the dead; anyone whose name was not written in the Book of Life will then be thrown into the lake of fire too but not until after the millennial.

"Then I saw an angel standing in the sun, and he cried out in a loud voice to all the birds flying overhead, 'Come, gather together for the great supper of God, so that you may eat the flesh of kings and commanders and mighty men, of horses and riders, of everyone slave and free, small and great.' Then I saw the beast and the kings of the earth with their armies assembled to wage war against the One seated on the horse, and against His army. But the beast was captured along with the false prophet, who on its behalf had performed signs deceiving those who had the mark of the beast and worshiped its image. Both the beast and the false prophet were thrown alive into the fiery lake of burning sulfur. And the rest were killed with the sword that proceeded from the mouth of the One seated on the horse. And all the birds gorged themselves on their flesh" (Rev. 20:10 BSB).

"When the thousand years are complete, Satan will be released from his prison, and will go out to deceive the nations in the four corners of the earth—Gog and Magog—to assemble them for battle. Their number is like the sand of the seashore. And they marched across the broad expanse of the earth and surrounded the camp of the saints and the beloved city. But fire came down from heaven and consumed them (Rev. 20:7–9 BSB). And the devil who had deceived them was thrown into the lake of fire and sulfur, into which the beast and the false prophet had already been thrown. There they will be tormented day and night forever and ever" (Rev. 20:7–10, BSB).

Notice that the nonbelievers are dealt with *after* the millennial reign. When "Satan is released from his prison, he goes out to deceive the nations…" I think "the nations" have to still be there on the battered earth, outside the gates of the new Jerusalem. Satan, otherwise, would have no one to "gather for battle and march across the broad expanse of the earth and surround the camp of the saints and beloved city" with. It is after God thwarts the planned battle of the deceiver and his armed forces that judgment finally occurs.

"Then I saw a great white throne and the One seated on it. Earth and heaven fled from His presence, and no place was found for them. And I saw the dead, great and small, standing before the throne. And there were open books, and one of them was the Book of Life. And the dead were judged according to their deeds, as recorded in the books. The sea gave up its dead, and Death and Hades gave up their dead, and each one was judged according to his deeds. Then Death and Hades were thrown into the lake of fire. This is the second death—the lake of fire. And if anyone was found whose name was not written in the Book of Life, he was thrown into the lake of fire" (Rev. 20:11–15, BSB). This is an eternal fire that lasts forever according to Matthew 18:8, Matthew 25:41 and Jude 7.

"We will all stand before God's judgment seat" (Rom. 14:10, BSB). "For we must all appear before the judgment seat of Christ, so that each one may receive what is due for what he has done in the body, whether good or evil" (2 Cor. 5:10, ESV). "There is therefore now no condemnation for those who are in Christ Jesus" (Rom. 8:1, ESV). "The result of God's gracious gift is very different from the result of that one man's sin. For Adam's sin led to condemnation, but God's free gift leads to our being made right with God, even though we are guilty of many sins" (Rom. 5:16, NLT). Believers will be judged according to their good works—and rewarded. This is imperative to know as we refute the hyper-grace movement teaching that doing good works is equivalent to a "works-based faith" or "living under the law instead of under grace." We are called to "be careful not to perform [our] righteous acts before men to be seen by them. If [we] do, [we] will have no reward from [our] Father in heaven" (Matt. 6:1, BSB). But we are called to good works and will be judged for all of those (that we didn't do and brag about or make sure others knew of).

We would be remiss not to talk about the judgment of those who are not saved from this wrath. Studying through Scripture, we can find that there will be degrees of punishment for people. Just as our rewards are based on works, so too are the punishments for the works of the lost and evil. We can first look at this in Matthew 11:20–22, BSB: "Jesus denounced the cities in which most of His miracles had been performed, because they did not repent. 'Woe to you, Chorazin! Woe to you Bethsaida! For if the miracles that were performed in you had been performed in Tyre and Sidon, they would have repented long ago in sackcloth and ashes. *But I tell you, it will be more bearable for Tyre and Sidon on the day of judgment than for you*" (emphasis added). There is another scripture in Matthew where Jesus tells us "it will be more tolerable for the land of Sodom and Gomorrah in the day of judgment than for that city" (Matt. 10:15, BSB). These two scriptures allude to the difference in degrees of punishments for these cities compared to others notably known for their sin and lack of repentance.

There is another stark warning for believers to stay true and holdfast to their faith. In the book of Luke, we find "that a slave who knew his master's will and did not get ready or act in accord with his will, will receive many lashes, but the one who did not know it, and committed deeds worthy of flogging, will receive but few. From everyone who has given much, much will be required; and to whom they entrusted much, of him they will ask all the more" (Luke 12:47–48, NASB). The slaves referred to here are those who are supposedly in Christ. Recall 1 Corinthians 7:22 (ESV): "For he who was called in the Lord as a slave is a freedman of the Lord. Likewise, he who was free when called is a slave to Christ." This verse in Luke refers to those who were once slaves to Christ who did not get ready or act in accord with his will. We know that true enduring believers have no condemnation in Christ, but these people will receive many lashes. It reminds me of the scripture in Hebrews: "It is impossible for those who have once been enlightened, who have tasted the heavenly gift, who have shared in the Holy Spirit, who have tasted the goodness of the word of God and the powers of the coming age—and then have fallen away—to be restored to repentance, because they themselves are crucifying the Son of God all over again and subjecting Him to open shame" (Heb. 6:4–6, BSB) Remember the beginning of this warning from (Luke 12:35–48): We know this is about the servant who says in his heart, 'My master will be a long time in coming,' and begins to beat the menservants and maidservants, and to eat and drink and get drunk. The master of that servant will come on a day he does not expect and at that hour he does not anticipate. Then he will cut him to pieces and assign him a place with the unbelievers.

In this case, the degree of punishment is harsher for the person who once knew Christ and the will of God but turns from it and goes his or her own way. Again, whether this person was once saved and fell away or was never truly saved doesn't matter. We can't know the heart, but we can read clearly the outcome for these such people.

Once the books are referenced and the judgments are complete, those who have endured will hear "Well done my good and faithful servant" (Matt. 25:21). They will be ushered into heaven. "The home of God is among mortals. He will dwell with them; they will be his peoples, and God himself will be with them; he will wipe every tear from their eyes. Death will be no more; mourning and crying and pain will be no more, for the first things have passed away" (Rev. 21:3–4, NRSV).

"Then I saw a new heaven and a new earth, for the first heaven and the first earth had passed away, and the sea was no more. And I saw the holy city, new Jerusalem, coming down out of heaven from God, prepared as a bride adorned for her husband. And I heard a loud voice from the throne saying: 'Behold, the dwelling place of God is with man. He will dwell with them, and they will be his people, and God himself will be with them as their God. He will wipe away every tear from their eyes, and death shall be no more, neither shall there be mourning nor crying, nor pain anymore, for the former things have passed away.' And he who was seated on the throne said, 'Behold, I am making all things new.' Also he said, 'Write this down for these words are trustworthy and true.' And he said to me, 'It is done! I am the Alpha and the Omega, the beginning and the end. To the thirsty, I will give from the spring of the water of life without payment. The one who conquers will have this heritage, and I will be his God and he will be my son. But as for the cowardly, the faithless, the detestable, as for murderers, the sexually immoral, sorcerers, idolaters, and all liars, their portion will be in the lake that burns with fire and sulfur, which is the second death'" (Rev. 21:1–14, BSB).

"Then the angel showed me the river of the water of life, bright as crystal, flowing from the throne of God and of the Lamb through the middle of the street of the city. On either side of the river is the tree of life with its twelve kinds of fruit, producing its fruit each month; and the leaves of the tree are for the healing of the nations. Nothing accursed will be found there anymore. But the throne of God and the Lamb will be in it, and his servants will worship him; they will see his face and his name will be on their foreheads. And there will be no more night; they will need no light of lamp or sun for the Lord God will be their light, and they will reign forever and ever" (Rev. 22:1–5, NRSV).

I wonder if the name of the Lord on the foreheads, described here, is the seal of God described back in the seventh chapter of Revelation.

"'I, Jesus, have sent My angel to give you this testimony for the churches. I am the Root and the Offspring of David, the bright Morning Star.' The Spirit and the bride say, 'Come!' Let the one who hears say, 'Come!' And let the one who is thirsty come, and the one who desires the water of life drink freely. I testify to everyone who hears the words of prophecy in this book: If anyone adds to them, God will add to him the plagues described in this book. And if anyone takes away from the words of this book of prophecy, God will take away his share in the tree of life and the holy city, which are described in this book. He who testifies to these things says, 'Yes, I am coming soon.' Amen. Come, Lord Jesus! The grace of the Lord Jesus be with all the saints. Amen'" (Rev. 22:16–21, BSB).

Abbreviated Version of a Time Line of the End-Times

The Antichrist comes
(not necessarily titled the Antichrist but more than likely as an acceptable messiah or world leader type—He will have to be someone who the Jews allow to build a third temple and sit on the throne as their messiah and be of Assyrian decent)

Worldwide chaos—no peace
(men slaying one another)

Famine
(Food will be scarce and overpriced.)

Death
(One-quarter of the world population will die by sword, famine, plague, and beasts of the earth.)

The Antichrist receives a fatal wound to the head—but will be healed miraculously.

The Antichrist will be given authority for forty-two months. The Antichrist will set up the abomination of desolation and abolish the daily sacrifice.

The Antichrist will bring world peace.

The Antichrist will make a seven-year covenant
with the world's nations for peace.

The mark of the beast will be rolled out and given to all who
will take it. (DON'T TAKE THE MARK OF THE BEAST.)
The Antichrist will wage war on the saints.
*(Believers will be betrayed by parents, brothers, relatives, and other
so-called believers—who will think they are doing good for the Lord.)*
Two witnesses will be on earth for 1,290 days.
The saints will be sealed with the seal of God.
There will be half an hour of silence in heaven.
Saint's prayers will go up to God like incense.
The people of God will be nourished for forty-two months.
Man will NOT be able to kill themselves.
Man will not repent of their sins.
Hail, fire, and blood will come from the sky,
and one-third of the earth will burn up.
Loathsome malignant sores break out on the ones who worship
the beast and his image and have taken the mark of the beast.
A great mountain will burn with fire and be thrown
into the sea. One-third of the sea creatures will die.
Wormwood falls from the sky and causes
bitter freshwater to turn into blood.
A supernova will occur, and one-third of
the sun and stars will go out.
For FIVE months—locusts with scorpion tails will
torment those with the mark of the beast.
One-third of mankind will be killed.
The Euphrates River will dry up.
The two witnesses will be killed, laid on the street for three
days, and then God will take them up to heaven with him.
The abomination of desolation will occur.
(The Antichrist will sit at the temple of God as God…)
Forty-five more days
The sun darkens.
The moon turns red.

Stars fall.
Great earthquakes
Mountains and islands removed
Man hides in caves and begs rocks to fall on them.
Flashes of lightning, peals of thunder, huge hail
Sky recedes like a scroll.
Christ comes in the clouds.
Rapture of the saints
(First those who have died before this time and then those who did not take the mark of the beast and lived through the Tribulation)
The final hour
(Babylon falls—who is modern-day Babylon?)
The marriage supper of the lamb
The Antichrist and the image are thrown into the lake of fire
Satan is chained for one thousand years.
The millennial reign of Christ
(With those who were martyrs during the Tribulation and those who survived the Great Tribulation alive and who endured to the end)
After the one-thousand-year reign—Satan is released from his chains and gathers the nations together to war against Christ.
Fire comes down and devours them!
Satan is cast into the LAKE of FIRE.
Judgment of all people
Hades and the sea give up their dead for judgment
Saints spend ETERNITY IN HEAVEN with God the Father, Christ the Son, and the precious Holy Spirit.

A Time Line of the End Times

Leading up to Tribulation

The Gospel must first be preached to all the nations. (Matt. 24:14, Mark 13:10)

'And in the last days it shall be, God declares, that I will pour out my Spirit on all flesh, and your sons and your daughters shall prophesy, and your young men shall see visions, and your old men shall dream dreams; (Acts 2:17)

As it was in the days of Noah, so will it be at the coming of the Son of Man. For in the days before the flood, people were eating and drinking, marrying and giving in marriage, up to the day Noah entered the ark. And they were oblivious, until the flood came and swept them all away. So will it be at the coming of the Son of Man. (Matt. 24:37–39)

Because of the multiplication of wickedness, the love of most will grow cold. (Matt. 24:12)

But the Spirit explicitly says that in later times some will fall away from the faith, paying attention to deceitful spirits and doctrines of demons, by means of the hypocrisy of liars seared in their own conscience as with a branding iron, (1 Tim. 4:1–2)

But realize this, that in the last days difficult times will come. For men will be lovers of self, lovers of money, boastful, arrogant, revilers, disobedient to parents, ungrateful, unholy, unloving, irreconcilable, malicious gossips, without self-control, brutal, haters of good, treacherous, reckless, conceited, lovers of pleasure rather than lovers of God, holding to a form of godliness, although they have denied its power; Avoid such men as these. (2 Tim. 3:1–5)

For the time will come when they will not endure sound doctrine; but wanting to have their ears tickled, they will accumulate for themselves teachers in accordance to their own desires, and will turn away their ears from the truth and will turn aside to myths. (2 Tim. 4:3–4)

No one should deceive you in any way, because it is not until the apostasy shall have come first, and the man of lawlessness shall have been revealed—the son of destruction, (2 Thess. 2:3)

World Unrest: Wars

You will hear of wars and rumors of wars, but see to it that you are not alarmed. These things must happen, but the end is still to come. Nation will rise against nation, and kingdom against kingdom. There will be famines and earthquakes in various places. All these are the beginning of birth pains. (Matt. 24:6–8)

The Beast/Antichrist Is Revealed (Seal 1)	World Unrest: Violence (Seal 2)	Food Prices Increase, Famine, Plague, Animals Killing People (Seals 3 and 4)
So I looked and saw a white horse, and its rider held a bow. And he was given a crown, and he rode out to overcome and conquer. (Rev. 6:2)	*Then another horse went forth. It was bright red, and its rider was granted permission to take away peace from the earth and to make men slay one another. And he was given a great sword.* (Rev. 6:4)	*…Then I looked and saw a black horse, and its rider held in his hand a pair of scales. And I heard what sounded like a voice from among the four living creatures, saying, "A quart of wheat for a denarius, and three quarts of barley for a denarius, and do not harm the oil and wine."* (Rev. 6:5–6)
"At the end time the king of the South will collide with him, and the king of the North will storm against him with chariots, with horsemen and with many ships; and he will enter countries, overflow them and pass through. "He will also enter the Beautiful Land, and many countries will fall; but these will be rescued out of his hand: Edom, Moab and the foremost of the sons of Ammon. "Then he will stretch out his hand against other countries, and the land of Egypt will not escape. "But he will gain control over the hidden treasures of gold and silver and over all the precious things of Egypt; and Libyans and Ethiopians will follow at his heels. "But rumors from the East and from the North will disturb him, and he will go forth with great wrath to destroy and annihilate many. (Dan 11:40–45)		*Then I looked and saw a pale green horse. Its rider's name was Death, and Hades followed close behind. And they were given authority over a fourth of the earth, to kill by sword, by famine, by plague, and by the beasts of the earth.* [According to www.census.gov/popclock/world, there are approximately 7.8 billion people on earth today. One-fourth of the population would be just under 2 billion people.] (Rev. 6:8)

The Beast

Then I saw a beast coming up out of the sea, having ten horns and seven heads, and on his horns were ten diadems, and on his heads were blasphemous names. And the beast which I saw was like a leopard, and his feet were like those of a bear, and his mouth like the mouth of a lion. And the dragon gave him his power and his throne and great authority. I saw one of his heads as if it had been slain, and his fatal wound was healed. And the whole earth was amazed and followed after the beast; they worshiped the dragon because he gave his authority to the beast; and they worshiped the beast, saying, "Who is like the beast, and who is able to wage war with him?" There was given to him a mouth speaking arrogant words and blasphemies, and authority to act for forty-two months was given to him. And he opened his mouth in blasphemies against God, to blaspheme His name and His tabernacle, that is, those who dwell in heaven. (Rev. 13:1–6)

"Here is the mind which has wisdom. The seven heads are seven mountains on which the woman sits, and they are seven kings; five have fallen, one is, the other has not yet come; and when he comes, he must remain a little while. "The beast which was and is not, is himself also an eighth and is one of the seven, and he goes to destruction. "The ten horns which you saw are ten kings who have not yet received a kingdom, but they receive authority as kings with the beast for one hour. "These have one purpose, and they give their power and authority to the beast. (Rev. 17:9–13)

Let no one deceive you in any way, for it will not come until the rebellion occurs and the man of lawlessness—the son of destruction—is revealed. (2 Thess. 2:3)

UNDESERVING YET ENTITLED

The Antichrist Comes to Power for Forty-Two Months (World Leader)	The Witnesses Have Power for Forty-Two Months	The People of God Will Be Nourished for Forty-Two Months
The beast was given a mouth to speak arrogant and blasphemous words, and authority to act for 42 months. And the beast opened its mouth to speak blasphemies against God and to slander His name and His tabernacle—those who dwell in heaven. Then the beast was permitted to wage war against the saints and to conquer them, and it was given authority over every tribe and people and tongue and nation. And all who dwell on the earth will worship the beast—all whose names have not been written from the foundation of the world in the Book of Life belonging to the Lamb who was slain. (Rev. 13:5-8)	*Then I was given a measuring rod like a staff and was told, "Go and measure the temple of God and the altar, and count the number of worshipers there. But exclude the courtyard outside the temple. Do not measure it, because it has been given over to the nations, and they will trample the holy city for 42 months. And I will empower my two witnesses, and they will prophesy for 1,260 days, clothed in sackcloth."* (Rev. 11:1-3) *"Behold, I will send you Elijah the prophet before the great and awesome day of the LORD comes.* (Mal. 4:5)	*And the woman fled into the wilderness, where God had prepared a place for her to be nourished for 1,260 days.* (Rev. 12:6)

This is what he said: 'The fourth beast is a fourth kingdom that will appear on the earth, different from all the other kingdoms, and it will devour the whole earth, trample it down, and crush it. And the ten horns are ten kings who will rise from this kingdom. After them another king, different from the earlier ones, will rise and subdue three kings. He will speak out against the Most High and oppress the saints of the Most High, intending to change the appointed times and laws; and the saints will be given into his hand for a time, and times, and half a time. (Dan. 7:23–25)

"*Then he shall confirm a covenant with many for one week; But in the middle of the week He shall bring an end to sacrifice and offering. And on the wing of abominations shall be one who makes desolate, even until the consummation, which is determined, is poured out on the desolate.*" (Dan. 9:27)

"*From the time that the regular sacrifice is abolished and the abomination of desolation is set up, there will be 1,290 days.* (Dan. 12:11)

UNDESERVING YET ENTITLED

The Beast Deceives the World to Believe He Is above God and Can Solve World Unrest* and Bring Peace	Mark of the Beast	Wages War Against the Saints	The Beast Sets Up the Abomination of Desolation
There was given to him a mouth speaking arrogant words and blasphemies, and authority to act for forty-two months was given to him. (Rev. 13:5) *And he deceives those who dwell on the earth because of the signs which it was given him to perform in the presence of the beast, telling those who dwell on the earth to make an image to the beast who had the wound of the sword and has come to life. And it was given to him to give breath to the image of the beast, so that the image of the beast would even speak and cause as many as do not worship the image of the beast to be killed.* (Rev. 13:14–15)	*And he causes all, the small and the great, and the rich and the poor, and the free men and the slaves, to be given a mark on their right hand or on their forehead, and he provides that no one will be able to buy or to sell, except the one who has the mark, either the name of the beast or the number of his name. Here is wisdom. Let him who has understanding calculate the number of the beast, for the number is that of a man; and his number is six hundred and sixty-six.* (Rev. 13:16–18)	*And the beast was allowed to wage war against God's holy people and to conquer them. And he was given authority to rule over every tribe and people and language and nation.* (Rev. 13:7) *Then I wanted to know the true meaning of the fourth beast, which was different from all the others—extremely terrifying—devouring and crushing with iron teeth and bronze claws, then trampling underfoot whatever was left. I also wanted to know about the ten horns on its head and the other horn that came up, before which three of them fell—the horn whose appearance was more imposing than the others, with eyes and with a mouth that spoke words of arrogance.*	*So when you see the abomination of desolation standing where it should not be (let the reader understand), then let those who are in Judea flee to the mountains.* (Mark 13:4) *So when you see standing in the holy place 'the abomination of desolation, described by the prophet Daniel (let the reader understand),* (Matthew 24:15) *But when you see Jerusalem surrounded by armies, you will know that her desolation is near.* (Luke 21:20)

*In the last days the mountain of the house of the L*ORD *will be established as the chief of the mountains; it will be raised above the hills, and all nations will stream to it. And many peoples will come and say: "Come, let us go up to the mountain of the L*ORD*, to the house of the God of Jacob. He will teach us His ways so that we may walk in His paths." For the law will go forth from Zion, and the word of the L*ORD *from Jerusalem. Then He will judge between the nations and arbitrate for many peoples. They will beat their swords into plowshares and their spears into pruning hooks. Nation will no longer take up the sword against nation, nor train anymore for war.* (Isa. 2:2–4)

As I watched, this horn was waging war against the saints and prevailing against them, until the Ancient of Days arrived and pronounced judgment in favor of the saints of the Most High, and the time came for them to possess the kingdom. This is what he said: 'The fourth beast is a fourth kingdom that will appear on the earth, different from all the other kingdoms, and it will devour the whole earth, trample it down, and crush it. And the ten horns are ten kings who will rise from this kingdom. After them another king, different from the earlier ones, will rise and subdue three kings. He will speak out against the Most High and oppress the saints of the Most High, intending to change the appointed times and laws; and the saints will be given into his hand for a time, and times, and half a time. (Dan. 7:19–25)

At the appointed time he will invade the South again, but this time will not be like the first. Ships of Kittim will come against him, and he will lose heart. Then he will turn back and rage against the holy covenant and do damage. So he will return and show favor to those who forsake the holy covenant. His forces will rise up and desecrate the temple fortress. They will abolish the daily sacrifice and set up the abomination of desolation. (Dan. 11:29–31)

"From the time that the regular sacrifice is abolished and the abomination of desolation is set up, there will be 1,290 days. "How blessed is he who keeps waiting and attains to the 1,335 days! "But as for you, go your way to the end; then you will enter into rest and rise again for your allotted portion at the end of the age." (Dan. 12:11–13)

UNDESERVING YET ENTITLED

With flattery he will corrupt those who violate the covenant, but the people who know their God will firmly resist him. Those with insight will instruct many, though for a time they will fall by sword or flame, or be captured or plundered. Now when they fall, they will be granted a little help, but many will join them insincerely. Some of the wise will fall, so that they may be refined, purified, and made spotless until the time of the end, for it will still come at the appointed time. "Then the king will do as he pleases, and he will exalt and magnify himself above every god and will speak monstrous things against the God of gods; and he will prosper until the indignation is finished, for that which is decreed will be done. "He will show no regard for the gods of his fathers or for the desire of women, nor will he show regard for any other god; for he will magnify himself above them all.

"At the appointed time he will return and come into the South, but this last time it will not turn out the way it did before. "For ships of Kittim will come against him; therefore he will be disheartened and will return and become enraged at the holy covenant and take action; so he will come back and show regard for those who forsake the holy covenant. "Forces from him will arise, desecrate the sanctuary fortress, and do away with the regular sacrifice. And they will set up the abomination of desolation. "By smooth words he will turn to godlessness those who act wickedly toward the covenant, but the people who know their God will display strength and take action.

"But instead he will honor a god of fortresses, a god whom his fathers did not know; he will honor him with gold, silver, costly stones and treasures. "He will take action against the strongest of fortresses with the help of a foreign god; he will give great honor to those who acknowledge him and will cause them to rule over the many, and will parcel out land for a price. (Daniel 11:32–39)

"Those who have insight among the people will give understanding to the many; yet they will fall by sword and by flame, by captivity and by plunder for many days. "Now when they fall they will be granted a little help, and many will join with them in hypocrisy. "Some of those who have insight will fall, in order to refine, purge and make them pure until the end time; because it is still to come at the appointed time. (Dan. 11:29–35)

You will be betrayed even by parents and brothers and relatives and friends, and some of you will be put to death. And you will be hated by everyone because of My name. Yet not even a hair of your head will perish. (Luke 21:16–18)

Seal 5
And when the Lamb opened the fifth seal, I saw under the altar the souls of those who had been slain for the word of God and for the testimony they had upheld. And they cried out in a loud voice, "How long, O Lord, holy and true, until You avenge our blood and judge those who dwell upon the earth?" Then each of them was given a white robe and told to rest a little while longer, until the full number of their fellow servants, their brothers, were killed, just as they had been killed. (Rev. 6:9–11)
Seal of God Put on the Foreheads of the Saints
After this I saw four angels standing at the four corners of the earth, holding back its four winds so that no wind would blow on land or sea or on any tree. And I saw another angel ascending from the east, with the seal of the living God. And he called out in a loud voice to the four angels who had been given power to harm the land and the sea: "Do not harm the land or sea or trees until we have sealed the foreheads of the servants of our God." (Rev. 7:1–3)
Those with the Seal of God
"These are the ones who have come out of the great tribulation; they have washed their robes and made them white in the blood of the Lamb. (Rev. 7:1–3)
Seal 7
…When the Lamb opened the seventh seal, there was silence in heaven for about half an hour. And I saw the seven angels who stand before God, and they were given seven trumpets. (Rev. 8:1)

*Note: The only way for trumpets 1 to 6 (and bowls 1 to 6) to occur is if seal 7 is only the seventh seal John saw but not opened since seal 6, trumpet 7, and bowl 7 all match in their description and lead in to the Rapture, the binding of Satan, the millennial reign, the Last Judgment, and heaven.

Another theory is that seals 1 to 7 are the opening scrolls that release the end-times events to unfold. If this is the case, the first and second seals usher in the beast/antichrist; the third and fourth are the ushering in of the trumpets and bowls of wrath; the fifth reminds us that the saints are persecuted, killed, and survive throughout the Tribulation; the sixth describes the final end before the Rapture; and the seventh releases the angels to blow the trumpets and pour out the bowls. Revelation 7 describes the saints being sealed by God on their foreheads. This must happen before the bowls and trumpets are blown and poured out because there is reference to those who are sealed: "They were told not to harm the grass of the earth or any plant or tree, but only those who did not have the seal of God on their foreheads" (Rev. 9:4).

I'm open to other options…

Just before the Trumpets Are Blown
And the smoke of the incense, with the prayers of the saints, went up before God out of the angel's hand. [The saints are still present to pray and for their prayers to go up before God.] (Rev. 8:4)
In those days men will seek death and will not find it; they will long to die, but death will escape them. (Rev. 9:6)
Trumpet 1
Then the first angel sounded his trumpet, and hail and fire mixed with blood were hurled down upon the earth. A third of the earth was burned up, along with a third of the trees and all the green grass. (Rev. 8:7)
Bowl 1
Then I heard a loud voice from the temple saying to the seven angels, <u>"Go, pour out on the earth the seven bowls of God's wrath."</u> So the first angel went and poured out his bowl on the earth, and loathsome, malignant sores broke out on those who had the mark of the beast and worshiped its image. (Rev. 16:2; emphasis added)
The Two Witnesses
These witnesses have power to shut the sky so that no rain will fall during the days of their prophecy, and power to turn the waters into blood and to strike the earth with every kind of plague as often as they wish. (Rev. 11:6)

Trumpet 2	Peter's Warning	Bowl 2
Then the second angel sounded his trumpet, and something like a great mountain burning with fire was thrown into the sea. A third of the sea turned to blood, a third of the living creatures in the sea died, and a third of the ships were destroyed. (Revelation 8:8–9)	*But the day of the Lord will come as unexpectedly as a thief. Then the heavens will pass away with a terrible noise, and the very elements themselves will disappear in fire, and the earth and everything on it will be found to deserve judgment.* (2 Pet. 3:10)	*The second angel poured out his bowl into the sea, and it became like the blood of a corpse, and every living thing died that was in the sea.* (Rev. 16:4)

Trumpet 3	Bowl 3
Then the third angel sounded his trumpet, and a great star burning like a torch fell from heaven and landed on a third of the rivers and on the springs of water. The name of the star is Wormwood. A third of the waters turned bitter like wormwood oil, and many people died from the bitter waters. (Rev. 8:10–11)	*And the third angel poured out his bowl into the rivers and springs of water, and they turned to blood. And I heard the angel of the waters say: "Righteous are You, O Holy One, who is and was, because You have brought these judgments. For they have spilled the blood of saints and prophets, and You have given them blood to drink, as they deserve."* (Rev. 16:4–6)
Bowl 4	**Trumpet 4**
Then the fourth angel poured out his bowl on the sun, and it was given power to scorch the people with fire. And the people were scorched by intense heat, and they cursed the name of God, who had authority over these plagues; <u>yet they did not repent and give Him glory.</u> (Rev. 16:8–9; emphasis added)	*Then the fourth angel sounded his trumpet, and a third of the sun and moon and stars were struck. A third of the stars were darkened, a third of the day was without light, and a third of the night as well.* (Rev. 8:12)
These two match if it is a supernova; first, it would scorch the	people with intense heat, then it would be darkened…
Trumpet 5	**Bowl 5**
Then the fifth angel sounded his trumpet, and I saw a star that had fallen from heaven [Satan is the fallen star] to earth, and it was given the key to the pit of the Abyss. The star opened the pit of the Abyss, and smoke rose out of it like the smoke of a great furnace, and the sun and the air were darkened by the smoke from the pit. (Rev. 9:1–2)	*And the fifth angel poured out his bowl on the throne of the beast, and its kingdom was plunged into darkness, and men began to gnaw their tongues in anguish and curse the God of heaven for their pains and sores; <u>yet they did not repent of their deeds.</u>* (Rev. 16:10–11; emphasis added)
The First Woe Has Passed	
The first woe has passed. Behold, two woes are still to follow. (Rev. 9:12)	

Notice no one is repenting of their deeds. Those with the seal of God were already believers who were living through the tribulation. The Rapture has not happened up to this point.

Ordered Not to Harm Those with the Seal of God

And out of the smoke, locusts descended on the earth, and they were given power like that of the scorpions of the earth. They were told not to harm the grass of the earth or any plant or tree, <u>but only those who did not have the seal of God on their foreheads</u>. The locusts were not given power to kill them, but only to torment them for five months, and their torment was like the stinging of a scorpion. In those days men will seek death and will not find it; they will long to die, but death will escape them. And the locusts looked like horses prepared for battle, with something like crowns of gold on their heads, and faces like the faces of men. They had hair like that of women, and teeth like those of lions. They also had thoraxes like breastplates of iron, and the sound of their wings was like the roar of many horses and chariots rushing into battle. They had tails with stingers like scorpions, which had the power to injure people for five months. They were ruled by a king, the angel of the Abyss. His name in Hebrew is Abaddon, and in Greek it is Apollyon. (Rev. 9:3–11; emphasis added)

Trumpet 6	Bowl 6
Then the sixth angel sounded his trumpet, and I heard a voice from the four horns of the golden altar before God saying to the sixth angel with the trumpet, "Release the four angels who are bound at the great river Euphrates." So the four angels who had been prepared for this hour and day and month and year were released to kill a third of mankind. And the number of mounted troops was two hundred million; I heard their number. (Rev. 9:13–16)	*And the sixth angel poured out his bowl on the great river Euphrates, and its water was dried up to prepare the way for the kings of the East.* (Rev. 16:12)

The End of the Two Witnesses on Earth

When the two witnesses have finished their testimony, the beast that comes up from the Abyss will wage war with them, and will overpower and kill them. Their bodies will lie in the street of the great city—figuratively called Sodom and Egypt—where their Lord was also crucified. For three and a half days all peoples and tribes and tongues and nations will view their bodies and will not permit them to be laid in a tomb. And those who dwell on the earth will gloat over them, and will celebrate and send one another gifts, because these two prophets had tormented them. But after the three and a half days, the breath of life from God entered the two witnesses, and they stood on their feet, and great fear fell upon those who saw them. And the witnesses heard a loud voice from heaven saying, "Come up here." And they went up to heaven in a cloud as their enemies watched them. And in that hour there was a great earthquake, and a tenth of the city collapsed. Seven thousand were killed in the quake, and the rest were terrified and gave glory to the God of heaven. <u>*The second woe has passed. Behold, the third woe is coming shortly.*</u> [The third woe is never specified after this.] (Rev. 11:7–14; emphasis added)

3 1/2 Years In

Abomination of Desolation

"Then he shall confirm a covenant with many for one week; But in the middle of the week He shall bring an end to sacrifice and offering. And on the wing of abominations shall be one who makes desolate, even until the consummation, which is determined, is poured out on the desolate." (Dan. 9:27)

Forces from him shall appear and profane the temple and fortress, and shall take away the regular burnt offering. And they shall set up the abomination that makes desolate." (Dan. 11:31)

But when you see Jerusalem surrounded by armies, you will know that her desolation is near. (Luke 21:20)

"From the time that the regular sacrifice is abolished and the abomination of desolation is set up, there will be 1,290 days. "How blessed is he who keeps waiting and attains to the 1,335 days! "But as for you, go your way to the end; then you will enter into rest and rise again for your allotted portion at the end of the age." There are 45 more days after the Abomination of Desolation… (Dan. 12:11–13)

After Tribulation

For then there will be <u>great tribulation, such as has not been from the beginning of the world until now,</u> no, <u>and never will be seen again</u>... "*Immediately after the tribulation of those days the sun will be darkened, and the moon will not give its light, and the stars will fall from heaven, and the powers of the heavens will be shaken.* (Matt. 24:21,29; emphasis added)

Because scripture tells us that this tribulation is greater than has ever been seen and will never be seen again, I conclude that all the seals, trumpets, and bowls must be included in the tribulation.

The Last Trumpet

In Revelation 8:1, seal 7 opens the trumpets.

Behold, I tell you a mystery; we will not all sleep, but we will all be changed, in a moment, in the twinkling of an eye, at the last trumpet; for the trumpet will sound, and the dead will be raised imperishable, and we will be changed. (1 Cor. 15:51–52)

At that time the sign of the Son of Man will appear in heaven, and all the tribes of the earth will mourn. They will see the Son of Man coming on the clouds of heaven, with power and great glory. And He will send out His angels with a loud trumpet call, and they will gather His elect from the four winds, from one end of the heavens to the other. (Matt. 24:30–31)

Seal 6 and Seal 7	Trumpet 7	Bowl 7
And when I saw the Lamb open the sixth seal, there was a great earthquake, and the **sun became black like sackcloth of goat hair, and the whole moon turned blood red, and the stars of the sky fell** to the earth like unripe figs dropping from a tree shaken by a great wind. The sky receded like a scroll being rolled up, and every **mountain and island was moved from its place.** Then the kings of the earth, the nobles, the commanders, the rich, the mighty, and every slave and free man hid in the caves and among the rocks of the mountains. And they said to the mountains and the rocks, "Fall on us and hide us from the face of the One seated on the throne, and from the wrath of the Lamb. For the great day of Their wrath has come, and who is able to withstand it?" (Rev. 6:12–17, 8:1; emphasis added)	But in the days of the voice of the seventh angel, when he is about to sound his trumpet, the mystery of God will be fulfilled, just as He proclaimed to His servants the prophets."... Then the seventh angel sounded his trumpet, and loud voices called out in heaven: ... Then the temple of God in heaven was opened, and the ark of His covenant appeared in His temple. And there were **flashes of lightning, and rumblings, and peals of thunder**, and an **earthquake**, and a great hailstorm. (Rev. 10:7, 11:15, 19; emphasis added)	Then the seventh angel poured out his bowl into the air, and a loud voice came from the throne in the temple, saying, "It is done!" And there were **flashes of lightning, and rumblings, and peals of thunder,** and a great earthquake the likes of which had not occurred since men were upon the earth—so mighty was the great quake. The great city was split into three parts, and the cities of the nations collapsed. And God remembered Babylon the great and gave her the cup of the wine of the fury of His wrath. **Then every island fled, and no mountain could be found**. And **great hailstones** weighing almost a hundred pounds each rained down on them from above. And men cursed God for the plague of hail, because it was so horrendous. (Rev. 16:17–20)

Sun, Moon, and Stars	Sky Recedes Like a Scroll	Flashes of Lightening, Rumblings, and Peals of Thunder	Great Earthquakes / Every Mountain and Island is Moved / Hail	Angels / Four Winds
Revelation 6:12–13	Revelation 6:14			Mark 13:27 Matthew 24:31
Seal 6 Joel 2:10, 31, 3:15 Amos 8:9 Matthew 24:29 Mark 13:24 Luke 21:25 Isaiah 13:10	Seal 6 Revelation 11:19 Trumpet 7 2 Peter 3:10	Revelation 8:5 Revelation 11:19 Trumpet 7 Revelation 16:17 Bowl 7 2 Peter 3:10	Revelation 8:5 Revelation 16:18–21 Bowl 7 Revelation 6:14 Seal 6 2 Peter 3:10	

Jesus Foretold the Details of His Second Coming

"Immediately *after the tribulation* of those days the sun will be darkened, and the moon will not give its light, and the stars will fall from heaven, and the powers of the heavens will be shaken. Then will appear in heaven the sign of the Son of Man, and then all the tribes of the earth will mourn, and they will see the Son of Man coming on the clouds of heaven with power and great glory. And he will send out his angels with a loud trumpet call, and they will gather his elect from the four winds, from one end of heaven to the other… So also, when you see all these things, you will know that He is near, right at the door. (Matthew 24:29-31, 33)

The Hour…

Because you have kept my word about patient endurance, I will keep you from the hour of trial that is coming on the whole world, to try those who dwell on the earth. (Rev. 3:10)

And he said with a loud voice, "Fear God and give him glory, because the hour of his judgment has come, and worship him who made heaven and earth, the sea and the springs of water." (Rev. 14:7)

But I have said these things to you, that when their hour comes you may remember that I told them to you. "I did not say these things to you from the beginning, because I was with you. (John 16:4)

UNDESERVING YET ENTITLED

Watch therefore, for you know neither the day nor the hour. (Matt. 25:13)

"You too, be ready; for the Son of Man is coming at an hour that you do not expect."…the master of that slave will come on a day when he does not expect him and at an hour he does not know, and will cut him in pieces, and assign him a place with the unbelievers. (Luke 12:40, 46)

He comes as a *thief*…

Remember, then, what you received and heard. Keep it, and repent. If you will not wake up, I will come like a thief, and you will not know at what hour I will come against you. (Rev. 3:3)

For you yourselves are fully aware that the day of the Lord will come like a thief in the night. (1 Thess. 5:2)

"Behold, I am coming like a thief. Blessed is the one who remains awake and clothed, so that he will not go naked and let his shame be exposed." (Rev. 16:15)

The Rider on the White Horse	Rapture	Battle with the Beast / Babylon Falls
And I saw heaven opened, and behold, a white horse, and He who sat on it is called Faithful and True, and in righteousness He judges and wages war. His eyes are a flame of fire, and on His head are many diadems; and He has a name written on Him which no one knows except Himself. He is clothed with a robe dipped in blood, and His name is called The Word of God.	For this we declare to you by a word from the Lord, that we who are alive, who are left until the coming of the Lord, will not precede those who have fallen asleep. For the Lord himself will descend from heaven with a cry of command, with the voice of an archangel, and with the sound of the trumpet of God. And the dead in Christ will rise first. Then we who are alive, who are left, will be caught up together with them in the clouds to meet the Lord in the air, and so we will always be with the Lord. (1 Thess. 4:15–17)	The ten horns you saw are ten kings who have not yet received a kingdom, but who for one hour will receive authority as kings along with the beast. (Rev. 17:12)

*And the armies which are in heaven, clothed in fine linen, white and clean, were following Him on white horses. From His mouth comes a sharp sword, so that with it He may strike down the nations, and He will rule them with a rod of iron; and He treads the wine press of the fierce wrath of God, the Almighty. And on His robe and on His thigh He has a name written, "*K<small>ING</small> <small>OF</small> <small>KINGS</small>, <small>AND</small> L<small>ORD</small> <small>OF</small> <small>LORDS</small>.*" Then I saw an angel standing in the sun, and he cried out with a loud voice, saying to all the birds which fly in midheaven, "Come, assemble for the great supper of God, so that you may eat the flesh of kings and the flesh of commanders and the flesh of mighty men and the flesh of horses and of those who sit on them and the flesh of all men, both free men and slaves, and small and great." And I saw the beast and the kings of the earth and their armies assembled to make war against Him who sat on the horse and against His army.* (Rev. 19:11–19)

Then there will be two men in the field; one will be taken and one will be left. (Matt. 24:40)

I tell you, on that night there will be two in one bed; one will be taken and the other will be left. (Luke 17:34)

Then I heard another voice from heaven say: "Come out of her, My people, so that you will not share in her sins or contract any of her plagues. (Rev. 18:4)

"Fallen, fallen is Babylon the great! She has become a lair for demons and a haunt for every unclean spirit, every unclean bird, and every detestable beast. All the nations have drunk the wine of the passion of her immorality. The kings of the earth were immoral with her, and the merchants of the earth have grown wealthy from the extravagance of her luxury."… For in a single hour your judgment has come."… For in a single hour such fabulous wealth has been destroyed!"… For in a single hour she has been destroyed." (Rev. 18:1–3, 10, 17, 19)

At that very hour there was a severe earthquake and a tenth of the city collapsed. Seven thousand people were killed in the earthquake, and the survivors were terrified and gave glory to the God of heaven. (Rev. 11:13)

> **Those with the Seal of God**
>
> *And I heard the number of those who were sealed, 144,000 from all the tribes of Israel: From the tribe of Judah 12,000 were sealed, from the tribe of Reuben 12,000, from the tribe of Gad 12,000, from the tribe of Asher 12,000, from the tribe of Naphtali 12,000, from the tribe of Manasseh 12,000, from the tribe of Simeon 12,000, from the tribe of Levi 12,000, from the tribe of Issachar 12,000, from the tribe of Zebulun 12,000, from the tribe of Joseph 12,000, and from the tribe of Benjamin 12,000. After this I looked and saw a multitude too large to count, from every nation and tribe and people and tongue, standing before the throne and before the Lamb. They were wearing white robes and holding palm branches in their hands. And they cried out in a loud voice: "Salvation to our God, who sits on the throne, and to the Lamb!" And all the angels stood around the throne and around the elders and the four living creatures. And they fell facedown before the throne and worshiped God, saying, "Amen! Blessing and glory and wisdom and thanks and honor and power and strength be to our God forever and ever! Amen." Then one of the elders addressed me: "These in white robes," he asked, "who are they, and where have they come from?" "Sir," I answered, "you know." So he replied, "These are the ones who have come out of the great tribulation; they have washed their robes and made them white in the blood of the Lamb. For this reason, they are before the throne of God and serve Him day and night in His temple; and the One seated on the throne will spread His tabernacle over them. 'Never again will they hunger, and never will they thirst; nor will the sun beat down upon them, nor any scorching heat.' For the Lamb in the center of the throne will be their shepherd. 'He will lead them to springs of living water, and 'God will wipe away every tear from their eyes.'"* (Rev. 7:1–12)

> **Marriage Supper of the Lamb**
>
> *And I heard a sound like the roar of a great multitude, like the rushing of many waters, and like a mighty rumbling of thunder, crying out: "Hallelujah! For the Lord our God the Almighty reigns. Let us rejoice and be glad and give Him the glory. For the marriage of the Lamb has come, and His bride has made herself ready. She was given clothing of fine linen, bright and pure." For the fine linen she wears is the righteous acts of the saints. Then the angel told me to write, "Blessed are those who are invited to the marriage supper of the Lamb." And he said to me, "These are the true words of God."* (Rev. 19:6–9)

Antichrist (Beast) and the False Prophet (His Image) Are Defeated

Then I saw an angel standing in the sun, and he cried out in a loud voice to all the birds flying overhead, "Come, gather together for the great supper of God, so that you may eat the flesh of kings and commanders and mighty men, of horses and riders, of everyone slave and free, small and great." Then I saw the beast and the kings of the earth with their armies assembled to wage war against the One seated on the horse, and against His army. But the beast was captured along with the false prophet, who on its behalf had performed signs deceiving those who had the mark of the beast and worshiped its image. Both the beast and the false prophet were thrown alive into the fiery lake of burning sulfur. And the rest were killed with the sword that proceeded from the mouth of the One seated on the horse. And all the birds gorged themselves on their flesh. (Rev. 19:17–21)

Satan is Bound to Prison for One Thousand Years

Then I saw an angel coming down from heaven with the key to the Abyss, holding in his hand a great chain. He seized the dragon, that ancient serpent who is the devil and Satan, and bound him for a thousand years. And he threw him into the Abyss, shut it, and sealed it over him, so that he could not deceive the nations until the thousand years were complete. After that, he must be released for a brief period of time. (Rev. 20:1–3)

Millennial Reign of Christ

Then I saw thrones, and they sat on them, and judgment was given to them. And I saw the souls of those who had been beheaded because of their testimony of Jesus and because of the word of God, and those who had not worshiped the beast or his image, and had not received the mark on their forehead and on their hand; and they came to life and reigned with Christ for a thousand years. The rest of the dead did not come to life until the thousand years were completed. This is the first resurrection. Blessed and holy is the one who has a part in the first resurrection; over these the second death has no power, but they will be priests of God and of Christ and will reign with Him for a thousand years. (Rev. 20:4–6)

Then one of the seven angels with the seven bowls full of the seven final plagues came and said to me, "Come, I will show you the bride, the wife of the Lamb." And he carried me away in the Spirit to a mountain great and high, and showed me the holy city of Jerusalem coming down out of heaven from God, shining with the glory of God. Its radiance was like a most precious jewel, like a jasper, as clear as crystal. The city had a great and high wall with twelve gates inscribed with the names of the twelve tribes of Israel, and twelve angels at the gates. There were three gates on the east, three on the north, three on the south, and three on the west. The wall of the city had twelve foundations bearing the names of the twelve apostles of the Lamb. The angel who spoke with me had a golden measuring rod to measure the city and its gates and walls. The city lies foursquare, with its width the same as its length. And he measured the city with the rod, and all its dimensions were equal—12,000 stadia in length and width and height. And he measured its wall to be 144 cubits, by the human measure the angel was using. The wall was made of jasper, and the city itself of pure gold, as pure as glass. The foundations of the city walls were adorned with every kind of precious stone: The first foundation was jasper, the second sapphire, the third chalcedony, the fourth emerald, the fifth sardonyx, the sixth carnelian, the seventh chrysolite, the eighth beryl, the ninth topaz, the tenth chrysoprase, the eleventh jacinth, and the twelfth amethyst. And the twelve gates were twelve pearls, with each gate consisting of a single pearl. The main street of the city was pure gold, as clear as glass. But I saw no temple in the city, because the Lord God Almighty and the Lamb are its temple. And the city has no need of sun or moon to shine on it, because the glory of God illuminates the city, and the Lamb is its lamp. By its light the nations will walk, and into it the kings of the earth will bring their glory. Its gates will never be shut at the end of the day, because there will be no night there. And into the city will be brought the glory and honor of the nations. But nothing unclean will ever enter it, nor anyone who practices an abomination or a lie, but only those whose names are written in the Lamb's Book of Life. (Rev. 21:9–27)

"But be glad and rejoice forever in what I create; For behold, I create Jerusalem for rejoicing And her people for gladness. "I will also rejoice in Jerusalem and be glad in My people; And there will no longer be heard in her The voice of weeping and the sound of crying. "No longer will there be in it an infant who lives but a few days, Or an old man who does not live out his days; For the youth will die at the age of one hundred And the one who does not reach the age of one hundred Will be thought accursed. "They will build houses and inhabit them, They will also plant vineyards and eat their fruit. "They will not build and another inhabit, They will not plant and another eat; For as the lifetime of a tree, so will be the days of My people, And My chosen ones will wear out the work of their hands. "They will not labor in vain, Or bear children for calamity; For they are the offspring of those blessed by the LORD, *And their descendants with them. "It will also come to pass that before they call, I will answer; and while they are still speaking, I will ear. "The wolf and the lamb will graze together, and the lion will eat straw like the ox; and dust will be the serpent's food. They will do no evil or harm in all My holy mountain," says the* LORD. (Isa. 65:18–25)

Then the word of the Lord *of hosts came, saying, "Thus says the* Lord *of hosts, 'I am exceedingly jealous for Zion, yes, with great wrath I am jealous for her.' "Thus says the* Lord*, 'I will return to Zion and will dwell in the midst of Jerusalem. Then Jerusalem will be called the City of Truth, and the mountain of the* Lord *of hosts will be called the Holy Mountain.' "Thus says the* Lord *of hosts, 'Old men and old women will again sit in the streets of Jerusalem, each man with his staff in his hand because of age. 'And the streets of the city will be filled with boys and girls playing in its streets.' "Thus says the* Lord *of hosts, 'If it is too difficult in the sight of the remnant of this people in those days, will it also be too difficult in My sight?' declares the* Lord *of hosts.* (Zech. 8:1–6)

But the court will convene, and his dominion will be taken away and completely destroyed forever. Then the sovereignty, dominion, and greatness of the kingdoms under all of heaven will be given to the people, the saints of the Most High. His kingdom will be an everlasting kingdom, and all rulers will serve and obey Him.' (Dan. 7:26–27)

Satan is Cast into the Lake of Fire

When the thousand years are completed, Satan will be released from his prison, and will come out to deceive the nations which are in the four corners of the earth, Gog and Magog, to gather them together for the war; the number of them is like the sand of the seashore. And they came up on the broad plain of the earth and surrounded the camp of the saints and the beloved city, and fire came down from heaven and devoured them. And the devil who deceived them was thrown into the lake of fire and brimstone, where the beast and the false prophet are also; and they will be tormented day and night forever and ever. (Rev. 20:7–10)

Judgment According to the Books

Then I saw a great white throne and the One seated on it. Earth and heaven fled from His presence, and no place was found for them. And I saw the dead, great and small, standing before the throne. And there were open books, and one of them was the Book of Life. And the dead were judged according to their deeds, as recorded in the books. The sea gave up its dead, and Death and Hades gave up their dead, and each one was judged according to his deeds. Then Death and Hades were thrown into the lake of fire. This is the second death—the lake of fire. And if anyone was found whose name was not written in the Book of Life, he was thrown into the lake of fire. (Rev. 20:11–15)

But to the cowardly and unbelieving and abominable and murderers and sexually immoral and sorcerers and idolaters and all liars, their place will be in the lake that burns with fire and sulfur. This is the second death." (Rev. 21:8)

Then another angel, a third one, followed them, saying with a loud voice, "If anyone worships the beast and his image, and receives a mark on his forehead or on his hand, he also will drink of the wine of the wrath of God, which is mixed in full strength in the cup of His anger; and he will be tormented with fire and brimstone in the presence of the holy angels and in the presence of the Lamb. "And the smoke of their torment goes up forever and ever; they have no rest day and night, those who worship the beast and his image, and whoever receives the mark of his name." (Rev. 14:9–12)

Including the Saints…

Why, then, do you judge your brother? Or why do you belittle your brother? For we will all stand before God's judgment seat. It is written: "As surely as I live, says the Lord, every knee will bow before Me; every tongue will confess to God." So then, each of us will give an account of himself to God. (Rom. 14:10–12)

For we must all appear before the judgment seat of Christ, that each one may receive his due for the things done in the body, whether good or bad. (2 Cor. 5:10)

Eternity: A New Heaven and Earth

Then I saw a new heaven and a new earth, for the first heaven and earth had passed away, and the sea was no more. I saw the holy city, the new Jerusalem, coming down out of heaven from God, prepared as a bride adorned for her husband. And I heard a loud voice from the throne saying: "Behold, the dwelling place of God is with man, and He will dwell with them. They will be His people, and God Himself will be with them as their God. 'He will wipe away every tear from their eyes,' and there will be no more death or mourning or crying or pain, for the former things have passed away." And the One seated on the throne said, "Behold, I make all things new." Then He said, "Write this down, for these words are faithful and true." And He told me, "It is done! I am the Alpha and the Omega, the Beginning and the End. To the thirsty I will give freely from the spring of the water of life. The one who overcomes will inherit all things, and I will be his God, and he will be My son. But to the cowardly and unbelieving and abominable and murderers and sexually immoral and sorcerers and idolaters and all liars, their place will be in the lake that burns with fire and sulfur. This is the second death." (Rev. 21:1–8)

BIBLIOGRAPHY

◇◇

Andrew Farley, May 2019, Twisted Scripture: Untangling 45 Lies Christians Have Been Told, Salem Books, Washington D.C.)

Berean Literal Bible (BLB) © 2016 by Bible Hub and Berean.Bible Used by Permission. All rights Reserved.

Holman Christian Standard Bible®, Copyright © 1999, 2000, 2002, 2003, 2009 by Holman Bible Publishers. Used by permission.

Holy Bible, New International Version®, NIV® Copyright © 1973, 1978, 1984, 2011 by Biblica, Inc.® used by permission. All rights reserved worldwide.

Holy Bible, New Living Translation, copyright © 1996, 2004, 2015 by Tyndale House Foundation. Used by permission of Tyndale House Publishers, Inc., Carol Stream, Illinois 60188. All rights reserved.

King James Bible Text courtesy of BibleProtector.com Section Headings Courtesy INT Bible © 2012, Used by Permission

New American Standard Bible Copyright © 1960, 1971, 1977, 1995, 2020 by The Lockman Foundation, La Habra, Calif. All rights reserved. For Permission to Quote Information visit www.lockman.org

New Revised Standard Version, Fully Rev. 4th ed, © 2010 by Oxford University Press, Oxford (England) Used by Permission. All rights Reserved

The Berean Bible (www.Berean.Bible) Berean Study Bible (BSB) © 2016, 2020 by Bible Hub and Berean.Bible. Used by Permission. All rights Reserved. Free downloads and licensing available. See also the Berean Literal Bible and Berean Interlinear Bible.

The ESV® Bible (The Holy Bible, English Standard Version®) copyright © 2001 by Crossway Bibles, a publishing ministry of

Good News Publishers. The ESV® text has been reproduced in cooperation with and by permission of Good News Publishers. Unauthorized reproduction of this publication is prohibited. All rights reserved.

The ESV® Bible (The Holy Bible, English Standard Version®) is adapted from the Revised Standard Version of the Bible, copyright Division of Christian Education of the National Council of the Churches of Christ in the U.S.A. All rights reserved.

The Holy Bible, New King James Version, Copyright © 1982 Thomas Nelson. All rights reserved.

John F. Kennedy's Inaugural Address, January 20, 1961, www.bible-studytools.com/lexicons/hebrew/nas/shalach.html

www. census.gov/popclock/ world

www.merriam-webster.com/ dictionary/

www.pursuegod.org/rules-pharisees/

About the Author

◇◇◇

Lisa Ann Samara Jones has a profound passion to share the gospel, challenging others to push deeper into a more meaningful and authentic faith in Christ through the Holy Spirit.

Born and raised in upstate New York, with her parents, an older sister, a twin sister, and a younger brother, she excelled in academics and received two full scholarships for her associate's and master's degrees. She is a believer, wife, mother, friend, and teacher, with three degrees in the field of education. Lisa has taught in both public and private schools from preschool level through seniors in high school, spending most of these years privately homeschooling her own children and dozens of others.

Having moved to the deep south in her late twenties, she now happily resides outside of Little Rock, Arkansas, with her cherished husband and their youngest children. Together, they've created a small farm with dozens of animals and enjoy life at the top of their mountain ridge.

Her insatiable desire to write this book began years ago, but the burning need to do so pushed her to spend this past summer writing. Feeling led by the Spirit of God, she'd sit from morning to evening with a cup of coffee nearby and fingers ferociously typing away. She didn't know what her next chapter would hold until she finished the previous and even surprised herself with content as the verses came to mind, leading her in an entirely different direction than she'd first thought it would go.

CPSIA information can be obtained
at www.ICGtesting.com
Printed in the USA
JSHW080759090223
37405JS00001B/7